Counseling Overweight Adults:

The Lifestyle Patterns Approach and Toolkit

Robert F. Kushner, MD
Nancy Kushner, MSN, RN
Dawn Jackson Blatner, RD

American Dietetic Association
Chicago, Illinois

Diana Faulhaber, Publisher
Laura Pelehach and Kristen Short, Acquisitions and Development Managers
Elizabeth Nishiura, Production Manager

American Dietetic Association
120 South Riverside Plaza, Suite 2000
Chicago, IL 60606

10 9 8 7 6 5 4 3 2 1

Library of Congress Cataloging-in-Publication Data
Kushner, Robert F., 1953-
    Counseling overweight adults: the lifestyle patterns approach and toolkit / Robert F. Kushner, Nancy Kushner, Dawn Jackson Blatner.
        p. ; cm.
    Includes bibliographical references and index.
    ISBN 978-0-88091-422-2
1. Obesity—Treatment. 2. Overweight persons—Counseling of. 3. Behavior modification. 4. Lifestyles—Health aspects.
5. Health behavior. I. Kushner, Nancy. II. Blatner, Dawn Jackson. III. American Dietetic Association. IV. Title.
[DNLM: 1. Overweight—therapy. 2. Counseling—methods. 3. Life Style. 4. Obesity—therapy. WD 210 K97c 2009]

RC628.K92 2009
362.196'398—dc22

2008014267

Contents

◆ ◆ ◆

Chapter 4: Counseling for Eating Lifestyle Patterns   51

Chapter 5: Counseling for Exercise Lifestyle Patterns   95

CD-ROM Contents

✦ ✦ ✦

Note: The Lifestyles Pattern Quiz is available as a computer program (which generates the Eating, Exercise, and Coping Patterns Quiz Bar Graph Results) and as a printer-ready PDF document. All other materials on the CD-ROM are printer-ready files.

Quizzes

- Lifestyle Patterns Quiz
- Eating Mini-Quiz
- Exercise Mini-Quiz
- Coping Mini-Quiz

Forms

- Health Assessment Patient Questionnaire
- Weight Flow Sheet
- Food and Activity Log
- Lifestyle Patterns Progress Note
- Health Care Provider Letter
- Progress Tracking Chart

Patient Education Handouts

Eating Patterns
- The Meal Skipper
- The Nighttime Nibbler
- The Convenient Diner
- The Fruitless Feaster
- The Steady Snacker
- The Hearty Portioner
- The Swing Eater

Exercise Patterns
- The Couch Champion
- The Uneasy Participant
- The Fresh Starter
- The All-or-Nothing Doer
- The Set-Routine Repeater
- The Tender Bender
- The Rain Check Athlete

Coping Patterns
- The Emotional Eater
- The Self-scrutinizer
- The Persistent Procrastinator
- The People Pleaser
- The Fast Pacer
- The Doubtful Dieter
- The Overreaching Achiever

Acknowledgments

✦ ✦ ✦

We would like to thank the publishing team of the American Dietetic Association, specifically Diana Faulhaber, Kristen Short, Laura Pelehach, and Elizabeth Nishiura, for their enthusiasm and excitement from the start for our project and their wise guidance along the way. Thanks also to Ed Przyzycki from Ed Edited It Productions, who produced the CD-ROM that allows clinicians to implement the Lifestyle Patterns Program as a turn-key operation in their workplace. We would also like to thank the anonymous reviewers who took the time to critique the hundreds of pages of the original manuscript. Your comments helped us refine and improve the final product.

We have other reviewers to thank as well—Peggy Mitchell and Dr. Brad Saks for their review and help with the exercise and coping chapters. We would also like to thank the staff from the Wellness Institute at Northwestern Memorial Hospital who helped implement the Lifestyle Patterns Approach in a professional manner and always gave welcome feedback. Thanks also to our patients who teach us every day and whose positive responses to this approach gave us the confidence to move forward with this project.

Thank you to Dr. Mike Zhang, president of Diet.com, who has had faith in the Lifestyle Patterns Approach from the time he read about it in the *Personality Type Diet* years ago and has supported the continuing education of registered dietitians in this approach, through teleconferences.

Nancy and Bob also want to thank Dawn for being an exemplary professional partner. Thanks also to our parents who always inspire us—little did they know when we married 30 years ago that we would end up being writing partners in addition to being life partners. To our children, Sarah and Steven, who make us proud every day for the young adults they've become, thank you for taking paths that reinforce our beliefs about fulfilling life passions and helping others. To our daily walking partner, Cooper, who helped our minds stay fresh and our bodies stay active during our much-needed computer breaks, thank you.

Dawn wants to thank Nancy and Bob for inviting her to be a part of this project and mentoring her through the writing process—this experience has been invaluable. A special thank you to my husband, Chris, and stepson, Christian, for their love and understanding when I was hidden in my office researching and writing. Thanks to my parents, Herb and Nancy, and my brother, Herb, for encouraging and supporting all of my personal and professional endeavors.

A final thanks to all the health care providers who are using the information in this book to help their patients live healthier and happier lives—health is a precious commodity.

Reviewers

✦ ✦ ✦

Christina Biesemeier, MS, RD, FADA
Vanderbilt University Medical Center
Franklin, TN

Mary Pat Bolton, MA, RD
Houston, TX

Ruth Ann Carpenter, MS, RD
The Cooper Institute
Dallas, TX

Molly Gee, MEd, RD
Baylor College of Medicine
Houston, TX

Lori F. Greene, MS, RD
University of Alabama
Northport, AL

Laurie Grubbs, PhD, ARNP
Florida State University College of Nursing
Tallahassee, FL

Rachel Huber, MPH, RD
The Cooper Institute
Dallas, TX

Eileen S. Myers, MPH, RD, FADA
Scales Nutrition & Wellness
Nashville, TN

Rebecca S. Reeves, DrPH, RD
Baylor College of Medicine
Houston, TX

Lynn Umbreit, MS, RD
Southwest Endocrinology Weight Management Center
Albuquerque, NM

Foreword

✦ ✦ ✦

With more than 65% of adults and 15% of children and adolescents in the United States currently categorized as overweight or obese, treating patients effectively to lose and maintain weight remains a great challenge. Because of the high risk of recidivism among clients who lose weight, registered dietitians (RDs) and other health care professionals are faced with motivating clients to assume responsibility for their own care. Nutrition counselors are challenged to guide clients to recognize the eating patterns and habits that have caused their weight gain over the years and then help them establish their own goals for changing their lifestyles to improve their health. Conducting counseling sessions with an understanding of the client's patterns and characteristics of eating is important so that the client is empowered to make the changes necessary to achieve a more healthful lifestyle.

This publication, *Counseling Overweight Adults: The Lifestyle Patterns Approach and Toolkit,* provides RDs and other health care professionals with the content, tools, and materials to conduct counseling sessions with this focus. This innovative counseling approach highlights an individual's lifestyle patterns for eating, exercise, and coping. The lead author, Robert F. Kushner, MD, developed and implemented this approach to counseling at the Northwestern Memorial Hospital Wellness Institute in Chicago. His coauthors and colleagues, Nancy Kushner, MSN, RN, and Dawn Jackson Blatner, RD, are experienced health professionals who helped refine the Lifestyle Patterns Approach. The basis for this counseling approach is that each person has his or her own lifestyle habits that have contributed to weight gain over time. The practitioner identifies the different patterns exhibited by a client and individualizes the counseling to match the client's habits.

Detailed information and techniques for conducting this creative counseling program are found in this book. Specific chapters discuss the actual counseling interventions and provide the Lifestyle Pattern descriptions, patient case studies, examples of dialogue, strategies, and counseling tips and techniques. A full explanation of the Lifestyle Patterns Quiz, which can categorize clients by their eating, exercise, and coping habits, is included along with methods to score the quiz. The book also explains how to monitor clients and track their progress. Information on applying the Lifestyle Patterns Approach to specific patient populations and group settings is included in later chapters.

A CD-ROM accompanies the book. It contains all the tools necessary to implement this counseling approach, including a program to score the Lifestyle Patterns Quiz and graphically present a patient's results. Forms, such as tools for tracking weight and logs to enter food and physical activity minutes, and patient education handouts are also found on the CD-ROM.

If you are looking for a counseling approach that identifies your client's habits, then this publication should satisfy your needs. Everything you require to implement this counseling approach is within the covers of this book.

Rebecca S. Reeves, DrPH, RD, FADA
President
American Dietetic Association, 2005–2006

Introduction

✦ ✦ ✦

The Epidemic of Adult Overweight

According to the 2003–2004 National Health and Nutrition Examination Survey (NHANES), more than two thirds of Americans are overweight or obese (1). Between1960 and 2002, the prevalence of obesity (body mass index ≥ 30) increased by 1.36 times among men (from 22.8% to 31.1% of the population) and 1.29 times among women (from 25.7% to 33.2%). This translates into an average weight gain of more than 24 pounds for each person in four decades (2). This alarming rise in overweight and obesity in the United States is not caused by a change in the gene pool. Rather, it is primarily due to the response to our environment, in which excessive energy intake, shifting eating patterns, and limited physical activity predominate.

The consequences of overweight and obesity are serious. Being overweight or obese can lead to diabetes, hypertension, dyslipidemia, coronary artery disease, and metabolic syndrome, among other diseases (3). Additionally, overweight and obesity negatively affect the individual's overall physical and psychological health and can diminish one's quality of life on a daily basis. Patients often feel desperate as they search for help.

The process of treating overweight and obese patients can be daunting. Health care professionals face many barriers, including limited resources, inadequate reimbursement, time constraints, competing demands, insufficient training in counseling, and a lack of confidence in their ability to treat and change behaviors (4). Clinicians need resources to help them quickly and easily identify each patient's weight-loss needs, tools to identify patients' primary barriers and obstacles to losing weight, and a method for developing individualized messages and strategies to enable patients to successfully lose weight and maintain weight loss. Accordingly, our objective in this publication is to provide health care professionals with resources and tools that will allow them to tailor a personalized weight management program for each weight-loss patient.

Why This Publication?

Our decision to write this book emerged over several years, beginning with the development of the Lifestyle Patterns Approach to weight management and the 2003 publication of the consumer title *Dr. Kushner's Personality Type Diet* (5). In recent years, Lifestyle Patterns educational programs have become popular among professionals in the weight management field. More than 200 registered dietitians (RDs) have participated in continuing education teleconferences sponsored by Diet.com, and Lifestyle Patterns educational programs have also been presented to professionals attending annual meetings of the American Association of Diabetes Educators and to physician groups at Harvard Medical School and Mayo Clinic conferences. Through these programs, Robert Kushner, MD, and Dawn Jackson Blatner, RD, stimulated a groundswell of interest among RDs, nurses, and physicians for a weight loss approach that considers an individual's lifestyle patterns for eating, physical activity, and coping.

During our various educational sessions, we heard clinicians express a common theme: counseling overweight adults is a challenge due to limited time, insufficient resources, and a lack of an organized structure. After presenting the Lifestyle Patterns Quiz and program, we received a great deal of positive feedback. The following are some of the things that clinicians said they liked about our approach:

- It helps the health professional to quickly identify problem patient areas.

- The Lifestyle Patterns Quiz results are printed in a visual format that patients can appreciate—they are able to see their progress and successes in a graphic, tangible format.

- The treatment plan handouts are both realistic for patients to follow and easy for them to understand.

Because the Lifestyle Patterns Approach had been successfully used at the Northwestern Memorial Hospital Wellness Institute since 2001, we believed that both patients and clinicians alike would appreciate these benefits. What surprised us, however, was the extent of the enthusiasm and positive comments expressed about our approach. The following comments received over the years from RDs, physicians, and nurses became our impetus to write this book:

- "The tool you have developed is wonderful and perfectly addresses my frustration in trying to get at the real issues of people's eating, exercise, and coping behaviors. I would be very interested in utilizing this in my practice."

- "Your method of 'diagnosing' the problem is exactly what we are searching for."

- "The original names for the lifestyle personality patterns are very catchy and pertinent. I feel clients can easily identify with those that fit their personality."

- "Your questionnaire enables the practitioner to give consistent care to all patients."

And so, *Counseling Overweight Adults: The Lifestyle Patterns Approach and Toolkit* was born.

How to Use This Publication

This publication has two separate components: the book and the CD-ROM. The book explains what you need to know to counsel patients using the Lifestyle Patterns Approach to weight management and provides numerous tips and resources to help make your counseling program a success. The CD-ROM gives you a variety of electronic tools so you can use this approach efficiently and quickly in your daily practice.

The Book

The book begins with a brief review of the basic counseling theories on which the Lifestyle Patterns Approach is based (Chapter 1). This review then leads into a discussion of how the Lifestyle Patterns Approach was developed (Chapter 2). In Chapter 3, we review how to use the Lifestyle Patterns Approach to evaluate and counsel overweight patients.

Chapters 4, 5, and 6 explain the counseling interventions for the three main dimensions of treatment—eating, exercise, and coping. These explanations are supported by full Lifestyle Pattern descriptions, patient case studies, examples of dialogue, pattern-specific strategies, and counseling tips and techniques for using this program.

In Chapter 7, we review the use of the Lifestyle Patterns Approach to monitor patients. This chapter outlines how to track patients' progress, provides approaches to deal with relapses and weight plateaus, and discusses ongoing monitoring considerations and family patterns. Chapters 8 and 9 contain what you need to know to apply this approach to specific patient populations and in group settings. The appendixes include the Lifestyle Patterns Quiz and Mini-quizzes, an explanation of how to score the quiz manually, sample patient education handouts, and a list of relevant resources.

The CD-ROM

The CD-ROM provides clinicians with an easy-to-use program to score the Lifestyle Patterns Quiz and generate bar graphs of patient-specific test results. These graphs illustrate patient profiles and can be easily printed for use in counseling sessions.

Additionally, the CD-ROM includes patient education handouts for each of the 21 Lifestyle Patterns. Each handout offers four goals for patients and numerous tips and resources for meeting these objectives.

Other documents on the CD-ROM include a printer-ready version of the Lifestyle Patterns Quiz, the three mini-quizzes, a daily food and activity log, records to track progress, a health care provider letter, and a health assessment form.

******

We hope this approach and convenient tools will put you and your patients on the path to a program that will easily fit into their lives.

References

1. Ogden CL, Carroll MD, Curtin LR, McDowell MA, Tabak CJ, Flegal KM. Prevalence of overweight and obesity in the United States, 1999—2004. *JAMA.* 2006;295:1549-1555.

2. Ogden CL, Fryar CD, Carroll MD, Flegal KM. Mean body weight, height, and body mass index, United States 1960-2002. *Adv Data VitalHealth Stat.* 2004;347(Oct 27):1-2.

3. Must A, Spadano J, Coakley E, Field AE, Colditz G, Dietz WH. The disease burden associated with overweight and obesity. *JAMA.* 1999;282:1523-1529.

4. Kushner RF. Barriers to providing nutrition counseling by physicians. A survey of primary care practitioners. *Prev Med.* 1995;24,546-552.

5. Kushner R, Kushner N. *Dr. Kushner's Personality Type Diet.* New York, NY: St. Martin's Press; 2003.

Chapter 1

✦ ✦ ✦

Counseling Basics

Overview

Although some clinicians have an innate ability to empathize and actively listen to their clients, none are born with the knowledge, skills, strategies, theories and techniques to help patients change their behavior. Rather, this set of "counseling basics" is a learning process that is honed by experience. This chapter provides an important primer on the importance of communication as well as the most commonly used theories and approaches for overweight adults, including the stages of change model, health belief model, self-determination and motivational interviewing, social cognitive theory/ecological models, theory of planned behavior, and cognitive behavioral therapy. These health behavior approaches help both experienced and less-experienced clinicians lay a foundation for good counseling techniques upon which the Lifestyle Patterns Approach in this book is based. Clinicians will periodically see snapshots of these approaches and communication techniques used in subsequent chapters.

This chapter can also serve as an excellent resource when clinicians need extra help with difficult patients. In this chapter, case examples and vignettes are used, when appropriate, to illustrate application of these methods during the process of counseling overweight adults. For further reading regarding the counseling process, clinicians are encouraged to pay particular attention to the resources cited at the end of this chapter.

Patient Communication

At its most basic level, good counseling requires good communication. A cornerstone of effective treatment for obesity is grounded in empathetic and skillful provider-patient communication. Because the primary aim of obesity counseling is to influence what the patient does outside of the office, the time spent in the office needs to be structured and meaningful.

In clinical practice, *empathy* is the ability to understand the patient's situation, perspectives, and feelings and to communicate that understanding to the patient (1). The feeling of being understood is intrinsically therapeutic. Patients with obesity typically share emotionally laden tales of the frustration, anger, and shame of losing (and gaining) weight, the discrimination they feel in the workplace and from society for being overweight, and the ridicule they may have experienced with other health care providers. Recognizing and acknowledging the patient's concerns and experiences is an extremely

1

important element in communication. It is important for patients to have the opportunity to tell the story of their weight journey in their own words and for the clinician to validate the patient's experiences. The dialogue in Box 1.1 illustrates the use of empathetic communication. In this example, the clinician expresses empathy for the patient's earlier experience of insensitive teasing and commends her on her ability to use humor as a coping strategy.

In addition to being empathetic, six other model communication behaviors were identified in a Mayo Clinic study as being important to patients (2). A provider who was confident, humane, personal, forthright, respectful, thorough (and empathetic) was considered ideal. These interpersonal skills are critical to establishing a trusting and professional rapport.

The optimal therapeutic relationship between the patient and provider is that of mutuality. Sometimes called *patient-centered* or *relationship-centered* communication, this type of relationship allows the patient to be an active participant in setting the agenda and having his or her concerns heard (3). Other terms for this mutual relationship are *shared decision-making* and *collaborative care*. In this type of intervention, the provider and patient work as partners, and patient choice and autonomy are always emphasized. The counselor and patient develop strategies that give the patient the best chance to manage his or her own weight problem. Such a relationship demands active participation from both patient and clinician. These principles of effective communication are central underpinnings for all encounters. The dialogue in Box 1.2 illustrates relationship-centered communication. In this example, the clinician provides specific suggestions for breakfast and guides the patient toward a specific action plan.

Box 1.1 ✦ Expressing Empathy

B: "When I was in high school, they used to call me thunder thighs. I always carried my weight in my thighs, butt, and hips. No matter how much weight I lost, my thighs didn't seem to lose even an inch. Every time I look in the mirror, I see my thunder thighs and can still hear the girls in the locker room laughing."

Clinician: "That must have been very hurtful. And it seems that it has left a lasting impression with you about your body shape even today."

B: "It sure has and I hate it. Is there any way I can trade in body parts for a new model?"

Clinician: "It's nice to see that you have developed a sense of humor about it. Humor can go a long way toward healing and dealing with problems."

Box 1.2 ✦ Relationship-Centered Communication

Clinician: "We've discussed that having breakfast every morning is an important strategy to satisfy your intense hunger that hits by 11:00 AM. Have you given any thought to what you could have for breakfast that is quick and easy?"

N: "I'm not sure. I could use some ideas."

Clinician: "I have many patients who do well eating a meal replacement bar or a yogurt with some high-fiber cereal; it's not only quick but quite filling as well. Have you ever tried these?"

N: "No, but I can give it a try."

Clinician: "Okay. I would recommend that you stop by your grocery store this weekend and check out the variety of meal replacement bars on the shelf. Pick a few that look good to you and read the label for calories. And be sure to monitor your hunger over the course of the morning."

Behavior-Change Theories

In the next sections, we discuss six behavior-change theories.

Stages of Change

Counseling an overweight patient begins with assessing whether the patient is ready to make changes in behavior. One model, the transtheoretical or stages of change (SOC) model, clarifies this process. It proposes that at any specific time, patients change problem behaviors by moving through a series of stages representing several levels of readiness to change. There are five distinct stages of change: precontemplation, contemplation, preparation, action, and maintenance (4,5). Patients move from one stage to the next in the process of change, and it is likely that they may repeat stages several times before lasting change occurs. Within the SOC model, the clinician's tasks include both assessing the patient's stage of change and using behavioral counseling strategies to help advance the patient from one stage to the next. Table 1.1 (6) shows samples of how to assess stages of change, describes the characteristics of each stage, identifies appropriate cognitive and behavioral counseling strategies, and provides helpful dialogues for each stage.

Table 1.1 ✦ Applying the Stages of Change Model to Assess Readiness

Stage	Characteristics	Patient Verbal Cues	Appropriate Intervention	Sample of Dialogue
Precontemplation	Unaware of problem, no interest in change	"I'm not really interested in weight loss. It's not a problem."	Provide information about health risks and benefits of weight loss.	"Would you like to read some information about the health aspects of being overweight?"
Contemplation	Aware of problem, beginning to think of changing	"I need to lose weight but with all that's going on in my life right now, I'm not sure I can."	Help resolve ambivalence; discuss barriers.	"Let's look at the benefits of weight loss, as well as what you may need to change."
Preparation	Realizes benefits of making changes and thinking about how to change	"I have to lose weight, and I'm planning to do that."	Teach behavior modification; provide education.	"Let's take a closer look at how you can reduce some of the calories and how to increase your activity during the day."
Action	Actively taking steps toward achieving the behavioral goal, but only for a brief period (less than 6 months)	"I'm doing my best. This is harder than I thought."	Provide support and guidance with a focus on the long term (relapse control).	"It's terrific that you're working so hard. What problems have you had so far? How have you solved them?"
Maintenance	Initial treatment and behavioral goals reached and sustained for a longer period of time (eg, more than 6 months)	"I've learned a lot through this process."	Relapse control.	"What situations continue to tempt you to overeat? What can be helpful for the next time you face such a situation?"

Source: Adapted with permission from Kushner RF. Roadmaps for Clinical Practice: Case Studies in Disease Prevention and Health Promotion—Assessment and Management of Adult Obesity: A Primer for Physicians. Chicago, IL: American Medical Association; 2003. http://www.ama-assn.org/ama/pub/category/10931.html. Accessed September 8, 2007.

It is important to remember that stages of change often reflect distinct behaviors. For instance, a patient may be in the preparation stage for making changes to her diet, such as adding more fruits and vegetables to each meal, but be in the precontemplation stage for engaging in more physical activity. In this case, you would praise the patient and provide specific advice about adding more fruits and vegetables while encouraging the patient to think about how to add small bouts of physical activity in the course of the day.

The SOC model incorporates 10 specific processes of change—ie, the activities and experiences in which individuals engage when they attempt to modify problem behaviors. Successful changers employ different processes at each particular stage of change. The basic skill for the clinician is to listen for these experiential verbal statements to determine where a patient is in the five stages of change. Four of the most useful processes of change with examples specific to weight management follow (7).

- **Consciousness-raising:** Patients actively seek new information and gain understanding and feedback about behavior change. For example, in her counseling session, S explains that she has talked to people who have been successful in losing weight and that this has made her a bit more hopeful that she can lose weight too. The clinician determines that S is moving from precontemplation to contemplation.

- **Environmental reevaluation:** Patients consider and assess how diet, physical activity, and coping are affected by their physical and social environments. For example, J remarks that he almost always grabs some candy every time he passes his secretary's desk—and he's not even hungry! The clinician determines that J is moving from contemplation to preparation.

- **Helping relationships:** Patients trust, accept, and utilize the support of others in their attempts to change behavior. For example, K explains that talking to a friend, someone she can count on, has been very important when she feels depressed—the time when she often turns to food for comfort. K explains that her friend has helped her to control her emotional urges for eating for the past 4 months. The clinician determines that K has moved from preparation to action.

- **Self-reevaluation:** Patients conduct emotional and cognitive reappraisal of individual values with respect to their behavior-change goals. For example, P explains that despite losing and keeping off 10% of her body weight, she still struggles with her body shape. She has learned to replace negative self-talk with more positive statements, such as "I am 16 pounds lighter now and have a new wardrobe that looks pretty darn good. Even though I still want to take off another 15 pounds, I'm going to celebrate my success along the way. I'm going to continue the healthy eating and physical activity plan I have been on for the past 8 months." The clinician determines that P is moving from action to maintenance.

Many of these processes are embedded in other behavior-change models. The role of the clinician is to guide the patient through these behavioral or thought processes, depending on their particular stage of change for a specific behavior.

Part of the decision for individuals to move from one stage to the next is based on the relative emphasis given to the pros and cons of changing behavior. The pros represent positive aspects of changing behavior while the cons represent negative aspects of changing behavior, which may be thought of as barriers to change (8). The clinician-patient dialogue in Box 1.3 illustrates an evaluation of the pros and cons of beginning an exercise routine. In this example, the patient moves from the preparation stage to the action stage with the help of the clinician.

Health Belief Model

What about the patient who doesn't seem to understand the need to lose weight? This is another situation that can arise when counseling an overweight patient. A model that describes this, the health belief model, holds the principle that health behavior change is a function of the individual's perceptions regarding his or her vulnerability to illness and the possible effectiveness of treatment (9,10). Behavior change is determined by individuals who:

- Perceive themselves to be susceptible to a particular health problem
- Identify the problem as serious
- Are convinced that treatment/prevention is effective and not overly costly in regard to money, effort, or pain
- Are exposed to a cue to take health action
- Have confidence that they can perform a specific behavior (self-efficacy)

The basic skill for the clinician is to help patients understand these behavior-change factors. This model is particularly useful when a patient is perceived to be in the precontemplation stage of change for initiating weight loss. The dialogue in Box 1.4 illustrates use of the health belief model.

Box 1.3 ✦ Weighing the Pros and Cons of Behavior Change

Clinician: "B, do you think you can exercise at least two times this week?"

B: "I'd like to, but time has always been a major issue."

Clinician: "Okay, I know that you want to exercise since we have talked about this before. And I know that you have a treadmill in the basement. What are the factors that make it hard for you to get started?"

B: "It's really all about time. Knowing myself, I would need to exercise in the morning. That means getting up a half hour earlier."

Clinician: "Is that doable?"

B: "Yes, it is. If I took my workout clothes out the night before and laid them on the chair, it would be even easier. I guess I could also make a point of going to sleep on time the night before."

Clinician: "Well the benefits are pretty clear—feel better during the day, get off to a good start, and burn more calories. Is there any downside to the plan?"

B: "The only downside is losing a half hour of sleep twice a week, and making sure I get my workout clothes ready the night before. I can do this."

Box 1.4 ✦ Using the Health Belief Model to Encourage Weight Loss

Clinician: "J, what do you know about the health risks of being overweight?"

J: "Everybody is telling me that I am too fat, but I feel all right as I am. My dad was my size and lived to be 85 years old!"

Clinician: "I see. While it is true that you are not severely overweight, your weight does concern me. You do meet the criteria for moderate obesity, and your weight does affect your joint pain, blood pressure, and cholesterol levels, which puts you at higher risk for heart disease. This is a serious problem."

(continued)

Box 1.4 ✦ (continued)

J: "I didn't know that. But I think this is the weight I am supposed to be. I've never been thin."

Clinician: "J, you've never tried to lose weight, and I think you can modify your eating and physical activity levels to make a difference. We know that losing as little as 5% to 10% of your weight can make a big difference in your health problems and will likely lower your risk for heart disease. What do you think about our developing a weight loss plan for you together?"

J: "If it's that serious and you can help me, I'll give it a try."

When using the health belief model for behavior change, it is important to give feedback to the patient and to continually link the patient's behavior changes to positive internal cues of health by pointing out that the changes the patient is making are directly leading to improved physical or mental well-being. In a weight-loss or weight-management setting, examples of improved physical or mental well-being include reduced blood pressure or cholesterol levels, climbing a flight of stairs without becoming breathless, or improved mood. These positive outcomes are intended to strengthen the "cause and effect" relationship between behavior and health and to reinforce motivation.

Self-Determination and Motivational Interviewing

In clinical care, one of the most frustrating and distressing situations is when a patient seems to lack motivation for change. Even after the clinician has addressed all of the benefits and obstacles to change and has laid out specific strategies to take action, the patient seems to be stuck in inertia (the inability or unwillingness to move or act). It is therefore not surprising that one of the most frequently asked questions by clinicians is, "How do I motivate my patient?" The theory of self-determination and the counseling process of motivational interviewing (MI) are particularly useful for these patients who seem to lack motivation for change.

According to the theory of self-determination, people are motivated to act by very different types of factors, either because they value a particular activity (internal/intrinsic motivation) or because there is strong external coercion (external motivation) (11). People will be internally motivated only when a change holds personal interest for them, such as enjoyment, satisfaction, and intrinsic reward.

Although powerful in its own right, intrinsic motivation requires supportive conditions (eg, people and an environment that are positive influences on behavior change) and can be readily disrupted by various less-supportive conditions. For example, let's consider a patient who wants to reduce the size of his dinner meal but whose wife serves family style (all food is presented in large serving dishes on the table), uses large plates, and encourages him to finish the food so there are no leftovers. In this case, the nonsupportive condition (the way dinner meals are served) will likely trump intrinsic motivation. In other words, patients must not only be ready, willing, and able to make change, there must also be a supportive condition.

At the other end of the spectrum are nonmotivated patients who don't see any value in changing, don't feel competent to change, or are not expecting the change to yield a desired outcome. Use of the health belief model as discussed previously may be useful for these patients. The basic skill of the clinician is to identify whether patients' motivation is internal or external and to help patients find supportive conditions for health behavior change.

Between these two extremes is a continuum of externally motivated patients who are prompted to change by their significant others or by their own need to feel connected to or valued by others. The more a person is externally motivated, the less he or she shows interest, value, and action toward achievement of change and the more he or she tends to blame others for a negative outcome. In a weight-loss setting, one end of this continuum includes patients who present themselves for weight loss solely because of the prompting of their physician or spouse. These patients will likely just "go through the motions" to satisfy these external demands. At the other end of the continuum are externally motivated patients who make changes to avoid guilt or anxiety or to achieve pride in themselves. An example would be a binge eater who feels bad about herself whenever she binges alone. Although an externally motivated patient can make positive behavior changes, the ultimate goal is to help patients become self-determined, ie, to internalize and assimilate the changes to the self so that they experience greater autonomy in their actions.

According to Watson and Tharp, all behaviors pass through the following sequence—control by others, control by self, and automatization (12). When patients achieve internal motivation, changes become more automatic and patients are authentic to their own goals. For example, a patient gains the assertiveness to say "no" to many of the peripheral demands asked of her and learns to prioritize her time to exercise on a regular schedule. This newly acquired sense of autonomy and control reinforces her internal motivation to carve out precious time for herself.

So how do clinicians assess motivation and facilitate behavior change? Motivational interviewing is defined as "a client-centered, directive method for enhancing intrinsic motivation to change by exploring and resolving ambivalence" (13). It focuses on what the patient wants and how the patient thinks and feels. According to MI, "motivation to change is viewed as something which is evoked in the patient rather, than imposed. It is the patient's task (not the practitioner's) to articulate and resolve his or her own ambivalence" (14). Readiness is viewed as the balance of two opposing forces: motivation or the patient's desire to change, and resistance or the patient's struggle against changing (15). Readiness for change is seen as the extent to which the patient has contemplated the need for change, having considered the pros and cons of changing.

Intrinsic to this model is the concept that most patients are ambivalent about changing long-standing lifestyle behaviors, fearing that change will be difficult, uncomfortable, or depriving. Initiating a change plan when the patient is not ready often leads to frustration and disappointment. Patients frequently misattribute their lack of success to either a failure of effort (low willpower) or a poorly conceived diet. Patients who are ready and have thought about the benefits and difficulties of weight management are more likely to succeed. One helpful, simple, and rapid method to begin a readiness assessment is to "anchor" the patient's interest and confidence to change on a numerical scale (for example, Figure 1.1). Simply ask the patient (16), "On a scale from zero to 10, with zero being not important and 10 being very important, how *important* is it for you to lose weight at this time?" and "Also on a scale from zero to 10, with zero being not confident and 10 being very confident, how *confident* are you that you can lose weight at this time?" This is a very useful exercise to initiate further discussion.

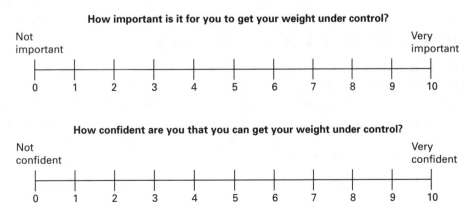

Figure 1.1 Weight control importance and patient confidence scales.

The dialogue in Box 1.5 demonstrates the use of this technique. In this example, the clinician is able to quickly identify two targets of opportunity to deal with behavior change. The ensuing discussion (Box 1.6) demonstrates how this technique helps to narrow the focus of counseling. In this example, two quick questions allow the clinician to gain a better appreciation of what L is thinking and the issues that will need to be addressed in more detail.

MI uses four general principles to help clinicians explore and resolve ambivalence (13):

- **Express empathy.** As previously discussed, empathy refers to understanding the patient's feelings and perspectives without judging, criticizing, or blaming.

Box 1.5 ✦ Using Weight Control Importance and Patient Confidence Scales to Identify Areas for Behavior Change

Clinician: "G, you've told me M has been encouraging you to lose weight. On a scale from zero to 10, with zero being not important and 10 being very important, how interested are you in losing weight?"

G: "I'm about an 8."

Clinician: "Okay, now I'd like to know how confident you are, again on a scale from zero to 10, with zero being not confident and 10 being very confident, that you can make the changes necessary to lose weight?"

G: "I'm about a 3."

Clinician: "That's interesting. You rate the importance pretty high, at an 8, but your confidence is much lower, at a 3. What would need to happen to raise your confidence score to a 5 or 6?"

G: "Boy, I can think of a few things. First, M needs to get off my back. She constantly reminds me of what I should and should not be eating. That just makes me eat more. Second, Sundays are always difficult. We have the entire family over after church for a huge lunch. I can't seem to control myself. Maybe if I had some ideas on how to control myself, I wouldn't feel so bad about dieting."

Clinician: "Those are two very important concerns and seem like a good place to start. Have you talked to M about her comments and how they make you feel?"

G: "Not really. I guess I just get so mad I shut her out."

Clinician: "What can you say that would be helpful?"

G: "I guess I could ask her not to comment on my eating and that I am trying to make better choices."

Box 1.6 ✦ Using Weight Control Importance and Patient Confidence Scales to Focus Behavior Change Counseling

Clinician: "L, you've ranked the importance of losing weight at a 7 and your confidence at a 4. What would have to happen for you to raise the importance of losing weight to an 8 or 9?"

L: "I guess if my doctor told me that I needed to go on insulin for my diabetes."

Clinician: "And what would it take to increase your confidence score from a 4 to an 8 or 9?"

L: "I really need the support of my family. They don't seem to understand how difficult this is for me. They expect me to simply not eat all of the junk food they bring into the house."

- **Develop discrepancy.** The second principle is to create and amplify the discrepancy between present behavior and the patient's broader goals and values. Discrepancy has to do with the importance of change and the distance that the patient's behavior would need to travel to reach the desired level. This is called the "behavioral gap" (12). The approach is one that results in the patient reflecting on the actions and reasons for change.

- **Support self-efficacy.** Self-efficacy refers to a person's belief in his or her ability to carry out and succeed with a specific task. Other common terms are *hope* and *faith*. A general goal of MI is to enhance the patient's confidence in her capacity to cope with obstacles and to succeed in change. The confidence scale represented in Figure 1.1 quickly assesses the patient's level of confidence for a particular behavior change. The dialogue in Box 1.7 illustrates this principle. In this example, the clinician lays out the behavioral discrepancy for the patient in clear terms. The patient is able to articulate the problem and verbalize a solution.

- **Roll with resistance.** Although reluctance to change is to be expected in weight control, resistance (denial, arguing, putting up objections, "yes, but" statements) arises from the interpersonal interaction between the clinician and patient. In this case, the therapeutic relationship is endangered and the counseling process becomes dysfunctional. It is a signal that the patient-clinician rapport is damaged. If this occurs, the clinician's task is to double-back, understand the reason for resistance behavior, and redirect counseling. When you roll with resistance, you do not confront patients; instead, you allow them to express themselves. Using a reflective response serves to acknowledge the person's feelings or perceptions. The dialogue in Box 1.8 illustrates this technique.

Box 1.7 ✦ Supporting Self-Efficacy

Clinician: "F, we've discussed how important it is for you to reduce your calories by at least 500 per day to lose 1 pound per week. We've also discussed strategies and options you can use at dinner, the most difficult time for you. However, it still sounds like your portions are too large, you're filling up on dinner rolls, and you're snacking into the evening. I know you want to lose weight. Help me understand—what is making it difficult for you to choose a healthier dinner?"

F: "I know I need to get my dinner under better control. If I did better planning before dinner, like having a late-afternoon snack to reduce my hunger or ordering half-size entrées, I would do a better job."

Clinician: "That sounds right on target. I'd like you to focus on those strategies this week."

Box 1.8 ✦ Rolling with Resistance

D: "I'm trying as hard as I can, but I'm not losing weight!"

Clinician: "It's frustrating to work hard and not see the results you expect."

D: "That is so true. It's hard to imagine how I can work any harder. I lost 40 pounds the last time I went on a diet, but I can't seem to lose a pound now. What's the use?"

Clinician: "I can see how you are discouraged and even a bit confused about what is going on. Let's take a closer look at your food logs and see if we can find some answers."

Social Cognitive Theory/Ecological Models

Clinicians need to know about the resources that patients have to support behavior change as well as any barriers that may prevent change. Social cognitive theory (SCT) emphasizes the interactions between the person and his or her environment. Behavior, therefore, is a function of aspects of both the environment and the person, all of which are in constant reciprocal interaction (17). The behavioral choices we make regarding what we eat or what we do are determined, in part, by whether resources for acquiring healthy food and engaging in physical activity are accessible, affordable, and available. Ecological models expand our definition of environmental influences to include interpersonal relationships, family, and community. The "built environment," meaning the environment that humans build, is a new concept in viewing behavior (18). For example, patients may be more likely (or less likely) to take a walk depending on neighborhood safety, lighting, sidewalks, traffic, and if there is an enjoyable route. Diet may be determined, in part, by whether the patient has access to neighborhood grocery stores vs large supermarkets, fast-food chains vs sit-down restaurants, or fresh vs processed foods, and by the price of food. These are essential questions to ask the patient before establishing behavior-change goals.

Two central concepts of SCT are self-efficacy and outcome expectations:

- Self-efficacy or confidence, previously mentioned in the discussion of the health belief model and MI, refers to a patient's belief in his or her ability to change or maintain a specific behavior under a variety of circumstances. It is not a general belief about oneself, but a specific belief that is tied to a particular task (12). Higher levels of self-efficacy are predictive of improved treatment outcomes (19). Low self-efficacy may be due to either perceived or actual deficits in personal knowledge, skills, resources, or environmental supports (20).

- Outcome expectations are the degree to which a patient believes that a given course of action will lead to a particular outcome. This is also a central feature of the health belief model. Outcome expectations must be favorable for behavior change to occur. Expectations are typically described as an individual's anticipation of the effects of future experiences (19). The dialogue in Box 1.9 illustrates the assessment of self-efficacy and outcome expectation.

Box 1.9 ✦ Assessing Self-Efficacy and Outcome Expectation

Clinician: "K, you need to reduce your calories by at least 500 every day to lose weight. Based on what I have learned about your diet so far, there are many changes you can make to cut out 500 calories. Do you have any thoughts on what you can do?"

K: "Well, although restaurant eating is probably my biggest problem, that's going to be tough to change. It's really hard for me to cut back when I'm entertaining all the time."

Clinician: "Okay, where do you think you can make a change?"

K: "Starting at home would be better. I can count on my wife to help me. I can ask her to serve me smaller portions and keep some fruit around for snacking. If the fruit is there, I'm more likely to eat it."

Clinician: "Sounds like a plan."

K: "So if I consistently reduce my calories by at least 500 every day, how much weight can I expect to lose?"

Clinician: "As a rule of thumb, it should translate into losing about a pound a week, but results can vary. We'll see how you do when I see you back in a month."

Theory of Planned Behavior

Considering the patient's perceived control over behavior change is also important. This is where the theory of planned behavior (TPB) comes in. According to the TPB, the intention to act is guided by three belief considerations—behavioral beliefs, normative beliefs, and control beliefs (21). Behavioral beliefs refer to the patient's perceived outcomes (benefits and rewards) and attitudes toward engaging in the behavior. Normative beliefs refer to the subjective norms or pressure of others in the family or community regarding the behavior change. Control beliefs refer to the presence of factors that may facilitate or impede performance of the behavior and the perceived power of these factors. In combination, "these three beliefs lead to the formation of a behavioral *intention* to take action" (21), similar to the support provided by a three-legged stool. A key principle of TPB is that behavior change (an observed action) is immediately preceded by intention. Applying this model, "the more favorable the attitude and subjective norm, and the greater the perceived control, the stronger should be the patient's intention to change behavior" (21). This concept is illustrated in Figure 1.2.

However, intention may not be enough. Behavior change will only occur if the patient has a sufficient degree of perceived *and* actual control over the behavior. This is illustrated by an additional direct arrow between perceived behavioral control and behavior. Studies have identified the importance of the TPB in explaining intended behavior change (22-25).

The dialogue in Box 1.10 illustrates the importance of identifying normative beliefs and perceived and actual behavioral control.

Cognitive Behavioral Therapy

When it comes to helping patients take action, cognitive behavioral therapy (CBT) is the most common behavioral therapy used in obesity counseling. It incorporates various strategies intended to help change and reinforce new dietary and physical activity behaviors as well as thoughts and attitudes (26,27). Rather than exploring the psychological underpinning for behavior that may be rooted in childhood (the past), CBT focuses on short-term, problem-oriented treatments that address the present and future. The primary aim of CBT is to produce cognitive change, that is, attention to inner thoughts, attitudes, and emotions as well as to the events that both trigger and result from our actions (28).

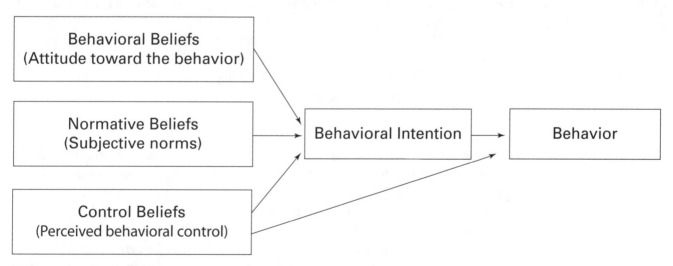

Figure 1.2 Theory of planned behavior model.

Box 1.10 ✦ Identifying Normative Beliefs and Perceived and Actual Behavioral Control

Clinician: "We've talked about how the food around the office and on everyone's desk is problematic for you. By keeping food diaries over the past 2 weeks, we've identified that you are getting about 500 extra calories by eating candy and other munchies every day. What's the likelihood that you can change the office environment?"

P: "That's going to be a problem. First of all, my coworkers like having food around. None of them have the same weight problem I have or don't seem to care. My boss is the one who fills the candy dish every Monday morning. I've already talked to the coworkers immediately around me, and they said they would try to be more conscientious about limiting the treats. I'm thinking about this all day long. I can't tell people what they can or cannot do."

Clinician: "Here's an idea. Perhaps you can help change what people bring into the office. Instead of a candy dish, what about a fruit bowl? You can make it a community effort where everyone who wants to contribute can. At least there would be an alternative to the candy and nuts. Who knows, maybe it will catch on."

P: "That's really a good idea. I'm going to try it."

Clinicians need to guide patients to think about behavior changes in specific terms, such as when, where, how, and with whom the change will occur. It is not enough for the patient to say "I am going to exercise some more." The patient needs to think about when (first thing in the morning), where (in the basement), how and how often (using the treadmill for 30 minutes three times per week). This constitutes a specific plan of action. By instructing patients on an assortment of specific strategies, they are able to more successfully self-manage their behavior.

Behavior is a function of the person in interaction with the environment; this is in contrast to "willpower," which implies that some entity, inner strength, or psychological makeup is all that is needed to lose weight. CBT is based on the need to cultivate skills that are developed through knowledge and practice vs just needing good intentions to succeed (12). Patients may come for treatment interested in losing weight (in the contemplation stage of change), but they will need to consciously apply learned techniques and strategies to make something happen.

There are three key traditional CBT techniques for treating patients with obesity: self-monitoring, stimulus control, and cognitive restructuring. We have found that all of these techniques can be helpful when used selectively. We review each briefly. Three other CBT strategies—stress management, social support, and problem solving—are addressed throughout this book.

Self-Monitoring

The purposes of self-monitoring are to increase awareness of habits; assess eating and exercise habits; reflect on habits; plan; restrain unhealthful habits; and assess the patient's motivation, engagement in, and adherence to the weight loss process. Typical examples of self-monitoring include keeping a journal of one's diet (eg, food groups, total calories, fat grams) and physical activity (eg, type, duration, frequency, intensity), weighing and measuring food, monitoring emotional triggers for eating, recording hunger/satiety before and after eating, and measuring changes in body weight. Recording can be done using pen-and-paper, with a software program for the personal computer or PDA, or by using an Internet tracking program.

Because self-observation is fundamental to self-awareness and behavior change, self-monitoring is one of the most frequently used CBT techniques. Although the term CBT may not be familiar to patients, the experience and feeling of keeping a personal diary is fairly common. Any diary-keeper knows that relationships between activities and behavior become apparent as one observes oneself. Keeping a diary also affords an opportunity to reflect on situations, emotions, and thoughts. It is for this very reason that journaling is an important element in weight management. For patients to successfully change behavior, they have to know what they're currently doing.

Stimulus Control

Stimulus control refers to the influence of antecedent (trigger) conditions on subsequent behavior. These are events that incite or urge one to engage in another associated behavior. Triggers can be physical events, thoughts, emotions, or inner speech. For example, watching television at night in a favorite living room chair can be a signal that induces snacking, being anxious in a bar can lead to drinking alcohol, or seeing a display of candy bars in the grocery store checkout line can prompt a point-of-purchase. Sometimes there are multiple cues leading to a sequence of behaviors called *behavior chains*. For example, an argument with the boss can lead to the following chain of events: anger and frustration, taking a walk to let off some steam, passing a vending machine, seeing packaged cookies, and then purchasing and eating them—even though the patient may not have been hungry or thinking about cookies two minutes earlier. To change these associations, the stimulus control must be broken down and rebuilt (12). For example, changing chairs at home or setting up rules to only eat in the kitchen will reduce television snacking; choosing a different route home that does not pass by your favorite cookie store will reduce temptation. Within a chain of behaviors, such as between an argument and purchasing a snack out of a vending machine, it may be useful to insert a reflective pause by counting to 5 or taking several slow, deep breaths. The goal for patients is always to develop a new behavior, not merely to suppress old behaviors.

Cognitive Restructuring

Cognitive restructuring involves having patients become more aware of their destructive or distorted thoughts and beliefs about themselves and teaching them to actively challenge and change their internal dialogue (26). These thoughts tend to occur in three principal areas—(a) dealing with setbacks, (b) self-criticism regarding self-esteem and body image issues, and (c) difficulty accepting less than desired weight loss (29). Examples of common cognitive distortions include:

- All-or-nothing thinking ("I've blown my diet so I might as well eat whatever I want.")
- Overgeneralization ("I've only lost 5 pounds this month so what's the use?")
- Discounting the positives ("I'm so fat, how can anybody stand to look at me?")

As patients are taught to directly challenge these irrational thoughts, they learn to "restructure" their beliefs. The dialogue in Box 1.11 exemplifies this technique. In this example, the patient has a short-term lapse in behaviors due to a change in her environment. She catastrophizes the situation and generalizes her failure. The clinician is able to help her rationalize the events and reinforce her ability to resume positive self-care strategies.

Box 1.11 ✦ Counseling a Patient to Restructure Beliefs

T: "I had a miserable week. I stopped doing everything we have been working on for the past few months and my weight shows it—I'm up 1 pound! This is not working."

Clinician: "What happened this week?"

T: "My in-laws stayed with us. I was catering to them day and night. We were out every day including lunch and dinner."

Clinician: "That's understandable. For all the eating out you did, I think it's pretty good that you only gained 1 pound. You must have been doing many things right to hold your own this week."

T: "Well, I tried to eat as healthy as I could. I was particularly careful about portion sizes and split entrées with my husband. I also did not eat any fried foods."

Clinician: "Kudos to you! So what did you stop doing which you are so concerned about?"

T: "I completely stopped keeping the food diary. And I didn't have time to have my usual breakfast. Many mornings we rushed out of the house."

Clinician: "T, it actually sounds like you are being too hard on yourself. Whenever guests stay in the home, the usual routine is disrupted. Now that they are gone, can you resume the strategies that you have been using successfully?"

T: "Yes, I guess so."

Clinician: "Do you have any concerns that they will not work again?"

T: "No. They should work. I really feel more in control when I keep a food diary and I can plan my day."

Clinician: "Good. Let's review the goals for this week. . . ."

Behavioral Attributes of Individuals Who Are Successful in Weight Loss

Although there is no such thing as an ideal patient, the following change-predisposing attributes typically lead to behaviors that promote weight loss:

- Strongly wants and intends to change for clear, personal reasons
- Faces a minimum of obstacles (information-processing, physical, logistical, or environmental barriers) to change
- Has the requisite skills and self-confidence to make a change
- Feels positively about the change and believes it will result in meaningful benefit(s)
- Perceives the change as congruent with his or her self-image and social group norms
- Receives reminders, encouragement, and support to change at appropriate times and places from valued individuals and community sources, and is in a largely supportive community/environment for the change

By assessing these qualities, the clinician can determine whether an individual is a ready candidate for lifestyle modification. Although it is unlikely that every patient will display all six qualities, they provide a useful benchmark for assessment. These attributes are a summation from the health behavior-change theories and models that predispose an individual to successful behavior change (30).

Summing It Up

Behavior-change theories are intended to explain the biological, cognitive, behavioral, psychological, environmental, and motivational determinants of human behavior. Thus, they also define interventions to produce changes in knowledge, attitudes, motivation, self-confidence, skills, and social support required for behavior change and maintenance (30). As previously mentioned, a skilled clinician mixes and matches all of these behavior-change principles, strategies, and techniques during obesity counseling. Often, a clinician will use several methods with a single patient, with the selection of counseling approaches determined by the targeted behavior and course of treatment. In the following chapters, these state-of-the-art methods will be applied using a Lifestyle Pattern–specific approach to eating, physical activity, and coping behaviors.

References

1. Coulehan JL, Platt FW, Egener B, Frankel R, Lin CT, Lown B, Salazar WH. "Let me see if I have this right . . . ": words that help build empathy. *Ann Intern Med.* 2001;135:221-227.

2. Bendapudi NM, Berry LL, Frey KA, Parish JT, Rayburn WL. Patients' perspectives on ideal physician behaviors. *Mayo Clin Proc.* 2006;81:338-344.

3. Roter D. The enduring and evolving nature of the patient-physician relationship. *Patient Educ Couns.* 2000;39:5-15.

4. Prochaska JO, DiClemente CC. Stages and processes of self-change of smoking: toward an integrative model of change. *J Consult Clin Psychol.* 1983;51:390-395.

5. Prochaska JO, DiClemente CC. Toward a comprehensive model of change. In: Miller WR, ed. *Treating Addictive Behaviors.* New York, NY: Plenum Press;1986:3-27.

6. Kushner RF. Roadmaps for Clinical Practice: Case Studies in Disease Prevention and Health Promotion—Assessment and Management of Adult Obesity: A Primer for Physicians. Chicago, IL: American Medical Association; 2003. http://www.ama-assn.org/ama/pub/category/10931.html. Accessed September 8, 2007.

7. Prochaska JO, Velicer WF. The transtheoretical model of health behavior change. *Am J Health Promot.* 1997;12:38-48.

8. Levenson W, Cohen MS, Brandy D, Duffy ED. To change or not to change: "Sounds like you have a dilemma." *Ann Intern Med.* 2001;135:386-390.

9. Becker MH. The health belief model and sick-role behavior. *Health Ed Monographs.* 1974;2:409-419.

10. Janz NK, Champion VL, Strecher VJ. The health belief model. In: Glanz K, Rimer BK, Lewis FM, eds. *Health Behavior and Health Education: Theory, Research, and Practice.* 3rd ed. San Francisco, CA: Jossey-Bass; 2002:45-66.

11. Ryan RM, Deci EL. Self-determination theory and the facilitation of intrinsic motivation, social development, and well-being. *Am Psychol.* 2000;55:68-78.

12. Watson DL, Tharp RG, eds. *Self-Directed Behavior. Self-Modification for Personal Adjustment.* 8th ed. Belmont, CA: Wadsworth Group; 2002.

13. Miller WR, Rollnick S, eds. *Motivational Interviewing: Preparing People for Change.* 2nd ed. New York, NY: Guilford Press; 2002.

14. Britt E, Hudson SM, Blampied NM. Motivational interviewing in health settings: a review. *Patient Educ Couns.* 2004;53:147-155.

15. Katz DL. Behavior modification in primary care: the pressure system model. *Prev Med.* 2001;32:66-72.

16. Rollnick S, Mason P, Butler C. *Health Behavior Change: A Guide for Practitioners.* London: Churchill Livingstone; 1999.

17. Baranowski T, Cullen KW, Nicklas T, Thompson D, Baranowski J. Are current health behavioral change models helpful in guiding prevention of weight gain efforts? *Obes Res.* 2003;11(Suppl):23S-43S.

18. Booth KM, Pinkston MM, Poston WS. Obesity and the built environment. *J Am Diet Assoc.* 2005;105(5 Suppl 1):S110-S117.

19. Witkiewitz K, Marlatt GA. Relapse prevention for alcohol and drug problems: that was zen, this is tao. *Am Psychol.* 2004;59:224-235.

20. Rosal MC, Ebbeling CB, Lofgren I, Ockene JK, Ockene IS, Herbert JR. Facilitating dietary change: the patient-centered counseling model. *J Am Diet Assoc.* 2001;101:332-338,341.

21. Aizen I. Theory of Planned Behavior. http://www.people.umass.edu/aizen/tpb.html. Accessed September 7, 2008.

22. Brickell TA, Chatzisarantis NL, Pretty GM. Autonomy and control: augmenting the validity of the theory of planned behaviour in predicting exercise. *J Health Psychol.* 2006;11:51-63.

23. Rhodes RE, Bianchard CM, Matheson DH. A multicomponent model of the theory of planned behaviour. *Br J Health Psychol.* 2006;11:119-137.

24. Brug J, De Vet E, de Nooijer J, Verplanken B. Predicting fruit consumption; cognitions, intention, and habits. *J Nutr Educ Behav.* 2006;38:73-81.

25. Armitage CJ, Conner M. Efficacy of the theory of planned behaviour: a meta-analytic review. *Br J Soc Psychol.* 2001;40:471-499.

26. Foreyt JP, Poston WS 2nd. What is the role of cognitive-behavior therapy in patient management? *Obes Res.* 1998;6(Suppl 1):18S-22S.

27. Wadden TA, Foster GD. Behavioral treatment of obesity. *Med Clin North Am.* 2000;84:441-446.

28. Williamson DA, Perrin LA. Behavioral therapy for obesity. *Endocrinol Metab Clin North Am.* 1996;25:943-954.

29. Wadden TA, Crerand CE, Brock J. Behavioral treatment of obesity. *Psychiatr Clin North Am.* 2005;28:151-170.

30. Whitlock EP, Orleans CT, Pender N, Allan J. Evaluating primary care behavioral counseling interventions: an evidence-based approach. *Am J Prev Med.* 2002;22:267-284.

Chapter 2

✦ ✦ ✦

An Introduction to the Lifestyle Patterns Approach

Overview

Lifestyle modification, which includes the three components of diet, physical activity, and behavior change, is the standard of care for treating overweight and obesity (1). Although clinicians generally know this, the concept of a lifestyle modification program may be new to many patients, especially those who are "chronic dieters" who have tried and failed popular, food-only fad diets.

Commonly, lifestyle modification is delivered to patients either individually or in small groups, in a series of planned lessons or using another standardized format, and by professionals who have differing skills. Because every clinician tries to "connect" with his or her patient to provide pertinent and meaningful guidance, the most significant challenge is to deliver obesity care specific to the patient's lifestyle—that is, provide a treatment that is tailored and individualized to each person's preferences, habits, priorities, time availability, likes and dislikes, style, attitudes, abilities, and culture. When general medical patients were asked to rank 28 expectations of care prior to seeing their clinician, Kravitz found that "discussion of [the patients'] own ideas about how to manage [their] condition" was ranked as the highest item (2). As explained in Chapter 1, an individualized approach uses "patient-centered" or "relationship-centered" communication (3). This chapter describes the process by which our patient-centered Lifestyle Patterns Approach was developed. Although this approach offers clinicians a new way to think about and manage overweight clients, all of the treatment strategies used reflect evidence-based recommendations for weight loss and behavior change.

Development

For more than two decades, Robert Kushner, MD, has been counseling overweight and obese patients about how to choose more healthful behaviors and incorporate them into their lifestyle. From the start of his career, he has been using an individualized, collaborative-care approach based on each patient's strengths and goals. He listened to the weight gain, loss, and regain stories of thousands of overweight

17

adults, and even though they were on different diets, he began to identify common themes in their stories. Patients would go on a new diet and initially lose weight. Then, before they knew it, their old lifestyle habits (or patterns) would slowly creep back into their lives and they would regain the weight.

For some time, clinicians have understood how recidivism and weight regain affect overall weight-loss outcomes. In the publication *Weighing the Options: Criteria for Evaluating Weight-Management Programs,* Thomas states that "those who complete weight loss programs lose approximately 10% of their body weight, only to regain two thirds of it back within 1 year and almost all of it back within 5 years" (4, p.1). Thus far, behavior and obesity specialists have primarily focused on defining the high-risk situations (emotional and physical events) that cause recidivism and developing relapse-prevention strategies (effective coping response and increased self-efficacy) (5-7). Additional research has centered on the identification of overall dietary intake pattern structures (combination of food groups) that are associated with either weight gain or weight loss (8-10).

In 2001, Dr. Kushner took a different diagnostic and therapeutic direction. Rather than only looking at high-risk situations, teaching relapse-prevention techniques, or counseling on prudent nutritional food group choices, he looked at the lifestyle habits or patterns of individuals who drifted away from their weight control program. From his experiences at both Northwestern Memorial Hospital and the University of Chicago, he realized that these recidivist patients always slid back into old habits—they seldom, if ever, slid back into new habits. Dr. Kushner theorized that patients tended to return to ingrained, unhealthful habits at unguarded moments, particularly in times of stress and poor planning. Based on his understanding of the literature pertaining to one's eating, exercise, and emotional coping patterns of behavior, along with his empirical observations, he categorized these patterns or habits into distinct eating, exercise, and coping lifestyle patterns that contributed to weight gain—a central theme that had not been previously addressed in the recidivism literature. Figure 2.1 displays how Dr. Kushner has organized the 21 identified lifestyle patterns within the three lifestyle dimensions (definitions and descriptions of each pattern are explained in Chapters 4, 5, and 6).

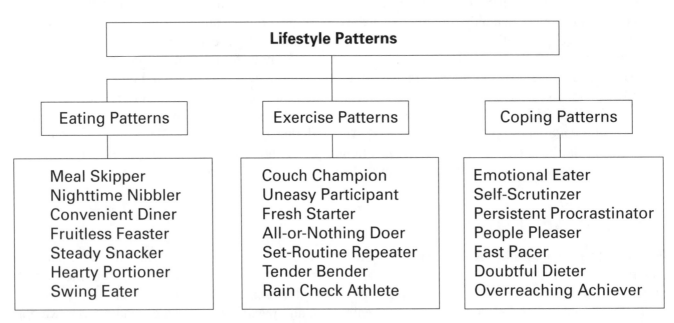

Figure 2.1 Lifestyle Patterns organizational chart.

Dr. Kushner proposed that the key to helping people take control of their body weight was not simply to instruct them on a new diet or a new behavior, but rather to help them first identify and then learn to manage their unique and relapsing lifestyle patterns that kept derailing their success. Furthermore, if a lapse did occur, Kushner believed his approach would prepare patients to be on guard for the reappearance of their old habits and be ready to take corrective action. He called this new method the Lifestyle Patterns Approach (11).

Key Principles of the Lifestyle Patterns Approach

The Lifestyle Patterns Approach is based on the following four principles:

- We live in an obesogenic society that causes people to develop specific weight-gaining lifestyle patterns or habits.
- Each person has his or her own personal weight-gain story to tell based on his or her own life events.
- A lifestyle pattern–specific approach (modeled after a symptom-pattern approach used in medicine) lets clinicians give individualized care to their overweight and obese clients.
- Treatment must be multidimensional.

Principle 1: We Live in an Obesogenic Society

Many people tend to blame themselves for being overweight or obese. However, as we have seen in Chapter 1, behavior and obesity researchers have tried to understand the epidemic of overweight and obesity using an ecological approach (12,13). Knowing that people adapt to and harmonize with their environment, it makes sense to expect that energy imbalance and weight gain will occur when large portions of high-calorie food are available 24/7 and technology has essentially engineered activity out of our daily lifestyle. Thus, overweight, obesity, and an unhealthful lifestyle could be considered the norm rather than the exception. As discussed previously, this supposition is supported by the latest statistics that show that people who can maintain a healthful body weight are in the minority.

As shown in Figures 2.2–2.4, the availability of inexpensive, unhealthful food, the advances of technology, and the pressures of time often trump patients' intentions to make healthful choices. Patients know that they need to eat more healthfully and be more active, but the pressures to do the opposite are sometimes too hard to overcome.

The Lifestyle Patterns Approach provides patients with specific strategies so they can tackle these pressures head-on. In accordance with the ecological approach to weight management, it's important that patients focus on three different settings that can affect their weight: their home, work, and social environments. As you will see in the case studies and patient dialogue examples presented in Chapters 4, 5, and 6, lifestyle pattern–specific strategies can easily target a patient's environment and be applied differently, depending on the patient's home life, work situation, or social circumstance.

Principle 2: Each Person Has His or Her Own Weight-Gain Story to Tell

The average American adult gains 1 to 2 pounds each year due to a subtle imbalance in the amount of calories consumed and the amount expended (14). The imbalance has multiple causes, including genetic, biological, environmental, social, cultural, and psychological factors. In Dr. Kushner's publication for consumers (15), he coined the term "Scaling Up Syndrome" to reflect the constellation of factors that adults experience throughout life that cause them to gain weight. This syndrome occurs while people are

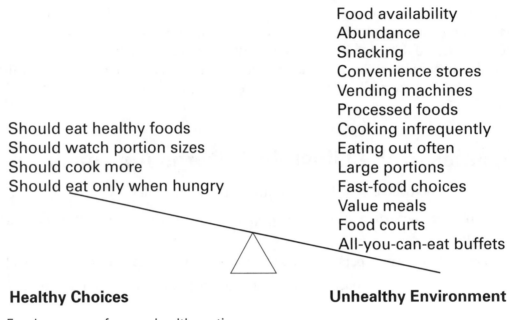

Figure 2.2   Food pressures favor unhealthy eating.

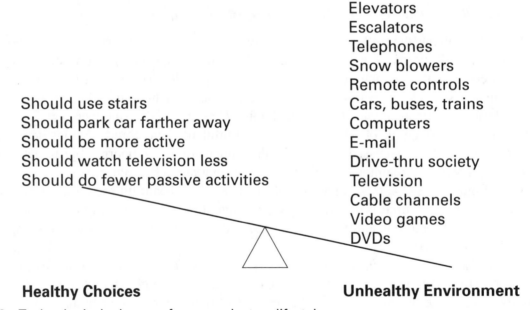

Figure 2.3   Technological advances favor a sedentary lifestyle.

maturing through the stages of adult life, focusing on their families and jobs, and putting their health on the backburner. Before they know it, with each passing year, they find themselves "scaling up" their weight (15). This weight gain is unintentional and unplanned.

Most patients can recall their approximate weight at different stages of life—upon entering college, when getting married, after each pregnancy, when starting a new job, when suffering an illness, quitting smoking, or going through menopause—the list goes on. Epidemiological and clinical studies have confirmed that weight gain is associated with key life events, including:

- Freshman year in college (16,17)
- Marriage (18,19)

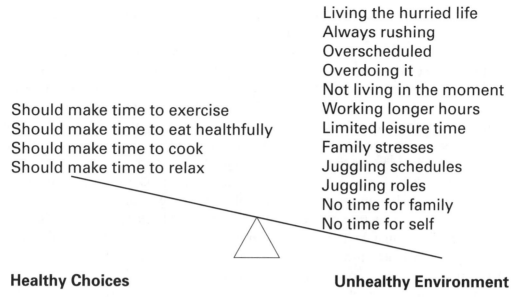

Living the hurried life
Always rushing
Overscheduled
Overdoing it
Not living in the moment
Should make time to exercise   Working longer hours
Should make time to eat healthfully   Limited leisure time
Should make time to cook   Family stresses
Should make time to relax   Juggling schedules
Juggling roles
No time for family
No time for self

Healthy Choices   **Unhealthy Environment**

Figure 2.4   Time pressures promote a hurried lifestyle.

- Pregnancy (20,21)

- Menopause (22)

- Smoking cessation (23,24)

- Holiday celebrations (25,26)

- Starting certain medications (27)

- Increased automobile commute time (28)

- Living in a low-income neighborhood (29)

The Lifestyle Patterns Approach helps people appreciate how specific life events have affected their lifestyle habits and weight gain. This awareness is key to helping people get control of their weight, as certain life events can be a red flag for weight regain. Chapter 3 provides examples of this syndrome in graphical form and explains how this information is used to begin the counseling process and establish a treatment plan.

Principle 3: Care Must Be Individualized

When helping patients lose weight, one size does not fit all in terms of treatment. For example, why should a 52-year-old traveling salesman who eats most meals on the road and hates exercise be given the same program as a 35-year-old mother of three who finishes her children's food and wants to exercise but can't find the time? Clearly, these individuals have different lifestyles, responsibilities, support systems, and obstacles. The Lifestyle Patterns Approach offers each patient a weight management program that fits his or her lifestyle.

The American Dietetic Association (ADA) and other reputable organizations (30,31) support individualized care as part of lifestyle modification counseling. ADA's Adult Weight Management Evidence-Based Nutrition Practice Guideline (published in 2006) discusses making a thorough clinical assessment to develop a more individualized therapeutic approach (32). An individualized treatment approach is also recommended for the management of people with diabetes who require counseling on lifestyle modification. The 2006 American Diabetes Association Standards of Medical Care states that "the management plan should be formulated as an individualized therapeutic alliance among the patient and family, the physician, and other members of the health care team" (33).

The use of pattern recognition to individualize treatment is an established therapeutic modality in medicine, but it has not been previously applied to the management of obesity. For example, diabetes management routinely includes a review of blood glucose patterns in relation to meal times, carbohydrate intake, and administration of diabetes medication. Individuals with asthma are routinely questioned about their symptom patterns of wheezing, coughing, or shortness of breath brought on by exercise or exposure to environmental allergens, cold air, or tobacco. In both examples, patterns are used to identify the problem, develop strategies to control or resolve the problem, and monitor response and progress. For example, if a blood glucose pattern reveals higher levels in the afternoon, the patient is instructed to limit the amount of carbohydrate consumed at lunch or increase the amount of short-acting insulin. The effect of the interaction is a normalized blood glucose pattern, and the result is improved diabetes control. In the case of asthma management, a bronchodilator may be prescribed for use prior to exercise. A beneficial response to treatment is confirmed by improvement in the exercise-induced symptom pattern, and the result is symptom-free exercise. Exacerbation of either condition can be explicitly monitored by a reoccurrence of the symptom patterns. This would then prompt the patient and clinician to take action. Using a patient's eating, exercise, and coping habits for symptom pattern recognition follows the same principles.

Principle 4: Treatment Must Be Multidimensional

Losing weight and living a more healthful lifestyle are not just about finding that perfect ratio of carbohydrate and protein in the foods on one's plate. Many patients can successfully lose weight following a food-only diet program, but successful weight maintenance over the long term usually requires addressing one's overall lifestyle habits and paying attention to how easily lifestyle habits can fluctuate with the normal ups and downs that life can bring.

Weight-management clinicians know very well the multiple influences that can quickly derail a dieter's program: for example, family or work stress can lead to emotional eating; a new job may require a long commute that steals away one's needed time for exercise; hosting family guests for a holiday celebration disrupts day-to-day eating and exercise routines. It is not unusual to find that yo-yo dieters can finally stop cycling once they learn to better cope with these types of stresses of daily life.

Use in Interdisciplinary Teams and Virtual Teams

The Lifestyle Patterns Approach is specifically designed to address the eating, exercise, and coping problems that health care providers are likely to encounter when working with patients. Many clinicians find that they do not need to work with other providers to use this holistic approach to help patients gain control of their weight. However, the complex health and psychosocial needs of overweight and obese adults often require services of more than one type of health care professional. Establishing an integrative team approach can be a useful strategy.

Effective counseling of overweight and obese adults requires that health care providers know when to refer patients to additional resources, such as a primary care physician or nurse practitioner, weight-loss surgeon, certified diabetes educator, registered dietitian (RD), health psychologist, psychiatrist, exercise specialist or personal trainer, commercial weight-loss group, or online program. Methods for working with other team members and when to refer patients will be discussed throughout the book.

Two key features of successful teams are communication and a shared philosophy. Teamwork entails coordination and delegation of tasks among providers and staff (34). A sense of "groupness," defined as the degree to which the group practice identifies itself and functions as a team, will enhance the quality and efficiency of care (35). As you learn the workings of the Lifestyle Patterns Approach, you will also learn a common language that can be used among professionals, how to foster continuity of care, and when to refer patients to other team members—even if the "team" you are working with is off-site.

Dr. Kushner's Lifestyle Patterns Approach has been used and studied in two different team-type settings: an interdisciplinary team setting in a hospital-based wellness program and an online virtual team setting. The Lifestyle Patterns Approach was used from 2001 through 2007 at Northwestern Memorial Hospital's Wellness Institute in Chicago where Dr. Kushner and Dawn Jackson Blatner both worked—Dr. Kushner as medical director and Jackson Blatner as an RD. The Wellness Institute was an interdisciplinary team setting of physicians, RDs, a nurse practitioner, exercise physiologists, and health psychologists who treated people with lifestyle-related disorders. Most of the initial research was done in this setting. Since leaving the Wellness Institute in August 2007, Dr. Kushner continues to use the Lifestyle Patterns Approach in his Lifestyle Medicine program at Northwestern Memorial Hospital.

Since June 2004, Dr. Kushner's Lifestyle Patterns Approach has been adapted as an online program on Diet.com (http://www.diet.com), where Dr. Kushner is medical director of the Diet.com premium program. Adapting the program to an online format required Dr. Kushner to change some of the original lifestyle-pattern names published in the *Personality Type Diet* book (15) to make them more user-friendly for a mass media, online format. These pattern name changes are included for your reference in Appendix D. The Diet.com virtual team includes Dr. Kushner, an RD, and a community support leader. This team is available by e-mail and on the message boards to answer member questions and guide them through the program. Diet.com also offers diet buddies and weight-loss challenge groups to provide social support.

Research

The Lifestyle Patterns Approach has been systematically studied. Validation of the patterns questionnaire was done with a convenience sample of 100 overweight and obese patients from the Wellness Institute (36). A 70-item self-assessment questionnaire was developed by Dr. Kushner to characterize the 21 eating, exercise, and coping patterns that were empirically identified in clinical practice. Participants were asked to use a six-point Likert scale to indicate their level of agreement or disagreement with each statement. Participants were then asked to complete a second questionnaire, which presented a brief description of all 21 lifestyle patterns and requested participants to identify their top three eating, exercise, and coping patterns. Agreement between the patterns questionnaire and validation measure was done using χ^2 tests. Statistically significant positive correlations were seen between body mass index (BMI) and number of patterns scored by both questionnaires. Agreement between subscales scored by both self-identified patterns was observed for 14 of 21 lifestyle patterns. Internal consistency reliabilities for the 21 lifestyle pattern subscales ranged from .35 to .90. On the basis of this analysis and further item analysis, seven items were deleted and three items were added to generate a revised 66-item questionnaire that has been used since 2003. To increase specificity, the questionnaire has been further refined to 50 items, as presented in this publication.

A prevalence study was subsequently done among 335 patients in the Wellness Institute who completed the lifestyle-patterns questionnaire (37). Seventy-eight percent were women with a mean age of 44 years and mean BMI of 40.3. For this study, a patterns scoring cutoff of 33% was designated as having a clinically meaningful pattern. The most prevalent set of patterns was related to the coping symptoms. All seven clinically relevant coping patterns were endorsed by more than 50% of the patients, compared with five eating patterns and three exercise patterns. These results suggest that while overweight and obese patients use a wide range of coping styles, their number of expressed eating and exercise patterns are more limited. Among all participants, the top three endorsed patterns were all coping patterns ("People Pleaser," "Persistent Procrastinator," and "Overreaching Achiever"). Compared with men, women scored significantly higher on four patterns: "Self Scrutinizer," "People Pleaser," "Couch Champion," and "Uneasy Participant." Men scored significantly higher than women on one pattern: "Hearty Portioner."

To assess the prevalence of patterns among a broader base of dieters, a convenience sample of 502,524 members of Diet.com was taken for an unpublished study. Among this sample, 87% were female with a mean age of 32.7 years and mean BMI of 30.5. For this study, a patterns scoring cutoff of 50% was designated as having a clinically meaningful pattern because the mean age and BMI of the sample was less than the study conducted in the Wellness Institute. On average, each dieter endorsed 3.4 eating patterns, 2.4 exercise patterns, and 3.8 coping patterns as their problem habits.

Kushner and associates also completed a 12-month prospective people and pets weight-loss study in which the Lifestyle Patterns Approach was used in a group format (38). In this study, 92 overweight men and women met weekly for the first 16 weeks (treatment phase), then once per month at months 5, 6, 9, and 12 (maintenance phase). Group sessions were led by Dawn Jackson Blatner and other RDs, who instructed participants in the Lifestyle Patterns Approach along with use of commercial meal-replacement products. Among the 61% who completed the study, percentage of weight loss at 6 months ranged from 6.6% to 8.2%; at 12 months, the range was 5.5% to 6.6%.

Although the Lifestyle Patterns Approach was developed empirically, the origin is founded on principles, observations, and research obtained from behavioral and medical literature. Pattern recognition is becoming increasingly important in epidemiological research and is linked to health outcomes (8-10). The patterns approach described in this publication is used therapeutically to provide a more targeted and patient-centered counseling process. Tables 2.1, 2.2, and 2.3 display the four distinct, targeted treatment strategies for each of the 21 lifestyle patterns within the three dimensions of eating, exercise, and coping. In the following chapters, we show you how to apply this treatment approach in the counseling process.

Table 2.1 ✦ Eating Pattern–Specific Strategies at a Glance

Meal Skipper	Nighttime Nibbler	Convenient Diner	Fruitless Feaster	Steady Snacker	Hearty Portioner	Swing Eater
Plan three meals each day	Spread calories evenly throughout the day	Eat smaller portions	Have produce ready and on hand	Keep a snacking log	Slow down your eating	Embrace all foods
Focus on your meal	Remove unhealthy foods from the home	Reduce added fat and beverage calories	Make fruits and vegetables flavorful	Pre-plan snacks—when and what	Eat more food for fewer calories	Add fiber and healthy fats for more eating pleasure
Track your hunger and fullness	Plan one nightly snack that satisfies	Use available nutrition information	Pick colorful produce	Stock up on healthy choices	Know serving sizes	Enjoy once off-limit foods in smaller portions
Fill up on water and fiber	Reset your nighttime routine	Practice quick cooking at home	Eat more vegetarian meals	Tame what triggers too much snacking	Avoid portion traps	Socialize and enjoy

Table 2.2 ✦ Exercise Pattern–Specific Strategies at a Glance

Couch Champion	Uneasy Participant	Fresh Starter	All-or-Nothing Doer	Set-Routine Repeater	Tender Bender	Rain Check Athlete
See benefits	Dress the part	Increase your confidence	Tone it down	Change the pace	Set limits	Fit in walking
Move more	Work out at home	Plan aerobic exercise	Be consistent	Vary workout type	Make activity time short and sweet	Schedule activity in a date book
Count steps	Sneak in walks	Build muscle	Enjoy building skills	Add weight lifting	Adapt your program	Combine activity with other things
Buddy up	Be mindful when moving	Improve flexibility	Prevent relapse	Try exercise tools	Seek expert advice	Ask for help

Table 2.3 ◆ Coping Pattern–Specific Strategies at a Glance

Emotional Eater	Self-Scrutinizer	Persistent Procrastinator	People Pleaser	Fast Pacer	Doubtful Dieter	Overreaching Achiever
Track your feelings	Be real about body image	List pros and cons	Commit to self-care	Take a new look at your life	Alter your fate	Describe weight goals
Know your triggers	Stop body-checking	Set mini-goals	Plan your yeses	Stay aware in the present	Confront your beliefs	Find new measures of success
Cope without food	Think positive thoughts	Prompt yourself	Say "no" like a pro	Seek support	Distract and dispute	Trim goals
De-stress	Enjoy your body	Use rewards	Assign tasks to others	Recharge and relax	Help yourself	Accept limits

Summing It Up

You will notice that symmetry was present in the design and development of the Lifestyle Patterns Approach: the three dimensions of eating, exercise, and coping; the seven patterns within each of the three dimensions; and the four strategies specific to each of the patterns. However, you will also see in the following chapters that what seems to be an exact, "cookie-cutter" approach actually allows for flexibility, variability, and personalization as clinicians and patients together can decide which patterns and strategies to work on. In the next chapter, we review how to use the Lifestyle Patterns Approach with your overweight clients.

References

1. National Heart, Lung, and Blood Institute. Clinical guidelines on the identification, evaluation, and treatment of overweight and obesity in adults: the evidence report. *Obes Res.* 1998;6(Suppl 2):51S-210S.

2. Kravitz RL. Measuring patients' expectations and requests. *Ann Intern Med.* 2001;134:881-888.

3. Roter D. The enduring and evolving nature of the patient-physician relationship. *Patient Educ Couns.* 2000;39:5-15.

4. Thomas PR, ed; Committee to Develop Criteria for Evaluating the Outcomes to Prevent and Treat Obesity, Institute of Medicine. *Weighing the Options: Criteria for Evaluating Weight-Management Programs.* Washington, DC: National Academy Press, 1995.

5. Grilo CM, Shiffman S, Wing RR. Relapse crises and coping among dieters. *J Consult Clin Psychol.* 1989;57:488-495.

6. Byrne S, Cooper Z, Fairburn C. Weight maintenance and relapse in obesity: a quantitative study. *Int J Obes Relat Metab Disord.* 2003;27:955-962.

7. Marlatt GA. Relapse prevention: theoretical rationale, and overview of the model. In: Marlatt GA, Gordon JR, eds. *Relapse Prevention.* New York, NY: Guilford Press; 1985:250-280.

8. Togo P, Osler M, Sorensen TI, Heitmann BL. Food intake patterns and body mass index in observational studies. *Int J Obes Relat Disord.* 2001;25:1741-1751.

9. Newby PK, Muller D, Hallfrisch J, Andres R, Tucker KL. Food patterns measured by factor analysis and anthropometric changes in adults. *Am J Clin Nutr.* 2004;80:504-513.

10. Schulze MB, Fung TT, Manson JE, Willett WC, Hu FB. Dietary patterns and changes in body weight in women. *Obesity.* 2006;14:1444-1453.

11. Kushner RF. Lifestyle patterns approach to weight management. *Obes Manage.* 2007;3:121-124.

12. Brug J, van Lenthe FJ, Kremers PJ. Revisiting Kurt Lewin: how to gain insight into environmental correlates of obesogenic behaviors. *Am J Prev Med.* 2006;31:1-5.

13. French SA, Story M, Jeffery RW. Environmental influences on eating and physical activity. *Annu Rev Public Health.* 2001;22:309-335.

14. Hill JO, Wyatt HR, Reed GW, Peters JC. Obesity and the environment: where do we go from here? *Science.* 2003;299:853-855.

15. Kushner R, Kushner N. *Dr. Kushner's Personality Type Diet.* New York, NY: St. Martin's Press; 2003.

16. Morrow ML, Heesch KC, Dinger MK, Hull HR, Kneehans AW, Fields DA. Freshman 15: fact or fiction? *Obesity.* 2006;14:1438-1443.

17. Hoffman DJ, Policastro P, Quick V, Lee SK. Changes in body weight and fat mass of men and women in the first year of college: a study of the "freshman 15." *J Am Coll Health.* 2006;55:41-45.

18. Sobal J, Rauschenbach B, Frongillo EA. Marital status change and body weight changes: a US longitudinal analysis. *Soc Sci Med.* 2003;56:1543-1555.

19. Lee S, Cho E, Grodstein F, Kawachi I, Hu FB, Colditz GA. Effects of marital transitions on changes in dietary and other health behaviors in US women. *Int J Epidemiol.* 2005;34:69-78.

20. Gunderson EP, Murtaugh MA, Lewis CE, Quesenberry CP, West DS, Sidney S. Excess gains in weight and waist circumference associated with childbearing: the Coronary Artery Risk Development in Young Adults Study (CARDIA). *Int J Obes Relat Metab Disord.* 2004;28:525-535.

21. Yeh J, Shelton JA. Increasing prepregnancy body mass index: analysis of trends and contributing variables. *Am J Obstet Gynecol.* 2005;193:1994-1998.

22. Wing RR, Matthews KA, Kuller LH, Meilahn EN, Plantinga PL. Weight gain at the time of menopause. *Arch Intern Med.* 1991;151:97-102.

23. Williamson DF, Madans J, Anda RF, Kleinman JC, Giovino GA, Byers T. Smoking cessation and severity of weight gain in a national cohort. *N Engl J Med.* 1991;324:739-745.

24. O'Hara P, Connett JE, Lee WW, Nides M, Murray R, Wise R. Early and late weight gain following smoking cessation in the Lung Health Study. *Am J Epidemiol.* 1998;148:821-830.

25. Yanovksi JA, Yanovski SZ, Sivik KN, Nguyen TT, O'Neil PM, Sebring NG. A prospective study of holiday weight gain. *N Engl J Med.* 2000;342:861-867.

26. Hull HR, Radley D, Dinger MK, Fields DA. The effect of the Thanksgiving holiday on weight gain. *Nutr J.* 2006;5:29.

27. Malone M. Medications associated with weight gain. *Ann Pharmacother.* 2005;39:2046-2055.

28. Lopez-Zetina J, Lee H, Friis R. The link between obesity and the built environment: evidence from an ecological analysis of obesity and vehicle miles of travel in California. *Health Place.* 2006;12:656-664.

29. Inagami S, Cohen DA, Finch BK, Asch SM. You are where you shop: grocery locations, weight, and neighborhoods. *Am J Prev Med.* 2006;31:10-17.

30. Position Statement of the American Dietetic Association: weight management, *J Am Diet Assoc.* 2002;102:1145-1155.

31. AHA Scientific Statement: diet and lifestyle recommendations. Revision 2006. *Circulation.* 2006; 114:82-96.

32. Adult Weight Management Evidence-based Nutrition Practice Guideline. May 2006. http://www.adaevidencelibrary.com/topic.cfm?cat=3014. Accessed November 26, 2007.

33. Standards of medical care in diabetes. *Diabetes Care.* 2006;29(Suppl):S4-S42.

34. Dickey LL, Gemson DH, Carney P. Office system interventions supporting primary care-based health behavior change counseling. *Am J Prev Med.* 1999;17:299-308.

35. Crabtree BF, Miller WL, Aita VA, Flocke SA, Stange KC. Primary care practice organization and preventive services delivery: a qualitative analysis. *J Fam Pract.* 1998;46:404-409.

36. Kushner RF, Mytko JJ, Kushner N. Using a new symptom pattern approach for management of obesity: development of an introductory questionnaire. *Am J Clin Nutr.* 2002;75(2 Suppl):368S.

37. Kushner R, Mytko J, Pelt J. Coping patterns predominate over eating and exercise patterns as the most prevalent self-identified problems among obese patients. *Obes Res.* 2003;11(Suppl):A103.

38. Kushner R, Jackson D, Jewell D, Rudloff K. The PPET Study—People and pets exercising together. *Obesity.* 2006;14:1762-1770.

Chapter 3

✦ ✦ ✦

Targeted Assessment and Treatment

Overview

The Lifestyle Patterns Approach for treating overweight adults can easily be incorporated into a busy clinician's practice. Both experienced and less experienced clinicians will appreciate its organized, streamlined, and focused counseling approach along with its time-saving benefits.

Patient Assessment

The first step in treating overweight and obese patients is a thorough clinical assessment focused on social, psychological, medical, environmental, and behavioral factors contributing to obesity (1). The information collected during a patient assessment is the springboard from which clinicians can develop empathy—an understanding for each patient's situation, perspectives, and feelings, and begin to individualize weight-management treatment. An assessment typically begins by having patients complete an extensive health assessment questionnaire that will be reviewed and discussed during the first appointment. Different types of questionnaires to assess lifestyle and weight, such as the Weight and Lifestyle Inventory (WALI) developed by Wadden and Foster, are available (2). We have also developed a full Health Assessment Patient Questionnaire, which is available on the CD-ROM for clinicians to use. Clinicians are encouraged to view the Health Assessment Patient Questionnaire on the CD-ROM and follow along as we discuss the different variables needed in an assessment questionnaire.

Clinical Assessment Form Variables

Demographics

The demographics section of the form asks for the patient's name, birthdate, contact information, occupation and work hours, marital status, living and family arrangements, and education level. From the outset, this descriptive information helps clinicians begin understanding each patient's individual situation, which factors into the treatment plan. For example, is the patient a nurse working odd hours or does the patient have his own business and work from home? The answers may potentially affect variables such as access to food, meal timing, or proximity to a gym. Does the patient live alone or with a large family? This may affect food availability and meal-planning issues.

General Health

The general health portion of the form asks for the following:

- Name and contact information of the current physician

- Recent physical examination results and blood work

- Perceived health rating (Patients circle perception of their current health status: poor, fair, good, or excellent.)

- Self-reported height and weight (Self-reported information gives the clinician an idea of the patient's own mindfulness and accuracy of weight-monitoring. Clinicians will measure accurate height and weight during the visit.)

- Review of major body systems: respiratory, cardiovascular, gastrointestinal, genitourinary, musculoskeletal, endocrine, skin, and psychiatric (This section asks patients to report their medical history. Clinician can use referral information, medications list, and laboratory test results to confirm conditions.)

- Family history

- Surgical history

- Tobacco and alcohol use

- Sleep habits (typical number of hours per night spent sleeping)

- Stress (On a scale from 1 to 5, patients circle perception of their current stress level.)

The review of systems is a vital element of the clinical assessment form because the specifics of the food and activity plan should be tailored to the patient's medical needs. For example, if a patient indicates she has high cholesterol or existing heart disease, incorporation of the Third Report of the National Cholesterol Education Program Adult Treatment Panel (NCEP ATP III) Therapeutic Lifestyle Change (TLC) diet may be implemented along with exercise recommendations consistent with guidelines from the American College of Sports Medicine (3,4). A letter to the patient's physician including an outline of the treatment plan can be sent to alert the physician that his/her patient is working with a weight-management professional. (See the Health Care Provider Letter on the CD-ROM.)

Medications and Supplements

The assessment form also asks the patient to report use of prescription medications, over-the-counter (OTC) medications, and dietary supplements (vitamins, minerals, and herbs). By reviewing the patient's current medications and supplements, clinicians can identify how health conditions are being managed and also identify any medications that may potentially contribute to weight gain (see Table 3.1) (5).

Many patients fail to disclose the use of OTC products to their health care providers. Instead of relying only on the patients' responses to the questionnaire, be sure to ask them whether they take any pills, herbs, vitamins, or other products bought from a supermarket, health food vendor, or drugstore. When discussing dietary supplements with patients, it is helpful to answer the following two questions for them:

- "Is there evidence that this supplement may hurt me?"

- "Is there evidence this supplement will help me?"

Table 3.1 ✦ Drugs That May Induce Weight Gain

Drug Category	Examples
Antidepressants	• tricyclic antidepressants (TCAs): amitriptyline (Elavil), imipramine (Tofranil), nortriptyline (Pamelor)
	• selective serotonin reuptake inhibitors (SSRIs): paroxetine (Paxil)
	• monoamine oxidase inhibitors (MAOIs): phenelzine (Nardil), tranylcypromine (Parnate)
	• other: mirtazepine (Remeron)
Mood stabilizers	• lithium
Typical antipsychotics	• chlorpromazine (Thorazine), haloperidol (Haldol)
Atypical antipsychotics	• clozapine (Clozaril), olanzapine (Zyprexa), risperidone (Risperdal)
Anti-epileptic	• valproate (Depakote)
	• gabapentin (Neurontin)
	• carbamazepine (Tegretol)
Diabetes medication	• insulin
	• sulfonylureas: glyburide (DiaBeta), glipizide (Glucotrol)
	• thiazolidinediones: pioglitazone (Actos), rosiglitazone (Avandia)
Steroid hormones	• prednisone, medroxyprogesterone (Depo-Provera)

Adapted from Pi-Sunyer X, Aronne L, Bray G. Weight gain induced by psychotropic drugs. *Obes Manage.* 2007;3:165-169. Used by permission.

Motivation

Patient motivation is a key component for success in a weight-loss program and is a prerequisite for weight-loss therapy. Although it is difficult to quantify, research suggests that patients who have high pretreatment motivation and self-efficacy (the belief and confidence in personal ability to manage life obstacles and successfully achieve goals) may lose more weight than patients with lower motivation and self-efficacy (6). A sense of motivation can be determined after reviewing the answers to such probing questions as:

- "How ready are you to commit time, energy, and resources to weight-loss therapy?"
- "How confident are you in your ability to lose weight and keep it off?"

Current Diet

The information gathered in this section helps clinicians identify potential opportunities for change and targets for dietary counseling. There is a 24-hour recall form to identify eating style, food preferences, and current habits, factors that must be understood at the start of an individualized dietary intervention.

The Current Diet section also asks, "What one or two things would you like to change about your diet?" This is one of the most time-effective questions to ask in a dietary assessment. As patients identify which areas they believe contribute to their weight gain, this streamlines the conversation about specific areas they are motivated to change and improve. The information in this section will be useful to cross-reference after your patient takes the Lifestyle Patterns Quiz described later in this chapter. In most cases, the information in this section will mirror the results of the Lifestyle Patterns Quiz.

Current Activity

This part of the form addresses:

- Activities of daily living
- Planned exercise
- Exercise safety concerns or medical limitations

One of the most enlightening questions clinicians can ask is: "What is the *most* physically active thing you do in an average day?" Patients' answers often help reveal their activity habits along with their attitudes about activity and exercise. Just as in the Current Diet section, you may find it useful to cross reference information in this part of the questionnaire after your patient takes the Lifestyle Patterns Quiz. In most cases, the information in this section will mirror the results of the Lifestyle Patterns Quiz.

Weight History

The second key principle of the Lifestyle Patterns Approach is "each person has his or her own weight gain story to tell based on his or her own life events." It is important for patients to have the opportunity to tell the story of their weight journey in their own words.

Using Graphs to Illustrate Weight History

Dr. Kushner and his staff find it helpful to have patients graph their recall of their weight history. This serves an important purpose of identifying the impact of specific life experiences on weight. Most patients can recall their approximate weight at different stages of life, such as when they got their first driver's license, entered college, started a new job, broke up with a boyfriend or girlfriend, cared for a sick parent, got injured while exercising, or got married. When patients plot these weights on a graph, they begin to appreciate and become aware of how life events have played a role in their personal weight-gain story. Perhaps most importantly, this activity helps clinicians get a better understanding of each patient's past diet attempts, barriers, pitfalls, and triggers.

A blank weight graph is included on the last page of the Health Assessment Patient Questionnaire on the CD-ROM. We strongly encourage clinicians to ask all patients to complete their own graph as part of the assessment process (even if clinicians use their own patient assessment forms).

Discussing Graphs with Patients

The weight graphing activity encourages patient-provider dialogue and the development of empathy (as discussed in Chapter 1). The following two dialogues demonstrate possible counseling approaches.

Clinician: "I would like to talk with you about the weight graph [Figure 3.1] so that I can better understand your situation. I see that your weight gain started in college, continued after two pregnancies, and most recently it appears job stress is contributing to your current weight gain. Tell me why you think your recent job change is causing weight gain?"

P: "I got a demotion. I work so hard and I feel so underappreciated. I have been eating much more junk food around the office to get through the days. I am looking for a new job, but right now I just hate being at work. Sometimes it seems like chocolate, donuts, muffins, and pizza help me tolerate the situation, but I know in the end overeating only hurts me. I am so frustrated with myself."

Clinician: "It sounds like work stress is very difficult for you and it sounds like you are taking charge by looking for a new job. I notice that in the past you have used diet and exercise to lose weight. What types of programs were these and what types of changes did you make?"

P: "Well, that first attempt was more like starvation and crazy exercise before my wedding. I didn't like what I was eating and couldn't keep up the exercise and started gaining weight the day after I got married. I think the second attempt was more realistic. I did a Weight Watchers–type plan although I never went to meetings. Just kept a log and talked to my sister who was going to the meetings. My sister and I gave each other great ideas and kept each other motivated."

Clinician: "That is great. Many people find social support to be helpful. As we develop your treatment plan, we will keep in mind that logging your food helped you in the past and that your sister was also a great support to you. When we review your Lifestyle Patterns, we'll be sure to note whether munching around the office led to a high score for the Steady Snacker eating pattern."

Please draw a graph of your weight gain. Mark *life events* and *diet attempts* that have contributed to your current weight.

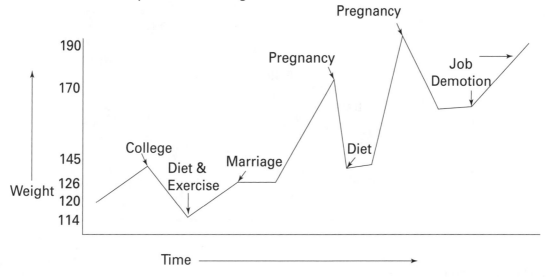

Figure 3.1   Weight graph example 1.

Clinician: "You did a thorough job filling out this weight graph [Figure 3.2]. Let's talk about it together so I can hear more about your weight gain and weight-loss attempts. I see that your weight gain started with traveling for work and continued due to dining out. I also see congratulations are in order because you quit smoking. Most recently, it appears your thyroid medication was changed. In addition to this medical condition, do you still think dining out plays a role in your weight gain?"

T: "Well, now that my thyroid is back to normal with medication, I guess my dining out contributes to my continued weight gain. I go out on business lunches many days during the week and in the evenings I just don't know how to cook so I tend to do take-out."

Clinician: "Okay, it sounds like you are a Convenient Diner when it comes to your diet pattern. We'll check that out when we review your Lifestyle Patterns profile. For now, I am going to make note of our conversation so we may talk about some menu maneuvers you can make for healthier dining out. I also will make a note that we can talk about some lunch and dinner solutions that take just a few minutes and require very little skill to make. Now, I am interested in how you have tried to lose weight in the past. I notice there is mostly exercise with one diet attempt, Atkins."

T: "Yep. I have to exercise to lose weight. The problem is that I go back and forth between frequent exercise and doing nothing. My exercise program never seems to stick."

Clinician: "It sounds like you're an All-or-Nothing Doer when it comes to exercise."

T: "Yes, exactly."

Clinician: "That's actually an exercise pattern that we'll talk about some more after I review your Lifestyle Patterns profile."

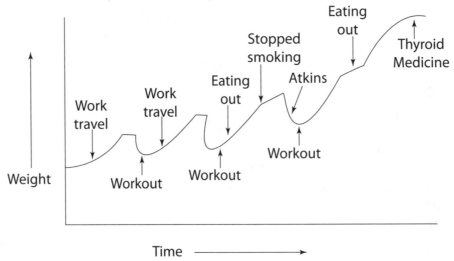

Please draw a graph of your weight gain. Mark life events and diet attempts that have contributed to your current weight.

Figure 3.2   Weight graph example 2.

Anthropometrics

In addition to the patient questionnaire, a complete patient assessment involves measurements and calculations such as:

- Measured height and weight
- Calculated body mass index (BMI)
- Measured waist circumference
- Measured or calculated resting metabolic rate (RMR)

A Weight Flow Sheet is available on the CD-ROM to document these measurements and calculations as part of the initial and follow-up visits. The Weight Flow Sheet offers clinicians an easy way to see a patient's weight progress from visit to visit. Clinicians are encouraged to view the Weight Flow Sheet on the CD-ROM as we discuss the different measurements and calculations.

Height, Weight, and Body Mass Index

To assess your patients' risk for developing obesity-associated diseases such as diabetes, hypertension, and cardiovascular disease, calculate their BMI by first measuring their height and weight. BMI should be calculated for every patient. Clinicians can calculate BMI using one of the following three methods:

- Checking a BMI table (see Table 3.2) (7)
- Using an online BMI calculator, such as the one from the National Heart, Lung, and Blood Institute (http://www.nhlbisupport.com/bmi)
- Using either of the following BMI equations:

$$BMI = \frac{\text{Weight (kg)}}{\text{Height (m)}^2}$$

$$BMI = \frac{\text{Weight (lb)}}{\text{Height (in)}^2} \times 703$$

A normal-weight BMI is 18.5 to 24.9, overweight is 25 to 29.9, and obesity is 30 and greater. Obesity has subcategories to further estimate health risk: Class I is 30 to 34.9, Class II is 35 to 39.9 and Class III is 40 and more (8). With each increasing category, there is an increased risk for developing obesity-related diseases.

Table 3.2 ◆ Body Mass Index

	Normal						Overweight					Obese										Extreme Obesity														
BMI	19	20	21	22	23	24	25	26	27	28	29	30	31	32	33	34	35	36	37	38	39	40	41	42	43	44	45	46	47	48	49	50	51	52	53	54
Height (inches)												Body Weight (pounds)																								
58	91	96	100	105	110	115	119	124	129	134	138	143	148	153	158	162	167	172	177	181	186	191	196	201	205	210	215	220	224	229	234	239	244	248	253	258
59	94	99	104	109	114	119	124	128	133	138	143	148	153	158	163	168	173	178	183	188	193	198	203	208	212	217	222	227	232	237	242	247	252	257	262	267
60	97	102	107	112	118	123	128	133	138	143	148	153	158	163	168	174	179	184	189	194	199	204	209	215	220	225	230	235	240	245	250	255	261	266	271	276
61	100	106	111	116	122	127	132	137	143	148	153	158	164	169	174	180	185	190	195	201	206	211	217	222	227	232	238	243	248	254	259	264	269	275	280	285
62	104	109	115	120	126	131	136	142	147	153	158	164	169	175	180	186	191	196	202	207	213	218	224	229	235	240	246	251	256	262	267	273	278	284	289	295
63	107	113	118	124	130	135	141	146	152	158	163	169	175	180	186	191	197	203	208	214	220	225	231	237	242	248	254	259	265	270	278	282	287	293	299	304
64	110	116	122	128	134	140	145	151	157	163	169	174	180	186	192	197	204	209	215	221	227	232	238	244	250	256	262	267	273	279	285	291	296	302	308	314
65	114	120	126	132	138	144	150	156	162	168	174	180	186	192	198	204	210	216	222	228	234	240	246	252	258	264	270	276	282	288	294	300	306	312	318	324
66	118	124	130	136	142	148	155	161	167	173	179	186	192	198	204	210	216	223	229	235	241	247	253	260	266	272	278	284	291	297	303	309	315	322	328	334
67	121	127	134	140	146	153	159	166	172	178	185	191	198	204	211	217	223	230	236	242	249	255	261	268	274	280	287	293	299	306	312	319	325	331	338	344
68	125	131	138	144	151	158	164	171	177	184	190	197	203	210	216	223	230	236	243	249	256	262	269	276	282	289	295	302	308	315	322	328	335	341	348	354
69	128	135	142	149	155	162	169	176	182	189	196	203	209	216	223	230	236	243	250	257	263	270	277	284	291	297	304	311	318	324	331	338	345	351	358	365
70	132	139	146	153	160	167	174	181	188	195	202	209	216	222	229	236	243	250	257	264	271	278	285	292	299	306	313	320	327	334	341	348	355	362	369	376
71	136	143	150	157	165	172	179	186	193	200	208	215	222	229	236	243	250	257	265	272	279	286	293	301	308	315	322	329	338	343	351	358	365	372	379	386
72	140	147	154	162	169	177	184	191	199	206	213	221	228	235	242	250	258	265	272	279	287	294	302	309	316	324	331	338	346	353	361	368	375	383	390	397
73	144	151	159	166	174	182	189	197	204	212	219	227	235	242	250	257	265	272	280	288	295	302	310	318	325	333	340	348	355	363	371	378	386	393	401	408
74	148	155	163	171	179	186	194	202	210	218	225	233	241	249	256	264	272	280	287	295	303	311	319	326	334	342	350	358	365	373	381	389	396	404	412	420
75	152	160	168	176	184	192	200	208	216	224	232	240	248	256	264	272	279	287	295	303	311	319	327	335	343	351	359	367	375	383	391	399	407	415	423	431
76	156	164	172	180	189	197	205	213	221	230	238	246	254	263	271	279	287	295	304	312	320	328	336	344	353	361	369	377	385	394	402	410	418	426	435	443

Source: Reprinted from National Heart, Lung, and Blood Institute. Body mass index table. http://www.nhlbi.nih.gov/guidelines/obesity/bmi_tbl.htm. Accessed December 7, 2007.

Waist Circumference

In addition to BMI, abdominal fat, which is measured by waist circumference, is an independent risk factor for morbidity and mortality. According to the ATP III report, high risk is associated with a waist circumference more than 40 inches (102 cm) for men and more than 35 inches (88 cm) for women. Lower cutpoints have been recommended for Asian ethnic groups (9). A waist circumference measurement is recommended in patients with a BMI 35 or less to determine whether their distribution of body fat (larger waist circumference) puts them at greater health risk than would be indicated from BMI alone.

To measure waist circumference, the NHLBI Practical Guide to the Identification, Evaluation, and Treatment of Overweight and Obesity in Adults (8) advises the clinician to:

> locate the upper hip bone and the top of the iliac crest. Place a measuring tape in a horizontal plane around the abdomen at the level of the iliac crest. Before reading the tape measure, ensure that the tape is snug, but does not compress the skin, and is parallel to the floor. The measure is made at the end of a normal expiration.

Resting Metabolic Rate

RMR is one component of the total amount of energy (calories) a person burns daily. RMR is the energy needed for daily housekeeping of vital organs and accounts for the majority of calories burned during the day (65% to75%). Thermic effect of food (energy needed to digest and absorb food) accounts for 5% to 10%, and physical activity accounts for 15% to 30% (depending on activity level) (10).

The American Dietetic Association (ADA) Evidence Analysis Library (11) recommends the use of indirect calorimetry to measure RMR for overweight and obese patients. Examples of office-sized indirect calorimetry devices include MedGem (Microlife. Dunedin, FLl http://www.microlife.com), REE-VUE (Korr Medical Technologies. Salt Lake City, UT; http://www.korr.com), or Fitmate (Cosmed. Chicago, IL; http://www.cosmed.it). When choosing an indirect calorimeter, the ADA Evidence Analysis Library recommends reviewing the safety features, ease of use, accuracy, precision, reliability, durability, and the machine's service/maintenance plan. To ensure accurate and reliable measurements, it is important to read the device instructions and follow a standard protocol, such as instructing patients prior to the test to fast (except water) overnight or for at least 5 hours; refrain from exercise for 24 to 48 hours; refrain from caffeine, alcohol, and nicotine for at least 2 hours; and rest lying down for 10 to 20 minutes (11).

Because indirect calorimeters can be quite expensive, measuring RMR is not always possible. In this case, the ADA Evidence Analysis Library (11) recommends that clinicians estimate RMR using the Mifflin-St. Jeor equation (12):

Women: $(9.99 \times \text{Weight [kg]}) + (6.25 \times \text{Height [cm]}) - (4.92 \times \text{Age [y]}) - 161$

Men: $(9.99 \times \text{Weight [kg]}) + (6.25 \times \text{Height [cm]}) - (4.92 \times \text{Age [y]}) + 5$

Once RMR is measured or estimated, the results are multiplied by the patient's typical activity factor to calculate total energy expenditure. See Table 3.3 to determine the appropriate activity factor for each patient (13). Multiplying RMR by an activity factor will estimate the daily energy requirement for weight *maintenance*. For weight *loss* of 1 to 2 pounds per week, clinicians typically subtract 500 to 1,000 kcal from the results (3,500 kcal ≈ 1 pound). Refer to Chapter 4 for more information about calorie balance and weight-loss dietary counseling.

Table 3.3 ✦ Physical Activity Factors

	Activity Factor	Definition
Sedentary	1.0 to <1.4	Includes RMR + thermic effect of food + physical activity for independent living
Low-Active	1.4 to <1.6	Walking 2 miles/day at 3.5 miles/hour
Active	1.6 to <1.9	Walking 7 miles/day at 3.5 miles/hour
Very Active	1.9 to <2.5	Walking > 16 miles/day at 3.5 miles/hour

Source: National Academy of Sciences Institute of Medicine (IOM) Food and Nutrition Board. DRI Physical Activity Factors. http://www.nap.edu/openbook.php?record_id=10490&page=895. Accessed February 12, 2008.

The Lifestyle Patterns Quiz

Whereas the Health Assessment Patient Questionnaire provides the background assessment information for your patient, the Lifestyle Patterns Quiz helps you target specific problematic behaviors. Each person struggles with a set of eating, exercise, and coping issues that are unique to his or her lifestyle. The quiz will assess each patient's dominant weight-gaining behaviors within three domains: eating, exercise, and coping. The following sections will explain how to discuss/introduce this approach to patients, how patients can take the quiz, and how the quiz can be scored.

The complete 50-question Lifestyle Patterns Quiz, which is made up of 17 questions related to eating, 17 related to physical activity, and 16 related to coping, is available on the CD-ROM and in Appendix A. We recommend that clinicians initially have patients take the complete Lifestyle Patterns Quiz. When asking patients to re-assess their progress, clinicians may choose to focus on just one of the three domains. See Chapter 7 for more information on re-administering the quiz. We encourage clinicians to review the Lifestyle Patterns Quiz now to get a better understanding of its format and directions.

Discussing the Lifestyle Patterns Approach

Once clinicians explain the individualized and targeted Lifestyle Patterns Approach, patients are eager to take the quiz and see their results. The following example shows how to introduce this approach to patients.

> **Clinician:** "When I talk to patients about their weight, most tell me that they are able to lose weight for a while by following a diet, but then they invariably slip back into old habits. It turns out that each person has his or her own unique eating, exercise, and coping habits that have caused weight gain. By focusing on these weight-gaining habits rather than simply giving you a diet to follow, we can address these recurring problematic areas. I would like you to complete a 50-item Lifestyle Patterns Quiz that will identify your own eating, exercise, and coping habits—these are the habits that cause *you* to gain weight. It will take about 20 minutes to complete the quiz, and we'll then review it together."

Administering and Scoring the Lifestyle Patterns Quiz

There are four primary ways to initially administer and score the quiz. Clinicians may choose the route that suits their practice and preferences as well as the particular patient's computer skills (see Table 3.4).

Table 3.4 ✦ Comparison of Administration and Scoring Method for Lifestyle Patterns Quiz

Method	Recommended for Clinicians Who . . .	Recommended for Patients Who . . .
Computerized full quiz with computer scoring	• Have computer available in the office for patient use • Want complete computer-generated printouts	• Have basic computer skills
Paper-and-pen full quiz with computer scoring	• Want to mail the quiz before the initial visit • Do not have computers for patient use • Want complete computer-generated printouts	• Do not have basic computer skills
Paper-and-pen quiz with hand scoring	• Want to mail the quiz before the initial visit • Do not have access to a computer	• Do not have basic computer skills
Mini-quizzes with no scoring	• Have limited time • Are using this approach in groups	• Have limited time • Have no computer skills

Computerized Full Quiz with Computer Scoring

For this method, the clinician puts the CD-ROM included with this publication in the CD drive of his or her computer and asks patients to complete the 50-question quiz on this computer when they arrive at their appointment. Results are immediately scored by the computer software. The computer-generated results appear as bar graphs that enable both clinicians and patients to have visual depictions of the behaviors to target for weight loss.

Paper-and-Pen Full Quiz with Computer Scoring

For this method, clinicians print a paper version of the quiz from the CD-ROM included with this publication. The quiz can then be mailed to patients to complete before the appointment, or given to patients at the appointment. Clinicians take the responses to the 50 questions and enter them into the software program on the CD-ROM. The computer-generated results appear as bar graphs that enable both clinicians and patients to have visual depictions of the behaviors to target for weight loss.

Paper-and-Pen Full Quiz with Hand Scoring

For this method, clinicians print a paper version of the quiz from the CD-ROM included with this publication. The quiz can then be mailed to patients to complete before the appointment, or given to patients at the appointment. The clinician then hand scores the responses to the 50 questions using the technique described in Appendix B. When the quiz is hand-scored, the results still identify which of the 21 Lifestyle Patterns should be targeted, but the disadvantage to this scoring method is that the computer-generated bar graphs will not be available.

Mini-Quizzes with No Scoring

Although the Lifestyle Patterns Approach is based on the results of the 50-question quiz, mini-quizzes are also available both on the CD-ROM and in Appendix C. Clinicians are encouraged to view the mini-quizzes now. These mini-quizzes are available as printer-ready forms only and the results cannot be scored on the computer. They're meant to be used to save time or when counseling groups. The mini-quizzes direct patients to briefly think about and reflect on which of the seven eating, seven exercise, and seven coping patterns best describe them. After reading a description of each of the 21 patterns, patients will simply check "yes" for any of the 21 patterns they believe to be a problematic behavior and contributing factor to their weight gain. Using the behaviors they have identified, treatment can begin by targeting those particular self-reported behaviors. A disadvantage of this approach is that no scoring or ranking of the patterns is available.

How to Interpret Quiz Results

After the test is scored with the CD-ROM software or by hand, certain patterns emerge, creating a diagnostic "portrait" specific to each patient. In our experience, the bar graph results definitely have more impact on patients than the scores alone because they're able to see an immediate visual snapshot of their problematic behaviors.

Patient results rarely showcase just one problematic pattern in each of the domains of eating, exercise, and coping. More often than not, patient results reveal multiple problematic areas with varying scores of the 21 total patterns within the three domains. Each patient's quiz results are as individual as their fingerprints—no two individual's pattern profiles look exactly alike. This section reviews how to interpret the Lifestyle Patterns Quiz results, prioritize the resulting dominant patterns to provide a clear treatment agenda for each patient, and discuss the results with patients.

Each patient's graphed results will display up to 21 bars, each corresponding to an eating, exercise, or coping pattern. The bars will be of varying heights ranging to a maximum of 100%. (A 0% pattern will not appear as a bar on the graph.) If a pattern score is close to or equal to 0%, the pattern is not likely to be a problematic behavior for the patient. The closer a pattern score is to 100%, the more likely that it identifies a problematic or dominant weight-gaining behavior. A pattern can be considered "dominant" when it scores at or more than the 33% threshold. This 33% grade is a guideline that has been used empirically by Dr. Kushner and his colleagues when treating patients. Such higher-percentage patterns should be targeted as a potential area to change.

It is likely that multiple dominant diagnostic patterns (behaviors at or more than the 33% threshold) will appear for each of the eating, exercise, and coping dimensions. In the example graphs used in this chapter, the patient has six dominant patterns: two eating patterns (Fruitless Feaster, Hearty Portioner), two exercise patterns (Uneasy Participant, Rain Check Athlete), and two coping patterns (People Pleaser, Unrealistic Achiever.)

Rather than trying to change all problematic behaviors at once, a more effective weight-management strategy is to set an agenda to tackle them in a gradual and systematic fashion (14). As discussed in Chapter 1, patient-centered counseling is a partnership. Therefore, the patient and clinician should discuss and mutually decide which pattern(s) to begin addressing first. After the clinician reviews the quiz results and explains the diagnostic dominant weight-gain behaviors to the patient, the following questions may be asked by the clinician to help set the agenda for behavior change:

- "Do you agree with this patterns profile? Does it reflect your habits?"

- "After reviewing your dominant patterns, are there any that you agree are most problematic areas? Are there any dominant patterns you do not agree represent your behaviors?"

- "Of the dominant patterns, which ones do you have the most confidence you can change?"

- "Are there one or more patterns we reviewed that you have been wanting to change?"

- "Which pattern do you think would be the easiest to change? Which would be the hardest to change?"

Clinicians may find that some patients need or want to focus on only one pattern at a time because it is their most problematic area, because they are easily overwhelmed, or because they aren't motivated or organized to work on more than one at a time. Other patients may work on multiple patterns at once, based on their motivation, dedication to practicing different behaviors, and capacity for dealing with change. However, the clinician should be alert to the ambitious, unrealistic patient who wants to change everything all at once. In this case, the clinician should guide the patient to be more realistic regarding behavior change. In general, anywhere from one to three patterns are chosen to target in the first session.

In subsequent sessions, patients may feel they have successfully changed a dominant behavior and feel confident to set a new agenda by choosing other dominant patterns to focus on. In other instances, patients may not have been successful changing the problematic behavior, or they do not feel confident to move on to other dominant patterns. In these cases, the same problematic behavior is discussed in even more detail to flush out the barriers to success and to ask the patient to consider what skills and strategies would be helpful to overcome barriers and accomplish the targeted changes. More information on how to assess patient progress and follow-up with patients using the Lifestyle Patterns Approach is discussed in Chapter 7.

Case Studies of the Interpretation and Discussion of Lifestyle Patterns Quiz

The following three case studies may illuminate the process of interpreting graphical test results and discussing them with clients to set an agenda of targeted treatment.

Eating Patterns Case Study

The Eating Patterns graph (Figure 3.3) is generated from the responses of patient "N" to the 17 eating questions in the Lifestyle Patterns Quiz.

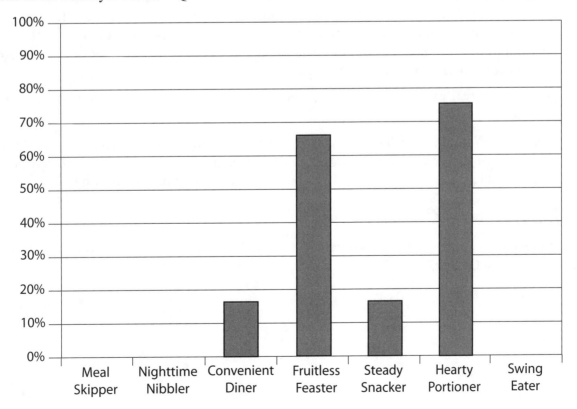

Figure 3.3 Eating Lifestyle Patterns Quiz results.

Clinician Considerations

When interpreting this graph, the clinician should consider the following:

- The dominant patterns are Fruitless Feaster and Hearty Portioner. Convenient Diner and Steady Snacker appear, but are below the 33% empirical threshold. The patient scored 0% for the Meal Skipper, Nighttime Nibbler, and Swing Eater patterns.

- The two dominant patterns may be interrelated. Teaching N to eat more fruits and vegetables can also help address the Hearty Portioner pattern because N can eat large portions of produce for very few calories.

- It can be helpful to cross-reference these results with responses on the Health Assessment Patient Questionnaire. Did N indicate on the assessment form a desire to increase fruits and vegetables or decrease portions?

Discussing Results with the Patient and Setting an Agenda

After interpreting the results, the following dialogue might unfold:

> **Clinician:** "Let's review your eating patterns first. The results show that you have two dominant patterns—Fruitless Feaster, who is a person who doesn't eat much produce, and Hearty Portioner, who is a person who eats large quantities of food at meals and snacks."

> **N (laughing and interrupting the clinician):** "I can't believe this! Yes, yes, yes. Those are my main problems. I tend to eat three meals a day and not snack much, but when I eat—oh, I eat. I joke that I belong to the clean plate club!"

> **Clinician:** "Okay, I was going to ask you if you agreed with the results, but I guess you answered that already. I also noticed on the initial patient questionnaire you filled out, you wrote that you "would like to eat more fruits and vegetables." So I get the feeling this is a behavior you and I should discuss in detail today and come up with some specific strategies to help you eat more fruits and veggies."

> **N:** "Absolutely. I would look forward to any ideas you have. I've struggled with this for a lifetime."

> **Clinician:** "Well, I have a handout with four specific strategies to help you with your Fruitless Feaster pattern, and eating more fruits and vegetables will even help your Hearty Portioner habit too. But let's first look over your exercise and coping pattern results."

Exercise Patterns Case Study

The Exercise Patterns graph (Figure 3.4) is generated from N's responses to the 17 exercise questions in the Lifestyle Patterns Quiz.

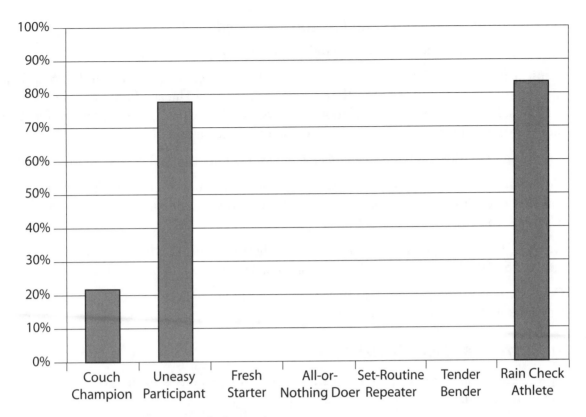

Figure 3.4 Exercise Lifestyle Patterns Quiz results.

Clinician Considerations

When interpreting this graph, the clinician should consider the following:

- The dominant patterns are Uneasy Participant and Rain Check Athlete. Couch Champion appears, but is below the 33% empirical threshold. The patient scored 0% for the Fresh Starter, All-or-Nothing Doer, Set-Routine Repeater, and Tender Bender patterns.

- Exercise suggestions for N should not involve large groups of people (because the Uneasy Participant is self-conscious when exercising around other people).

- Selection of activities will also need to be suited to the time constraints of busy people (because N is a Rain Check Athlete).

- N is not a novice (Fresh Starter) and does not have injuries that will restrict activity (Tender Bender). Patients like N may have ideas about types of exercise they have done in the past; that can be a place to start when brainstorming ideas and solutions.

Discussing Results with the Patient and Setting an Agenda

After interpreting the results, the following dialogue might unfold:

Clinician: "So, now on to the exercise patterns. You can see the results identify you primarily as an Uneasy Participant and Rain Check Athlete. The Uneasy Participant tends to be self-conscious about exercising in front of others and Rain Check Athletes tend to feel they don't have time to exercise. Do you see yourself in these patterns?"

N: "I do agree, 100%. What is that Couch Champion? It looks like I scored on that one too."

Clinician: "Well, yes, the results slightly indicate that you are a Couch Champion, a person who doesn't like exercise and would prefer the couch to being active. Do you feel that describes you?"

N: "Yes, I do, but I probably most agree with the Rain Check Athlete—I never feel like I have time to do the exercise and I know I should. That's going to be a problem for me."

Clinician: "We'll talk about that because it is so important. But before we address that, let's look at the last dimension of your results: coping.

Coping Patterns Case Study

The Coping Patterns graph (Figure 3.4) is generated from N's responses to the 16 coping questions in the Lifestyle Patterns Quiz.

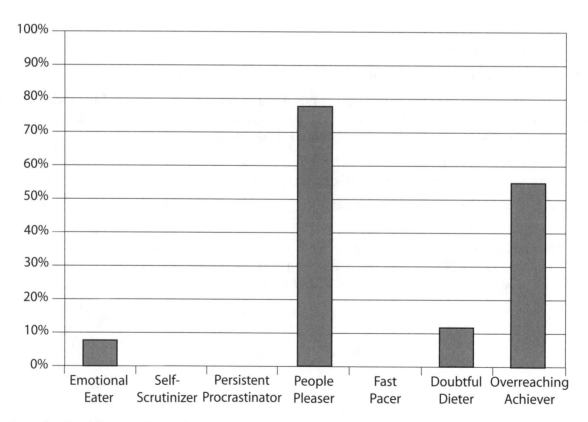

Figure 3.5 Coping Lifestyle Patterns Quiz results.

Clinician Considerations

When interpreting this graph, the clinician should consider the following:

- The two dominant coping patterns are People Pleaser and Overreaching Achiever. Emotional Eater and Doubtful Dieter appear, but are below the 33% empirical threshold. The patient scored 0% for the Self-Scrutinizer, Fast Pacer, and Persistent Procrastinator patterns.

- People Pleasing, putting other people's needs before one's own, may be why N never has time to exercise. (Rain Check Athlete was a dominant exercise pattern.)

- Unrealistic expectations are a main source of frustration and dropout in weight-management programs. It is especially important to review weight-loss expectations with Overreaching Achievers such as N. Help this patient understand that a reasonable goal may be 10% body weight reduction in 6 months.

Discussing Results with the Patient and Setting an Agenda

After interpreting the results, the following dialogue might unfold:

Clinician: "In the coping domain, it appears the most dominant patterns are People Pleaser and Overreaching Achiever."

N: "What do you mean by People Pleaser?"

Clinician: "That is when you put others ahead of yourself. That can be very altruistic and giving, but if it always means placing yourself on the bottom of the ladder and you don't get to take care of yourself, it is a problem."

N: "Okay, that is me. And the Overreaching Achiever, I don't know if that describes me."

Clinician: "Overreaching Achievers have unrealistic expectations about weight loss and behavior change, tend to get frustrated if they aren't able to achieve those lofty goals, and subsequently want to quit. Does that sound familiar from your past experiences with dieting and weight loss?"

N: "Now that you have explained it, it does sound like me—if you tell me I am supposed to lose 1 pound a week, I think I could probably lose closer to 3. I tend to think that way."

Clinician: "We'll keep that in mind as we work together. Let's first set the agenda for behavior change. Right now we have Fruitless Feaster as a key eating pattern you want to change and Rain Check Athlete as an exercise pattern you would like to discuss."

N: "I could do the People Pleaser one too."

Clinician: "My recommendation is to get started with one eating and one exercise pattern for now so we don't overload you at the start. Down the road you can choose one of the coping patterns to work on."

N: "I do agree, good point. Let's just pick those two and I will see how I do. Now what exactly should I do to correct these problematic behaviors?"

Clinician: "In this Lifestyle Patterns Approach, we will target the treatment of your problematic behaviors by using behavior change handouts. Each handout corresponds to the behavior we want to change and has four strategies for you to practice until our next appointment. At the next appointment, we will review how well you have done with each of these target areas. Let's review the information on each handout and make it more specific and individualized just for you."

N: "I am excited to get started."

Targeted Treatment Handouts

After setting an initial agenda to address one to three problematic patterns, the targeted treatment can begin. The Lifestyle Patterns Approach uses pattern-specific, action-oriented handouts to outline each patient's treatment plan. For each of the 21 identified dominant patterns, there is a corresponding two-page patient handout that includes four pattern-specific behavioral strategies. The four strategies on each treatment-plan handout give the patient ideas, tips, and tricks to correct the problematic behavior. With dedication to practicing these strategies, patients change weight-gaining behaviors into more healthful lifestyle habits for weight loss. The 21 Lifestyle Pattern handouts are available on the CD-ROM; selected sample handouts are available in Appendix E.

We encourage clinicians to view the handouts and follow along as we discuss the case studies. Please note that the handouts are designed to be personalized for each patient. Clinicians are encouraged to underline, highlight, or circle strategies and information which they want a client to focus on, and to write on the lines provided or add more information in the margins if needed. Clinicians can even cross out information that may not be pertinent to that particular patient. Following is an overview of how to use the targeted treatment plan handouts with patients as well as how to begin dialogue to further individualize each strategy.

In the case study of N, the patient and clinician have chosen two dominant behaviors or patterns as the initial focus: Fruitless Feaster and Rain Check Athlete. The two corresponding targeted treatment handouts should be discussed in detail to give N a clear understanding of exactly what needs to be practiced until the next appointment.

The four strategies covered in the handout to help the Fruitless Feaster are as follows:

- Have produce ready and on hand
- Make fruits and vegetables flavorful
- Pick colorful produce
- Eat more vegetarian meals

The following are the four strategies addressed in the Rain Check Athlete handout:

- Fit in walking
- Schedule activity in a date book
- Combine activity with other things
- Ask for help

N's "homework" is to practice these targeted strategies to gradually correct each problematic behavior, which will lead to a more healthful lifestyle and weight loss. The following dialogue illustrates how the clinician encourages and supports N's efforts.

> **Clinician:** "Okay, here are the two handouts that correspond to the dominant patterns we agreed to tackle for "homework": the Fruitless Feaster and the Rain Check Athlete. Each handout has four strategies to help you manage your weight-gaining behavior. As you prac-

tice these strategies, you will begin to take charge of your problematic behavior, which will lead to weight loss. I would like to read over each of the strategies and personalize them further with you."

N: "I am glad you are giving me handouts to summarize what we are talking about today. They will help remind me what I am supposed to be doing. It probably would be a good idea if I put them some place where I will remember to read them, like hanging on the fridge or on my nightstand."

Clinician: "It's a good idea to keep them in a place where you will see them and re-read them. Let's start by reading over the Fruitless Feaster treatment handout. I will briefly explain each of the four strategies and then we can talk in detail about how to apply them in your life: First, 'have produce ready and on hand': this is a key strategy because the first step in eating fruits and vegetables is buying them and having them easy to grab. Second, 'make fruits and vegetables flavorful': of course, learning to prepare good-tasting produce is important. Third, 'pick colorful produce': this strategy focuses on getting variety in your produce for the best nutrition and helping you avoid boredom. Finally, 'eat more vegetarian meals': this suggests that you have one or two vegetarian-type meals each week for a delicious change of pace and potentially fewer calories than meat-based meals. For homework, you can practice all four of these strategies or just a couple. Tell me, which ones are going to be the easiest and which will be the hardest for you to practice?"

N: "I definitely agree that buying more fruits and vegetables is the first step. I don't buy many fruits and vegetables. I will aim to buy more frozen vegetables because they are already cut and cleaned so all I have to do is microwave them, and I will keep a fruit bowl on the counter so I remember to grab it. I am going to have trouble with the meatless meals; I don't have any ideas of what I can cook that is vegetarian."

Clinician: "Let's note on your handout that you are going to buy more frozen vegetables and keep fruit out in a bowl on the counter. Let me give you two ideas of quick meatless meals and we will write them on the handout as well. Two of my favorites are low-fat refried bean burritos with lettuce, salsa, sliced bell peppers, and onions and grilled veggie burgers with a quick side salad with low-fat dressing."

N: "Oh, write those ideas down; they sound good and actually pretty easy to make—I will try them."

Clinician: "Next, let's read over the Rain Check Athlete handout together. 'Fit in walking' is about moving your body more during the course of your normal day's routine; this means at least 30 minutes of daily walking—maybe you can do that by parking farther away and taking the stairs instead of the elevator. The second point is 'schedule activity in a date book': the idea here is that you preschedule exercise by putting it in your calendar; this helps you reserve that time and not give it away to someone or something else. Third is 'combine activity with other things': for example, you could catch up on the news or think through a work project while you are exercising. And the fourth point is 'ask for help': ask a neighbor, friend, or coworker to help you watch your kids or do an errand so you have more time to put toward taking care of yourself and exercising. Which strategies do you think sound most effective to help you find more time to exercise?"

N: "They all sound good, but I'm going to focus on moving my body more each day—I can shoot for maybe 20 minutes daily to start—as well as making an appointment with myself. If I don't need time to drive to and from a health club, I think 20 minutes of walking is doable. Also, I never blow off appointments when I put them in my calendar. I never thought about scheduling my exercise like that."

Clinician: "Good, let's make a note on your handout that you are going to fit in 20 minutes of walking each day and start writing your exercise appointments in your calendar. At our next visit together I will check your calendar and see how it is going. You may want to record the time you spend walking each day in your calendar too. It helps to keep you on track if you write down how much you exercise."

N: "Okay, these are very specific and helpful behavior changes. I feel this is all very doable."

Other Forms

In addition to the Health Assessment Patient Questionnaire, the Weight Flow Sheet, the Lifestyle Patterns Quiz, the Mini-Quizzes, and the 21 pattern-specific handouts, the following forms are also available on the CD-ROM:

- Food and Activity Log
- Lifestyle Patterns Progress Note
- Health Care Provider Letter
- Progress Tracking Chart

Clinicians are encouraged to follow along and view the forms as we discuss each of these in the following sections.

Food and Activity Log

Self-monitoring is a fundamental skill to help individuals be more successful in losing weight. In Chapters 4, 5, and 6, we highlight the specific patterns for which tracking food, activity, or mood are particularly helpful. However, almost all patients could benefit from filling out the Food and Activity Log on a regular basis and bringing completed logs to future appointments. Some patients may do well completing daily logs, but this may be too time-intensive for others. Clinicians can help patients develop a self-monitoring plan that is realistic for them. A minimal goal should be to use the log for two days during the week and one weekend day. Also, the sooner patients complete the food log after eating, the more accurate their logs will be. For some patients, recording their log *before* they eat is a useful planning strategy. Each of the columns in the Food and Activity Log may seem self-explanatory, but it is a good idea to review each section with patients so they understand what's expected of them. Alternatively, patients may prefer to use one of the many free online tracking tools (many also calculate calorie contents of meals and snacks). See Appendix F for online resources that include free tracking tools.

Lifestyle Patterns Progress Note

The Lifestyle Patterns Progress Note can be used at each visit to document the patient's weight along with the specific patterns and strategies that were discussed. Thorough and time-efficient documentation is critical during and after each patient visit. Documentation using the Lifestyle Patterns Approach should include the dominant patterns discussed with the patient as well as the targeted strategies agreed upon for "homework." Keeping detailed accounts of each of the personalized strategies allows for targeted and seamless follow-up visits.

For example, our case study patient, N, is focusing on two dominant patterns: Fruitless Feaster and Rain Check Athlete. Specifically, the patient has identified strategies to practice for homework to target these two problematic areas, including:

- Purchase more produce, especially frozen vegetables for ease.
- Keep produce at eye-level in the fridge as a reminder to incorporate it in meals.
- Put a fruit bowl on the counter as a prompt to remember to eat it.
- Try a meatless meal on Mondays.
- Fit in 20 minutes of walking daily.
- Preschedule exercise on the calendar as an appointment and set a computer alarm reminder.
- Record time spent walking each day in a calendar.

Either during the patient visit or shortly after, the clinician should write down these strategies so they can be acknowledged, evaluated, and discussed at the follow-up appointment. If a patient does extremely well with a particular strategy, he or she should be congratulated on this success. If a particular strategy is neglected or not practiced successfully, further problem-solving should be done, including discussion of probable barriers and solutions to those barriers.

Health Care Provider Letter

Another recommended part of documentation is correspondence to the patient's physician and/or other involved health care providers. The correspondence serves to keep health care providers informed about their patient's goals and involvement in a weight-management program. Establishing communication between multiple providers allows patients to feel that their team of health professionals is connected and their messages are consistent. The letter should include information about the patient and the visit, such as the patient's name, height, weight, BMI, health goals, and basic treatment plan. The letter is intended for physicians, nurse practitioners, or other health care providers caring for the patient.

Progress Tracking Chart

This form is discussed in Chapter 7 when we address follow-up visits, tracking progress, retaking the Lifestyle Patterns Quiz, and dealing with lapse and relapse.

Summing Up Targeted Assessment and Treatment

In this chapter you have learned how to use the Lifestyle Patterns Approach to assess and target treatment to your overweight clients. In Chapters 4, 5, and 6, you will learn in greater detail how to counsel your patients to reshape their specific weight-gaining lifestyle patterns into weight-losing habits. In Chapter 7, you will learn how to follow-up and monitor patients using this approach.

References

1. American Dietetic Association. Position paper: weight management. *J Am Diet Assoc.* 2002;102:1145-1155. (Note: at press time, a 2008 update was pending.)
2. Wadden TA, Foster GD. Weight and Lifestyle Inventory (WALI). *Obesity.* 2006;14(Suppl 2):99S-118S.

3. Expert Panel on Detection, Evaluation, and Treatment of High Blood Cholesterol in Adults. Executive summary of the Third Report of the National Cholesterol Education Program (NCEP) Expert Panel on Detection, Evaluation, and Treatment of High Blood Cholesterol in Adults (Adult Treatment Panel III). *JAMA*. 2001;285:2486-2497. http://www.nhlbi.nih.gov/guidelines/cholesterol/atp3xsum.pdf. Accessed September 28, 2007.

4. Franklin BA, Whaley MH, Brubaker PH, Otto RM, eds. *American College of Sports Medicine's Guidelines for Exercise Testing and Prescription*. 7th ed. Philadelphia, PA: Lippincott Williams & Wilkins; 2006.

5. Pi-Sunyer X, Aronne L, Bray G. Weight gain induced by psychotropic drugs. *Obes Manage*. 2007;3:165-169.

6. Elfhag K, Rossner S. Who succeeds in maintaining weight loss? A conceptual review of factors associated with weight loss maintenance and weight regain. *Obes Rev*. 2005;6:67-85.

7. National Heart, Lung, and Blood Institute. Body mass index table. http://www.nhlbi.nih.gov/guidelines/obesity/bmi_tbl.htm. Accessed December 7, 2007.

8. National Heart, Lung, and Blood Institute (NHLBI) and North American Association for the Study of Obesity (NAASO). The Practical Guide:Identification, Evaluation, and Treatment of Overweight and Obesity in Adults. Bethesda, MD:National Institutes of Health; 2000. NIH publication 00-4084.

9. Alberti KGMM, Zimmet P, Shaw J, for the IDF Epidemiology Task Force Consensus Group. The metabolic syndrome—a new worldwide definition. *Lancet*. 2005;366:1059.

10. North American Association for the Study of Obesity (NAASO), the Obesity Society. Components of daily energy expenditure. http://www.obesityonline.org/slides/slide01.cfm?q=total+energy+expenditure&dpg=2. Accessed February 13, 2008.

11. American Dietetic Association Evidence Analysis Library. Adult Weight Management Evidence Analysis Project. http://adaevidencelibrary.com/topic.cfm?cat=1193&auth=1. Accessed September 28, 2007.

12. Mifflin MD, St. Jeor ST, Hill LA, Scott BJ, Daugherty SA, Koh YO. A new predictive equation for resting energy expenditure in healthy individuals. *Am J Clin Nutr*. 1990;51:241-247.

13. National Academy of Sciences Institute of Medicine (IOM) Food and Nutrition Board. DRI Physical Activity Factors. http://www.nap.edu/openbook.php?record_id=10490&page=895. Accessed February 12, 2008.

14. Hill JO. Understanding and addressing the epidemic of obesity: an energy balance perspective. *Endocr Rev*. 2006;27:750-761.

Chapter 4

✦ ✦ ✦

Counseling for Eating Lifestyle Patterns

Eating: The Foundation of Weight Management

The objective of weight-loss diet counseling is to teach patients how to consume fewer calories in a healthful, realistic, and consistent manner. The National Heart, Lung, and Blood Institute (NHLBI) guidelines recommend that patients initially set a target of consuming 500 to 1000 kcal less than their current daily diet to produce approximately a 1- to 2-pound weight loss per week (1). Keys to an individual diet prescription include attention to taste preferences, food cost, time management, and environmental and emotional eating triggers. Effective nutrition therapy is a balance of both nutrition information and individualized strategies to overcome barriers to change.

Even though health care providers know calorie control is the key to weight loss, many patients remain confused about this fundamental principle. According to the 2007 Food and Health Survey of 1,000 people conducted by International Food Information Council, only one in three people know that calories cause weight gain and only one out of 10 people know the correct number of calories per day that they should eat (2).

As part of the assessment process discussed in Chapter 3, clinicians should measure or calculate each patient's resting metabolic rate (RMR) and multiply it by an activity factor to estimate daily calorie needs. See Chapter 3 for more specifics about how to do this calculation to help patients achieve a predicted weight loss of 1 to 2 pounds per week.

Dietary Guidelines: Dietary Reference Intakes and USDA Dietary Guidelines

Although calories are the bottom line to weight management, the macronutrient (carbohydrates, protein, and fat) composition of the diet is important to overall health and wellness. The Institute of Medicine (IOM) recommends that adults consume 45% to 65% of daily calories from carbohydrates, 10% to 35% of calories from protein, and 20% to 35% of calories from fat (3). The macronutrient Dietary Reference Intakes (DRIs) offer a flexible range (instead of a single target amount), which supports the philosophy that one diet does *not* fit all. Diets should be tailored to each individual's taste preferences and lifestyle within these wide healthful ranges. See Table 4.1 for examples of calculated ranges. The IOM has set DRIs for vitamins, minerals, fiber, water, and other diet components. A complete set of DRI tables is available online from IOM (http://www.iom.edu/CMS/3788/4574/45132.aspx).

Table 4.1 ✦ Quick Macronutrient Reference

Macronutrient	% of Total Daily Energy Intake[a]	1200 kcal/d Diet	Daily Recommendations	
			1600 kcal/d Diet	2000 kcal/d Diet
Carbohydrate	45–65	540–780 kcal (135–195 g)	720–1040 kcal (180–260 g)	900–1300 kcal (225–325 g)
Protein	10–35	120–420 kcal (30–105 g)	160–560 kcal (40–140 g)	200–700 kcal (50–175 g)
Fat	20–35	240–420 kcal (27–47 g)	320–560 kcal (36–62 g)	400–700 kcal (44–78 g)

[a]Percentages are Acceptable Macronutrient Distribution Ranges from the Dietary Reference Intakes.

Source: Data are from reference 3.

The US Department of Agriculture (USDA) 2005 Dietary Guidelines are based on scientific evidence for reducing risk of chronic disease and promoting health and can be translated into patient-friendly advice. The objective of these guidelines is to encourage Americans to eat fewer calories, be more active, and make wiser food choices. The basic daily dietary guidelines (for Americans older than 2 years) include (4):

- Choose high-fiber foods such as a variety of colorful fruits and vegetables and whole grains.

- Choose three servings of low-fat dairy foods.

- Limit total fat to 20% to 35% calories and choose heart-healthy fats such as fish, nuts, and vegetable oils.

- Limit saturated fat to less than 10% of calories, *trans* fats to a minimum, and cholesterol to less than 300 mg.

- Prepare and select lean, low-fat, and fat-free meat, poultry, dry beans, and milk.

- Limit sodium to 2,300 mg (1 teaspoon of salt) or less.

- Choose foods and beverages with little added sugars or high-calorie sweeteners.

- For those who choose to drink alcohol, do so in moderation. Alcohol in moderation is one drink per day for women and two for men. (1 drink = 12 ounce beer, 5 ounces wine, or 1.5 ounces spirits.)

Comprehensive information about the USDA Dietary Guidelines for both health professionals and patients can be found on the MyPyramid Web site (http://www.mypyramid.gov). MyPyramid personalizes the general guidelines by calculating each individual's calorie needs using five variables—age, sex, weight, height, and activity level (using the IOM's Estimated Energy Requirement [EER] formulas). The site will fit each person in one of 12 calorie levels (from 1,000 to 3,200 calories per day) and provide a corresponding specific breakdown of daily food group servings needed for a well-balanced and healthful diet. There are other free tools on the MyPyramid Web site that patients may find helpful, such as a food and activity tracker and portion-size educational pictures. See Table 4.2 for examples of daily recommendations for specific food groups.

Healthy Eating Decisions

The four pillars, or driving forces, of food decisions are taste, price, health, and convenience. Results of the 2007 Food and Health Survey show that food decisions are based mostly on taste (53%), followed by price (37%), health (25%), and convenience (23%) (2). When counseling patients, it is important to dis-

Table 4.2 ✦ Dietary Guidelines 2005: Recommended Daily Amount of Food from Each Food Group for Adults

	1,600 kcal/d	2,000 kcal/d
Fruits	1.5 cups	2 cups
Vegetables	2 cups	2.5 cups
Grains	5 ounce-equivalents	6 ounce-equivalents
Meat and beans	5 ounce-equivalents	5.5 ounce-equivalents
Milk	3 cups	3 cups
Oils	5 teaspoons	6 teaspoons
Discretionary "extra" calories	132 calories	267 calories

Source: Data are from reference 4.

cuss these four factors because any of them can pose a barrier to making dietary change. For example, if a health care provider recommends that a patient eat a more healthful breakfast cereal but it doesn't taste good to the patient, is too expensive, or isn't convenient to purchase or use, the patient likely will not follow through with the change.

Additionally, patients' current internal emotions (mood), physical state (such as thirst), and present eating situation and environment (when, where, with whom, food availability) contribute to food decisions and the probability of making healthful dietary changes (5). It is the responsibility of the clinician to help patients identify and problem-solve potential barriers. Here are some open-ended questions to probe for barriers:

- What do you think will stand in your way of making healthy changes?
- What makes it hard for you to make diet changes?
- What in the past has stopped you from being successful with healthy food changes?
- What do you think is going to be your greatest challenge when making diet changes?

This chapter gives health care providers detailed advice about how to use the Lifestyle Patterns Approach to tailor nutrition strategies to match each patient's needs and overcome each patient's barriers. The information in this chapter will build provider skills and confidence in personalizing nutrition information and using targeted treatment strategies in an efficient and effective way.

Eating Lifestyle Patterns

As explained in Chapter 2, there are seven eating lifestyle patterns:

- Meal Skipper
- Nighttime Nibbler
- Convenient Diner
- Fruitless Feaster
- Steady Snacker
- Hearty Portioner
- Swing Eater

The discussion format of the seven eating lifestyle patterns that follows includes:

- A description of each eating pattern.
- A discussion of why each pattern is a problem, with supportive research.
- Four strategies to help patients reshape the problem pattern into a more healthful one (highlights of this information are included in the corresponding patient teaching handout).
- Questions clinicians can ask during counseling.
- Pattern-specific case studies. Please keep in mind that the case scenarios that follow each pattern should be viewed as excerpts taken from a longer counseling process. The primary intent of the case studies is to demonstrate dialogue and phraseology that are consistent with the particular pattern.

The Meal Skipper

Description

Meal Skippers have little structure when it comes to their eating routine. They don't plan their meals because food is an afterthought. When they skip meals, they become starved and reach for anything edible, healthful or not. Based on observations of patients' food recalls and logs from patients at Northwestern Memorial Hospital's Wellness Institute in Chicago, food intake differs each day depending on the Meal Skipper's schedule, whereabouts, and to-do list. At the end of the day, Meal Skippers have no idea what they ate or how much, because they're just not paying attention.

The Problem

Skipping meals and eating at irregular mealtimes can cause people to overeat (6). Skipping breakfast is a particular concern because including breakfast in one's diet has been shown to be an important strategy for successful weight loss and maintenance. The National Weight Control Registry has thousands of members who have lost an average of 70 pounds and kept it off for more than 5 years. Nearly four out of five registry members eat breakfast every day whereas only 4% never eat breakfast (7).

Research has found that people who have a regular meal schedule consume about 80 kcal fewer per day than those who eat irregular meals. In addition to decreased calorie consumption, other reported health benefits of regular mealtimes include increased calories burned after mealtime, improved insulin sensitivity, and improved cholesterol levels (6). Analysis of the Third National Health and Nutrition Examination Survey (NHANES III) found that people consuming regular meals had more healthful diets than those who had irregular meal patterns. Their diets had more vitamin C, calcium, magnesium, iron, potassium, and fiber, and less total fat, cholesterol, and sodium (8). Kruger et al found individuals successful at weight loss and maintenance planned their meals significantly more than those people who weren't successful (36% vs 25%) (9).

Strategies for Meal Skippers

The following strategies may help Meal Skippers succeed at weight loss and maintenance:

- Plan three meals each day
- Focus on your meal
- Track your hunger and fullness
- Fill up on water and fiber

Plan Three Meals Each Day

The adoption of a regular eating schedule is an extremely important strategy to teach your patients. Without a schedule in place, Meal Skippers are vulnerable to becoming so hungry during the day that they'll reach for anything edible, healthful or not. The following counseling suggestions may help Meal Skippers plan three meals each day:

- Explain to patients that a regular eating schedule will help them eat fewer calories each day and improve their overall diet quality (6,8).

- For Meal Skippers who are skeptical about developing *and sticking to* a set schedule, it may be beneficial to ask them:"What would your work be like if you didn't have a structure, routine, or plan every day? For example, would you find such randomness a productive and successful strategy for work?"

- Write the set mealtimes down on paper.

- Ask patients to structure their environment so that they are reminded of the set mealtimes. For example, patients can set their computer to remind them to eat breakfast, ask a friend or coworker to "drag" them to lunch, or set their cell phone alarm to prompt them at dinnertime. After a few weeks of practice, patients may enjoy the energy and satisfaction they get from eating regular meals.

- For patients who don't have typical 9 AM to 5 PM work hours, use the terms Meal 1, Meal 2, Meal 3 instead of breakfast, lunch, and dinner to ease confusion. Have the patient eat Meal 1 within the first hour or two of waking and set meals about 4 to 6 hours apart with a 100- to 200-kcal snack in between meals.

- For patients who say that they aren't hungry for breakfast, feel nauseous at breakfast time, or just don't like to eat at that time of day, suggest they start the day with something small, such as a protein bar or shake with a piece of fruit.

- Encourage patients to plan ahead for times when they cannot make a meal. A suggestion would be to try a meal replacement bar that meets the nutrition guidelines in Box 4.1.

Focus on Your Meal

Our surroundings and environmental stimuli affect what and how much we eat. These stimuli and external conditions are known as *ambience*. A review of the literature on ambience and food intake found that distracting factors, such as a large number of people, loud or soft music, and television viewing, increase food consumption (10). Hetherington et al specifically report that television distractions cause a 14% increase in calorie intake, relative to baseline (11). When blindfolded, obese subjects ate 24% fewer calories without feeling less full. This experiment supports the recommendation that limiting distractions can decrease calorie intake (12).

Box 4.1 ✦ Nutrition Guidelines for Meal Replacement Bars

As a general rule of thumb, patients should look for meal replacement bars with

- 220–350 kcal per bar (be sure to check label carefully to determine how many servings are in one bar)
- Less than 4 grams saturated fat per serving
- At least 10 grams protein per serving
- At least 3 grams of fiber per serving

The following counseling suggestions may help Meal Skippers focus on their meals:

- Ask patients to focus on their meal and postpone their e-mail, newspaper, Internet surfing, or television until mealtime is over.

- Recommend that patients eat at a dining room or kitchen table or in their office cafeteria where there are limited distractions, such as no computers or television.

- Encourage Meal Skippers to not eat while driving but rather to eat seated in a restaurant or pull over and park the car while eating.

- Ask patients to slow down the speed of eating to get the full pleasure out of each mealtime. One researcher suggests that making meals last 30 minutes may help decrease the amount of food eaten by about 70 kcal per meal (13).

- Discuss tips to help Meal Skippers slow down eating, such as putting less food on each forkful, chewing each bite thoroughly, and putting the fork down between bites.

Track Your Hunger and Fullness

Meal Skippers are seldom in touch with hunger and fullness cues. They don't notice hunger until it is too late and they are overly hungry and famished, which can lead to overeating. *The Appetite Awareness Workbook* by Craighead teaches patients to understand hunger and fullness sensations (14). Craighead uses a self-monitoring technique to help people regulate their eating behavior; the workbook includes daily appetite rating forms that are to be completed for each meal and snack with the goal of eating when moderately hungry and stopping when moderately full.

To help Meal Skippers develop hunger and fullness cues, clinicians should show patients how to monitor their appetite. A study by Drapeau and colleagues of 315 obese (BMI 30 to 35) dieting adults found that when people are aware that their hunger is minimal, they will eat a small meal (15). Clinicians may try asking patients to rate their hunger before each meal on a scale of 0 to 4 where:

- 0 = Not hungry
- 1 = Slightly hungry
- 2–3 = Moderate hunger
- 4 = Starving or overly hungry

Patients can either write this number on their food log or make a mental note. The goal is to have patients eat when they are between 2 and 3.

Teach patients that they should re-evaluate why they are eating if they eat when their hunger is at 0 to 1. They may eat for an emotional reason, such as anxiety, or for situational reasons, such as the food is just there or they were triggered by a food commercial on TV.

Remind patients who rank their hunger at a 4 that they are especially vulnerable to overeating when they are overly hungry, and therefore they need to pay extra close attention to eating slowly. Also remind them not to go long periods of time between meals and in the future to keep a snack, such as a piece of fruit or almonds, available to prevent high ratings. This self-monitoring activity will help the patient determine how different hunger levels feel.

Clinicians may also ask patients to rate fullness after a meal on a scale of 0 to 4 where:

- 0–1 = Not full
- 2–3 = Moderate fullness
- 4 = Stuffed or overly full

Similar to rating hunger, patients can either write down their fullness number on their food log or make a mental note of it. The goal is to have patients stop eating when they are a 2 or 3. If a patient pulls away from the table at a rating of 0 to 1 (before fullness), this may lead to feelings of deprivation and/or overeating later. If a patient eats until a 4 rating (overly full), the excess food will likely lead to weight gain.

Fill Up on Water and Fiber

Fiber and water can help keep patients full between meals. Together, fiber and water release the energy of food over several hours. Rolls et al have shown that when people increase consumption of foods with high amounts of water and fiber, they eat 30% fewer calories and do not feel deprived or hungry (16). Water needs vary based on weight, sex, age, activity level, and medications (17). Refer to Table 4.3 for the DRIs for fiber and fluids (3).

The following counseling suggestions may help Meal Skippers fill up on water and fiber:

- Ask patients to plan their meals so that each meal contains approximately 10 g of fiber or about one third of their daily fiber requirements. See Table 4.4 for fiber content of select foods (18,19). For a more complete list of fiber-rich foods, visit the USDA National Nutrient Database for Standard Reference Web site (http://www.ars.usda.gov/Services/docs.htm?docid=9673).

- Show patients how to read food labels for fiber and explain that products with 3 g per serving are a good source of fiber and products with more than 5 g per serving are an excellent source of fiber.

Questions to Ask During Counseling Sessions

The following are potential questions to help the clinician and the patient decide which of the four strategies or combination of strategies will best target the patient's needs. With practice, these strategies will lead your patient to more healthful eating habits.

- "Do you understand how meal skipping has caused you to gain weight?"

- "Why do you think you skip meals?"

- "What are the barriers that make it hard for you to eat at regular mealtimes each day?"

- "Given your schedule, what time of day do you think you should be eating each of your three meals?"

- "What can you do to reduce distractions while you eat?"

- "What physical signs do you notice when you are hungry or full?"

- "Do you know which kinds of foods are high in fiber?"

- "Of the four Meal Skipper strategies, which ones are you most confident you can adopt?"

- "Have you been successful at using any of these strategies in the past?"

Table 4.3 ✦ Dietary Reference Intakes for Fiber and Fluid[a]

	Men	Women
Fiber, g/d	Age ≤ 50 y: 38 Age > 50 y: 30	Age ≤ 50 y: 25 Age > 50 y: 21
Fluid, glasses/d (oz/d)	12.5 (100)	9 (72)

[a]Values are 80% Adequate Intakes (AIs) to reflect fluid needs in beverages only (not food).

Source: Data are from reference 3.

Table 4.4 ✦ Fiber Content of Select Foods

Food	Serving Size	Total Dietary Fiber, g
Fruits		
Apple, w/skin	1 large	3.7
Banana	1	2.8
Figs, dried	2	4.6
Orange	1	3.1
Peaches, canned	1/2	1.3
Pear	1	4.0
Prunes, dried	5	3.0
Raisins	1 small box (14 g)	0.6
Strawberries, sliced	1 cup	3.8
Vegetables		
Beans, canned (pinto, kidney, black, etc)	1/2 cup	4.5
Broccoli, raw	1/2 cup	1.3
Brussels sprouts, cooked	1/2 cup	2.0
Carrots, raw	1/2 cup	1.8
Celery, raw	1/2 cup	1.0
Lentils, cooked	1/2 cup	7.8
Lettuce, iceberg, shredded	1 cup	0.8
Peas, green, canned	1/2 cup	3.5
Peas, split, cooked	1/2 cup	8.1
Potatoes, boiled	1/2 cup	1.6
Spinach, cooked	1/2 cup	2.2
Grains		
Bread, white	1 slice	0.6
Bread, whole-wheat	1 slice	1.9
Cheerios	1 cup	2.6
Crackers, graham	2 squares	0.4
Cream of wheat	1 cup	2.9
Oat bran muffin	1	2.6
Oatmeal, cooked	3/4 cup	3.0
Raisin bran	1 cup	7.5
Rice, brown, cooked	1 cup	3.5
Rye crispbread	1 wafer	1.7

continued

Table 4.4 ✦ (continued)

Food	Serving Size	Total Dietary Fiber, g
Grains (continued)		
Shredded wheat	2 biscuits	5.0
Wheat bran flakes	3/4 cup	4.6
Others		
Nuts, mixed, dry roast	1 oz	2.6
Peanut butter	2 tablespoons	1.9

Source: Data are from reference 18. Table reprinted with permission from Position of the American Dietetic Association: health implications of dietary fiber. *J Am Diet Assoc.* 2002;102:993-1000.

Case Study

E is a 38-year-old male, 5′10″, who weighs 250 pounds with a BMI of 35.9. For his current job he travels to various client sites each day. He ends up eating only when he gets overly hungry, and then he will eat whatever the client site has available—leftover take-out, cookies, chips, and vending machine snacks. He will eat while he is working and seldom feels satisfied with what he is eating.

Clinician: "E, one of your dominant patterns is a Meal Skipper and you agreed that meal skipping is a pattern that you would like to change. Why do you think you skip meals?"

E: "I guess I get so busy during my work day and I don't feel hungry until it is too late and then I end up eating whatever is around me, which is usually doughnuts, cookies, or chips from a vending machine. I guess I just never come to work prepared to eat regular meals."

Clinician: "Well E, the first step for the Meal Skipper is to add structure to your eating, which will take some planning ahead on your part. Do you have any ideas of how you could be more prepared to eat regular meals when at your client sites?"

E: "Because my schedule changes day to day, I guess I could plan ahead each night before I go to work and figure out how to fit breakfast and lunch into the next day's routine. But whatever I do has to be quick and easy because I don't have a lot of time."

Clinician: "I have two suggestions that may work. First, if you keep some meal replacement bars in your home, you'll be able to grab a bar any time you're in a rush and that plus a piece of fruit can be your breakfast. And, if you get a cooler or a thermal lunch pack for your car, you could pack it when needed with fruit, yogurt, a sandwich, or some healthy snacks and bottled waters. This way you'll be prepared when visiting your client sites. Does this seem doable?"

E: "Yes it does. My wife actually does the shopping on the weekends and as long as I tell her the types of foods I need, I'll be all set for the week."

Clinician: "Take this Meal Skipper handout as a reminder of what you are working on until our next appointment. We only discussed the first strategy for the Meal Skipper, but I want you to feel successful following this strategy before we get into the other three strategies. I wrote down what to look for when purchasing a healthy meal replacement bar and I also listed some healthy lunch options that you can bring from home. At your next appointment we will see how well you have controlled meal skipping and, if you're ready and interested, we will discuss how the other three strategies might be helpful."

The Nighttime Nibbler

Description

Nighttime Nibblers find themselves eating most of their daily calories from dinnertime onward. Their night eating habit causes them to awaken without a morning appetite, which leads them to go through the day without eating much; then they approach night time ravenous, and the cycle continues.

The Problem

People with night eating behaviors are more likely to be obese, be depressed, and suffer from emotional eating, and they are less likely to adhere to a healthful diet and exercise plan (20). Gluck et al found that night eaters in a weight-loss study lost significantly less weight in a 1-month period than non–night eaters (9.7 pounds vs 16.1 pounds.) (21). Therefore, for increased quality of life and weight control, it is important to help patients learn to break the cycle of night eating. See Box 4.2 for information about when night eaters may need medical intervention (22,23).

Strategies for Nighttime Nibblers

Tips to help Nighttime Nibblers succeed at weight loss and maintenance include:

- Spread calories evenly throughout the day
- Remove unhealthy foods from the home
- Plan one nightly snack that satisfies
- Reset your nighttime routine

Spread Calories Evenly Throughout the Day

Normal-weight individuals are more likely to eat their calories evenly distributed throughout the day than are obese patients (24). Keim et al found that when people eat 70% of their calories early in the day, they lose about 1.5 pounds more in 6 weeks than those who eat 70% of their calories in the evening (25).

The following counseling suggestions may help Nighttime Nibblers evenly spread their calories through the day:

- Ask Nighttime Nibblers to add a light lunch to their schedule. Lunch is often the best place to begin because patients probably are not very hungry in the morning. Light lunch suggestions include lentil soup and a roll or a half turkey sandwich and a piece of fruit or baby carrots.

Box 4.2 ✦ When Night Eaters May Need Medical Intervention

"Nighttime nibbling" is different from conditions associated with sleep disturbances called "night eating syndrome" or "nocturnal eating" (22). Night eating syndrome is defined as overeating at night before bed with trouble getting to sleep, whereas nocturnal eating is defined as having trouble getting to sleep, trouble staying asleep, eating after having gone to bed, and potentially sleepwalking and eating (23). These conditions may need medical intervention and potentially medications. If your patient is having difficulty breaking the night-nibbling habit and is experiencing sleep disturbances, it may be necessary to refer him or her to a sleep expert.

- After patients have successfully added lunch to their schedule, ask them to plan an afternoon snack, such as apple slices with peanut butter or a 100-calorie bag of popcorn and a piece of string cheese.

- As your patients eat more during the day and less at night, they will start feeling hungry in the morning and it will be easier to add a morning meal. Breakfast suggestions include a quick bowl of cereal with skim milk or low-fat yogurt with a sprinkle of high-fiber cereal and fruit on top.

For feedback from an actual patient see Box 4.3.

Remove Unhealthy Foods from the Home

Patients will find it much easier to snack less in the evening if they completely remove high-calorie munchies such as chips, cookies, and ice cream. This concept of "out of sight, out of mouth" was verified in a 2006 study. In this study, consumption of candy increased when it was visible and in closer proximity to the study participants. The 40 secretaries in the study ate 2.2 more candies per day when the candy was visible in a clear bowl vs in an opaque one, and 1.8 more candies per day when the sweets were in close proximity on their desks vs 6.5 feet away (26).

The following counseling suggestions may help Nighttime Nibblers remove unhealthful snacks from their home:

- Encourage patients to completely remove any items they consider a "trigger" food (ie, those foods that are difficult to have just a small amount).

- Ask patients to restock their kitchens with more healthful, lower-calorie snacks such as low-fat microwave popcorn, crispy apples, low-fat ranch dip with peapods, string cheese and whole grain crackers, and low-fat yogurt.

- If patients are unwilling to remove all unhealthful snacks from the home, discuss a compromise in which they keep unhealthful snacks out of sight (in the back of their cabinets and fridge), in opaque containers, and not in plain view on the counter.

Plan One Nightly Snack That Satisfies

A snack after dinner can be a healthful way for your patients to end the evening. The key is to teach them to pre-plan the snack, in a portion- and calorie-controlled amount, and eat it slowly and mindfully. When patients were instructed to pre-plan a 200-calorie bowl of cereal in the evening, they reduced their evening snack calories by more than 100 and their total daily calories by almost 400 (27).

Box 4.3 ✦ Patient Feedback on Changing Nighttime Nibbling Habits

"Now that I am focusing on eating during the day, I am not as hungry at night. So, even though I want to snack, I tell myself I am not really hungry and I brew my favorite brand of herbal tea. It doesn't work every night, but most nights it does!"

—Patient quote

The following counseling suggestions may help Nighttime Nibblers plan one satisfying snack per evening:

- Ask patients to eat 200 or fewer calories for the evening snack.

- Have patients pre-plan their snack by writing out three to five choices on an index card. See Box 4.4 for snack suggestions.

- Remind patients to eat *mindfully* to increase their enjoyment. For example, instead of eating a low-fat vanilla pudding cup standing at the fridge, put it in a bowl, add some fresh strawberries, and sit down at the table to mindfully enjoy the snack.

- If patients find that they are still hungry for more food after eating the snack, ask them to practice activities to signal "doneness," such as brewing a cup of peppermint tea, brushing their teeth, and/or turning the lights off in the kitchen.

- Remind patients they need three things when eating: a table, a plate, and a chair. No more standing at the cabinet eating out of a package!

Reset Your Nighttime Routine

Many patients say it feels like they are on "autopilot" and just can't get a handle on the nighttime nibbling. In many instances, patients' unhealthful eating habits are triggered by their surroundings. When patients pair certain activities repeatedly with eating, it is difficult to break the routine. Sitting in that same chair, watching TV, *and* snacking makes them associate sitting in that chair and watching TV *with* snacking. The influence of the environment on behaviors has been extensively investigated in the psychology literature. Treatment protocols focus on a combination of reducing the exposure to environmental triggers associated with eating (eg, don't watch TV—read instead) and unlearning these associations with practice (eg, watch TV without food repeatedly) (28). Teach your patients to practice new evening traditions and rituals so they learn to untangle their "autopilot associations."

The following counseling suggestions may help Nighttime Nibblers reset their nighttime routine:

- Have patients try new locations for doing their evening activities, such as watching TV in another room or sitting in another chair.

- Ask patients to list out the chain of events in their typical evening; then review this chain with them and provide suggestions of what other options or activities they can try. For example, patients could try reading a book or magazine, using an exercise video, or doing puzzles instead of watching TV.

- Ask patients to add 20 minutes of relaxation, such as deep breathing, listening to calming music, or taking a bath, to their evening routine. In a 2003 study of 20 nondieting adults with Night Eating Syndrome, participants who practiced 20 minutes of muscle relaxation significantly decreased the number of nights they snacked (from 50% to 3% of nights) and lost almost 2 pounds in the first 8 days of adding relaxation before bed (29).

Box 4.4 ✦ Nighttime Snack Suggestions with Less than 200 kcal

- 3/4 cup wholegrain cereal with 4 ounces fat-free milk
- 5 whole grain crackers and 1 tablespoon peanut butter
- Portion-controlled, 150-calorie ice cream sandwich

See Box 4.5 for feedback from a Nighttime Nibbler.

Questions Clinicians Ask During Counseling Sessions

The following are potential questions to help the clinician and patient decide which of the four strategies (singly or in combination) will best target the patient's needs. With practice, these strategies will lead your patient to more healthful eating habits.

- "What are the reasons you don't eat much in the morning and afternoon?"
- "Are you usually ravenous when dinnertime approaches? Why do you think that happens?"
- "What triggers your evening snacking?"
- "What are the trigger foods you tend to eat for evening snacks?"
- "What healthy snacks do you enjoy eating?"
- "Where do you eat in the evening (table, couch, bed, etc)?"
- "What activities are you doing while you are eating/snacking at night?"
- "What activities do you enjoy that you are not doing now?"
- "Of the four Nighttime Nibbler strategies, which ones are you most confident you can adopt?"
- "Have you been successful at using any of these strategies in the past?"

Case Study

T is a 27-year-old woman, 5'2", who weighs 158 pounds with a BMI of 28.9. She works as a manager in a retail store. She eats something small, such as a piece of fruit, for breakfast because she isn't hungry. She tries to be "good" all day by eating very small portions at lunch and fights her urge to snack. She gets home tired and hungry and goes right to the fridge. Because T is starving, she regularly overeats at dinner. Her nighttime ritual is watching TV on the couch and continual snacking until bedtime. She isn't even sure she is actually hungry, but this habit seems ingrained into her nightly routine.

> **Clinician:** "T, how long has nighttime eating been a habit?"
>
> **T:** "For as long as I can remember. I guess because I don't eat much during the day, and am so hungry that once I start eating dinner I just can't stop. Snacking at night is kind of soothing to me—as is the TV."
>
> **Clinician:** "There are four strategies that we've discussed from this handout that can help control the evening eating. What do you think of these?"
>
> **T:** "It's the evening routine that really interests me."

Box 4.5 ✦ Patient Feedback on Changing Nighttime Habits

"Changing my evening routine has been the key to decreasing my Nighttime Nibbling. Instead of getting up during commercial breaks to get a snack, I now practice my golf putts while I am waiting for my show to come back on."

—Patient quote

Clinician: "Okay. We can start in the home. Resetting your evening routine means disentangling eating on the couch and watching TV. Would you be willing to make a new rule for yourself in the evenings? The rule would be: If you want to snack at night, you must do it in the kitchen. No more eating on the couch. And you have to sit down and eat off of a plate."

T: "And that will help me eat less at night?"

Clinician: "Actually, yes. Going through this activity will make you think twice whether you are hungry or not. And when you do want to have a snack at night, let's plan for it in advance. I want you to "calorie-proof" your home—that is, have only lower calorie snack choices, such as a 100-calorie bag of fig cookies or a single-portion ice cream sandwich, in the house."

T: "All right. I'll give it a try."

Clinician: "Take this Nighttime Nibbler handout as a reminder of what you are working on until our next appointment. A good place to keep this handout is posted on the fridge where you can see it and you will be reminded to not bring food to the couch in the TV room, but rather only eat in the kitchen, sitting down, with a plate."

The Convenient Diner

Description

Convenient Diners eat foods that are convenient, ready-made, packaged, frozen and microwavable, with most foods in their diet bearing a brand name that is posted on the box or bag. Convenient Diners grab for the phone to dial for take-out more often than they grab a cookbook to make a fresh homemade meal. They dine out at sit-down, buffet, or fast-casual restaurants and may even visit a fast-food drive-through on most days of the week. Their diets consist of foods higher in fat, calories, and sodium and lower in fiber than foods cooked at home. When they do eat at home, their meal is most often ordered-in or microwaved.

The Problem

From 1978 to 1996, consumption of food eaten away from home significantly increased, from 18% to 32% of total calories. Away-from-home meals typically contain more calories, saturated fat, sodium, and cholesterol, and less fiber, calcium, and iron than home-cooked meals. Of all dining-out categories, fast food is chosen more often than sit-down restaurants or other types of dining establishments (30). According to a 2004 study, one in six adults reported eating fast food on one of the two survey days in 1989-1991 vs one in four adults in 1994-1996. Adults consume 200 kcal more on days they dine at fast-food restaurants than on days they do not (31). Bottom line: the more frequently your patients dine out, the more calories they will eat. Kant and Graubard estimate that individuals who dine out less than once per week eat an average of 271 kcal less per day than people who dine out six or more times per week (32). Members of the National Weight Control Registry (NWCR) who have lost an average of 70 pounds and kept it off for more than 5 years tend to dine out no more than 2.5 meals/week in restaurants and less than once per week at fast-food restaurants (7).

The goals are to improve how Convenient Diners order at restaurants and/or decrease their frequency of dining out. The strategies used with the Convenient Diner assume that people will continue to dine out for many reasons and need information and skills to improve the quality of their dining-out occasions. People dine out because they are in a hurry, are too tired to cook, want a treat that tastes good, or feel they have no other choice (33).

Strategies for Convenient Diners

The following strategies may help Convenient Diners succeed at weight loss and maintenance:

- Eat smaller portions
- Reduce added fat and beverage calories
- Use available nutrition information
- Practice quick cooking at home

Eat Smaller Portions

Decreasing portion size when dining out is an extremely important strategy to teach patients. Diliberti et al found that when large entrées were served, people ate 43% more (over 700 kcal more!) than when smaller entrees were served (34). Whether it is fast-food restaurants or sit-down dining, large portions are an industry standard. According to a 2003 study, portions of away-from-home foods were two to eight times federal recommended serving sizes. For example, the Food Guide Pyramid recommended a cookie portion of 0.5 oz, but average cookies available in the marketplace were 4 oz, or eight times the recommended size (35).

The following counseling suggestions may help Convenient Diners eat smaller portions:

- Teach patients to order smaller portions so they can clean their plates without overeating. For example, instead of the four-taco entrée served with rice and beans, suggest they order three tacos a la carte; instead of the double cheeseburger, ask them to consider changing to a single; encourage them to choose a cup of soup instead of the bowl or a small latte instead of a large.

- Suggest that patients try ordering an appetizer portion paired with a broth soup or salad for their lunch and dinner meals. Most patients are surprised that the smaller portions satisfy their hunger and they appreciate not feeling overly full.

- Remind patients that splitting entrées with another person can be a great strategy to enjoy smaller versions of their favorites.

- If patients cannot split an entrée with someone, have them order an entrée with half wrapped to go and the other half on a plate to eat immediately.

Reduce Added Fat and Beverage Calories

Added fats, such as butter, salad dressings, and oil, are the primary sources of fat in the diet (25% fat calories) compared to fat from meats (21%), desserts (13%), cheese (10%), and salty snacks (6%) (36). It is estimated that beverage calories are increasing steadily. In 1965 Americans drank 236 calories per day whereas in 2002 beverage consumption had risen to 458 calories per day. The increase comes primarily from fruit drinks, alcohol, and soda. (37)

The following counseling suggestions may help Convenient Diners reduce added calories:

- Teach patients to ask for added fats such as sauces, cream, cheese, mayonnaise, salad dressings, and butter on the side, or to hold them altogether. When added fats are on the side, patients can use them sparingly, if at all. See tips for making healthful food choices when eating out in Table 4.5.

- Teach patients key words to use and not use when ordering food items, such as avoid the words *crispy*, *fried*, and *breaded* and look for the words *grilled*, *baked*, and *broiled*.

- Remind patients that lower-fat and lower-calorie foods can be easily substituted for higher-fat and higher-calorie foods. For example, an english muffin can be substituted for a biscuit or croissant. An extra steamed vegetable side can be substituted for fried rice. Low-fat salad dressing can be substituted for full-fat versions.

- Discuss added calories in beverages, such as soda, beer, wine, sweetened tea, specialty coffee drinks, and juice.

Table 4.5 ✦ Patient Tips for Making Healthy Food Choices When Eating Out

Type of Restaurant	Choose *More*	Choose *Less*	Special Requests:
Fast-food/ fast-casual	• Salads • Chili, bean, and broth soups • No-calorie drinks • Grilled chicken sandwiches • Single hamburger • Turkey sandwich	• Fries • Chips • Cream soups • Soft drinks • Fried or crispy sandwiches • Upsized burgers and sandwiches	• Light salad dressing • No mayonnaise • Hold the cheese • Grilled not fried • Extra vegetables on sandwich • Fruit on the side
Mexican	• Soft tacos • Chicken, vegetable, or shrimp fajitas • Bean soup • Black beans • Gazpacho • A la carte items • No- or low-calorie drinks, such as unsweetened iced tea or light beer	• Deep-fried items such as flautas, chimichangas, chips • Sour cream, cheese, guacamole • Full entrees and meal platters • Margaritas, sangria	• Salsa or jalapeño peppers instead of guacamole or sour cream • Easy on the cheese or hold the cheese • A la carte items instead of meal platter
Italian	• Bean and broth soup • Salad • Tomato-based sauces, such as marinara • Thin-crust pizza, easy on the cheese, extra vegetable, no meat toppings • Whole-grain pasta and crust when available	• Cream-based sauces • Deep-dish pizza with meat toppings • Fried eggplant parmesan • Garlic bread/bread with butter or oil • Cheese-based entrees such as ravioli or lasagna	• Light salad dressing • Remove bread basket • Glass of wine instead of bottle • Extra vegetables
Asian (Thai, Chinese, Japanese)	• Broth-based soup • Steamed tofu entrees • Edamame • Sushi • Fish dishes • Dishes with extra steamed vegetables • Steamed appetizers, such as spring rolls	• Soups made with coconut milk • Fried tofu • Deep-fried dishes, such as tempura • Fried crispy noodles • Fried and/or cheesy appetizers such as crab rangoon	• Extra vegetables • Chopsticks (for slower eating) • Cook in less oil • Brown rice instead of white when available
Greek	• Hummus and pita • Fish entrees • Bean- and lentil-based dishes • Chicken shish kebab	• Fried cheese	• Light on oil • Whole-grain pita when available
Indian	• Dishes with beans and lentils • Roasted meats/tandoori style	• Deep-fried bread and appetizers • Dishes with cheese	• Make without cream • Light on oil/butter/ghee

Use Available Nutrition Information

Restaurants are providing consumers with more healthful options, and increasing numbers of restaurants are providing nutrition information. Among nearly 300 restaurants surveyed in 2004, 54% of restaurants made some type of nutrition information available and more than 85% of restaurants provided information on their Web site (38). But although the information is being provided, most people are not likely to use nutrition information if it were available (39). Furthermore, about one in three people who use the nutrition information use it inaccurately (40).

The following counseling suggestions may help Convenient Diners use nutrition information, and use it accurately:

- Ask patients to gather the menus of their three favorite restaurants by either going to the restaurant or visiting the Web site; then review the menus with patients, and teach them specific maneuvers to practice the next time they dine in those restaurants.

- Have your patients print nutrition information from restaurant Web sites. They can keep it in a binder, or even in their car, for reference the next time they are dining out.

- Advise patients to ask for nutrition information provided at restaurants.

- Educate patients about calorie-counting Web sites (eg, http://www.calorieking.com) that have nutrition analyses for a variety of restaurant meals.

- Inform patients about Nutrition on the Go text messaging service offered by Diet.com. Using a cell phone and texting DIET1 (34381) with a menu item and restaurant name, individuals can get nutrition information on more than 36,000 menu items at 1,700 restaurants. This service is free (aside from the costs of text messaging). An online demonstration of this tool is available (http://diet.com/mobile).

- Because many people are unlikely to stop ordering high-fat foods at their favorite restaurants (41), encourage patients to try a new healthful entrée or side, such as a salad with light dressing, a cup of fruit, sliced apples, or light yogurt.

- Most importantly, provide patients with healthful guidelines for their restaurant meal. See Box 4.6.

Box 4.6 ✦ Nutrition Guidelines for Healthy Restaurant Meals

For individuals following a 1200- to 1599-calorie diet, their restaurant meal should be:
- 350–500 kcal (about 30% of total daily calories)
- < 5 g saturated fat (less than 10% of meal's calories)
- < 2 g *trans* fat (if any at all)
- < 800 mg sodium (about 30% of daily recommendation of 2,300 mg)

For individuals following a 1600- to 2000-calorie diet, a restaurant meal should be:
- 500–700 kcal (about 30% of total daily calories)
- < 7 g saturated fat (less than 10% of meal's calories)
- < 2 g *trans* fat (less than 1% of daily calories if any at all)
- < 800 mg sodium (about 30% of daily recommendation of 2,300 mg)

Practice Quick Cooking at Home

Cooking for enjoyment is a common strategy of people successful at losing weight and keeping it off (9). Help patients learn how to stock up on easy and quick meals they can enjoy making at home. Convenient Diners dine out because they are in a hurry, are too tired to cook, and want a meal or treat that tastes good, so it is important that cooking at home is fast, easy, and delicious.

The following counseling suggestions may help Convenient Diners practice quick home cooking:

- Ask patients what their favorite restaurant meals are and explain that at-home versions can be more healthful, lower in calories, and possibly just as quick. For example, if your patient's favorite meal is shrimp stir fry, suggest that they stock up on precooked frozen shrimp, frozen vegetable medleys, and microwaveable plain brown rice.

- Encourage patients to try at least one new convenient product at each trip to the grocery store. Convenience product suggestions include precooked chicken strips, precut and cleaned green beans, or whole grain couscous, which takes less than 10 minutes to cook.

- Suggest that patients time how long it takes to wait in a restaurant for their meal or for take-out to arrive. This will help patients realize that quick meals at home usually take the same amount of time or are even faster than restaurants.

- Have patients write down three to five quick meal ideas on index cards that they can hang on their fridge, and ask them to always keep recipe ingredients stocked so when they feel tired and can't think of what to prepare, they will have ideas ready to whip up that are quicker than calling for take-out. See quick meal lunch and dinner ideas in Box 4.7.

- Ask patients to visit Web sites (such as http://www.fruitsandveggiesmorematters.org) for new recipes, subscribe to weekly e-mail recipes online (eg, recipes from the American Institute for Cancer Research [http://www.aicr.org]), or purchase a healthy cooking magazine such as *Cooking Light*.

Box 4.7 ✦ Patient Tips: Five Quick Meal Lunch and Dinner Ideas

- **Salad in a Pita:** Stuff a whole wheat pita with spinach, shredded carrots, and cucumber slices, 3 ounces of precooked chicken strips. Top with 2 tablespoons of reduced fat salad dressing. Serve with a broth-based canned soup.
- **Bean Burrito:** In an 8-inch whole-wheat tortilla, place 1/2 cup canned low-fat refried beans, 1/3 cup low-fat shredded cheddar cheese, shredded romaine, and salsa. Microwave until warm, about 3 to 4 minutes. Enjoy with a side salad.
- **Shrimp Caesar:** Toss romaine lettuce with 3 ounces thawed precooked frozen shrimp, pre-sliced mushrooms, diced zucchini, and 2 tablespoons of reduced-fat Caesar dressing. Enjoy with 10 high-fiber crackers.
- **Better BLT:** Between 2 pieces of whole-wheat bread, place 4 strips of cooked turkey bacon, sliced tomatoes, romaine lettuce leaves, and 1 tablespoon of low-fat mayonnaise. Enjoy with a piece of fruit on the side.
- **Chili Cheese Potato and Broccoli:** Bake a potato in the microwave for 6 to 8 minutes until tender. Top with broccoli, 1/2 cup canned vegetarian chili, and 1/3 cup shredded low-fat shredded cheddar cheese.

Questions Clinicians Ask During Counseling Sessions

Following are potential questions to help the clinician and the patient decide which of the four strategies or combination of strategies will best target the patient's needs. With practice, these strategies will lead your patient to more healthful eating habits.

- "What are the reasons that you tend to dine out frequently?"
- "How many times do you dine out for business and social reasons vs just dining out for convenience?"
- "How and when do you decide what you are going to order at a restaurant?"
- "What are your favorite types of restaurants and what do you order?"
- "What healthy requests do you feel comfortable asking for?"
- "Do you think you can order smaller meals, split entrées with others, or order healthier foods at restaurants? What would be the difficulties in doing this?"
- "What limits you from cooking at home?"
- "Which strategies do you think would be the easiest for you to adopt? The hardest?"
- "Which strategies have you tried successfully in the past or have you seen someone else try?"

Case Study

A is a 34-year-old man, 5′9″, who weighs 196 pounds with a BMI of 29.0. He is single and lives alone but has many friends who live nearby. He received his first big promotion about two years ago and now goes to many business lunches during the week. Since he started making more money, he can afford to go out to nice restaurants for most of his dinner meals after work. On the weekends, because he doesn't keep much food in the house, he orders in or dines out with friends for almost all of his meals.

> **Clinician:** "A, your major eating pattern is a Convenient Diner and you agree that working on this pattern makes the most sense to start taking better control of calories. So let's start here. What are your favorite types of restaurants and what do you order?"
>
> **A:** "I love all types of restaurants, but I particularly love Italian restaurants—pasta is a favorite of mine. I usually am drawn to dishes with cheese fillings or cream sauce."
>
> **Clinician:** "There are three strategies that are useful when eating away from home: decrease portions, find extra calories, and use nutrition information when it's available. Are you willing to start focusing on reducing portions, finding added calories, and being more assertive when you're ordering your meal—having it 'my way' as the song says? Have you ever ordered off the appetizer side of the menu?"
>
> **A:** "Yes, I am up for trying new restaurant strategies. I haven't even thought of ordering off the appetizer menu. I could do that."
>
> **Clinician:** "Along with splitting entrées, that is probably one of the most useful strategies when eating in a restaurant. Just ask for an appetizer size of what you want. You've just cut the calories by one third or a half. When I say 'find added calories,' that primarily means the cream sauces, dressings, cheeses, and oils that are added to food. And the idea of having restaurant foods 'your way' means asking for sauces on the side or special ordering dishes to be light on oil and cheese—these modifications can significantly reduce the calories served."

A: "The last idea will be a bit harder, but I see where you are going with that suggestion. How about if I first work on reducing portions and I'll try to cut the fatty foods as well?"

Clinician: "Sounds good. I want you to remember that planning for what you're going to eat must begin before you walk into the restaurant. Have a game plan in mind before you open the door."

The Fruitless Feaster

Description

Fruitless Feasters don't eat enough fruits and vegetables, enjoying a diet mainly of proteins, breads, pastas, desserts, processed snacks and, of course, fats. They know they should be eating more fruits and vegetables than they do, but either they don't purchase fruits and vegetables at all; they sometimes buy produce but end up having to toss it because it rots before they eat it; or they never learned to enjoy fruits or vegetables as part of their diet.

The Problem

We can best understand the problem of not eating enough fruits and vegetables by the vast amount of information available on the benefits of eating produce. Increased consumption of fruits and vegetables has been found to be beneficial for weight loss and maintenance in both epidemiological research and intervention trials (42). In addition to being beneficial to weight management, diets high in fruits and vegetables may prevent about 20% of all cancer incidence, decrease heart disease by 15%, decrease stroke by 27%, and decrease blood pressure for those with hypertension by approximately 11.6 mm Hg systolic/5.3 mm Hg diastolic (43).

The goal is to help Fruitless Feasters consume at least 1.5 cups of fruit and 2 cups of vegetables each day (44). Patients trying to lose weight appreciate the satiety fruits and vegetables can provide as part of a low-calorie diet. Studies show that increasing amounts of produce decreases total daily calorie intake without increasing feelings of hunger or deprivation. Specifically, Shintani et al found that when participants were encouraged to eat more fruits and vegetables, they consumed 40% fewer calories (from 2,594 to 1,596 kcal per day) without increasing hunger (45). Advising patients to increase fruits and vegetables emphasizes a positive message of "adding to" their diet as opposed to focusing on restriction. Positive messaging is a key principle for effective nutrition communication and initiation of behavior change (46). For a discussion of counseling principles, see Chapter 1.

The strategies used for the Fruitless Feaster address the reported barriers to eating more fruits and vegetables. Barriers to eating more fruits and vegetables can be internal (taste, lack of skills/knowledge, digestive problems) or external (availability, accessibility, cost, time/effort, support system) (47).

Strategies for Fruitless Feasters

The following strategies may help Fruitless Feasters succeed at weight loss and maintenance:

- Have produce ready and on hand
- Make fruits and vegetables flavorful
- Pick colorful produce
- Eat more vegetarian meals

Have Produce Ready and On Hand

For most consumers, the challenge with fresh produce is that it needs to be bought regularly to maintain its freshness. For Fruitless Feasters, some produce also needs a bit of preparation time to encourage them to eat it. However, frozen fruits and vegetables offer Fruitless Feasters a convenient way to eat produce with less prep work.

The following counseling suggestions may help Fruitless Feasters have produce available and accessible:

- Encourage patients to *buy* more produce to have available in the home. This is the first step to helping them eat more produce.

- Advise patients to go to the grocery store regularly, at least once a week, to stock up on produce and other healthful foods.

- Ask patients to do the "grocery cart check"—making sure their cart is filled with 50% produce before checking out.

- Because cost may be a perceived barrier for certain patients, encourage them to check circulars and newspaper ads for sales on fresh produce, comparison shop between fresh and frozen versions, shop for produce at discount fruit markets or warehouse clubs like Costco or Sam's Club, and buy produce that is in season.

- Teach patients to have produce available and accessible (ready-to-eat.) (48). For example, tell your patients to make produce easy to grab by keeping a fruit bowl out on the counter and a cut vegetable tray at eye-level in the refrigerator.

- Talk to patients about purchasing precut fresh and frozen produce and spending time on the weekend to get ready for the week. Because many patients report time as being a barrier to eating more fruits and vegetables, it is important to make them especially convenient.

- Review with patients specific ways to conveniently and easily add fruits and vegetables through the day. See examples in Box 4.8.

Box 4.8 ✦ Patient Tips: Adding Fruits and Vegetables to Meals

Breakfast

- Add fresh or thawed frozen strawberries, blueberries, or raspberries to cereal or on top of low-fat yogurt or cottage cheese.
- Add bell peppers, onions, salsa, or spinach to morning omelets.
- Eat sliced tomato and cucumber on a bagel.
- Add chopped apple and cinnamon or canned pumpkin to a bowl of oatmeal.

Lunch and Dinner

- Pack grape tomatoes, peapods, baby carrots, cucumber slices, or celery sticks to dip in low-fat ranch dressing.
- Add shredded broccoli and carrots, spinach, or pear slices to a sandwich.
- Choose a side salad or fruit instead of fries when eating at a restaurant.
- Ask for an extra vegetable-of-the-day or vegetable soup at a restaurant.
- Microwave a bag of frozen vegetables and top with a handful of chopped almonds or walnuts, lemon pepper, or low-fat Italian dressing for a quick side dish.
- Add more vegetables (fresh or frozen) to family-favorite entrées that typically contain few to no vegetables, such as casseroles, pasta, and soups.

Make Fruits and Vegetables Flavorful

Taste is one of the most important factors when discussing food and nutrition with your patients. Many patients may have never purchased or tasted certain fruits or vegetables and don't know how to eat them or prepare them.

The following counseling suggestions may help Fruitless Feasters learn how to prepare delicious produce:

- Encourage patients to enhance the flavor of produce by trying a variety of fresh and dried herbs and spices. They can purchase them at local grocery stores or spice shops, or visit online stores to have them delivered right to their door.

- Advise patients to purchase prepared low-fat marinades and dressings, which are available in many different styles and flavors.

- Talk with patients about the sodium content in seasonings and marinades and instruct them to aim to have 2,300 mg of sodium (equivalent to 1 teaspoon of salt) or less per day as recommended by the USDA 2005 Dietary Guidelines (4).

- Encourage patients to look for low-sodium seasonings (those that have 140 mg sodium or less per serving) (49).

- Have patients try new recipes. They may want to subscribe to magazines such as *Cooking Light,* find produce recipes online, or ask a friend for recipes.

- Encourage patients to take a cooking class or watch a cooking program on TV. Improved cooking skills have been shown to increase fruit consumption by 40% and vegetables by 30% (50).

- Suggest that patients learn and try different cooking methods (boiling and steaming can get boring!) such as roasting to bring out the sweetness of vegetables or grilling for new flavor experiences.

- Review with patients previous positive dining experiences with fruits and vegetables and have them re-create those recipes. For example, if your patient has had delicious green beans with pine nuts and lemon zest at a restaurant, encouraging him or her to sprinkle lemon pepper and toasted pine nuts on sautéed green beans at home.

Clinicians should note the following:

- Research shows there are taste and preference differences between fruit lovers and vegetable lovers. If patients say they like spicy foods and/or drinking wine with dinner, they are candidates for increasing vegetables before fruits. If patients say they do not like trying new recipes, focus on increasing fruits before vegetables (51).

- About 25% of the population are "super tasters," people who are extra-sensitive to bitter tastes found in foods such as vegetables (52). To help combat the bitter taste, have your patients add fat or sugar. Just like cream and sugar "de-bitter" black coffee, a little bit of cheese, reduced-fat salad dressing, barbecue sauce, or sweet–and-sour sauce can make vegetables taste less bitter.

Pick Colorful Produce

For the first time in history, the United States Department of Agriculture (USDA) 2005 Dietary Guidelines include recommendations for target amounts of specific produce. For example, on an 1,800-calorie diet, the goal is 2.5 cups of vegetables each day, *but* the specific breakdown each week should be 3 cups of dark green vegetables, 2 cups of orange vegetables, 3 cups of legumes, 3 cups of starchy vegetables, and 6.5 cups of others (44).

Americans do not eat enough fruits and vegetables, and they are particularly unlikely to eat enough dark-green and orange produce (53). Phytochemicals give plants their color and have been found to help prevent chronic disease. The color of a fruit or vegetable indicates which phytochemicals it provides. For example, red is associated with lycopene, yellow-green foods with lutein and zeaxanthin, red-purple with anthocyanins, orange with flavonoids, green with glucosinolates, and white-green with allyl sulfides (54). As clinicians, teaching patients to eat a wide variety of produce based on color is an easy and positive message that can have health benefits.

The following counseling suggestions may help Fruitless Feasters pick colorful produce:

- Have patients check their grocery cart to see whether they purchased all the colors: red, orange, yellow, green, purple, and white.

- Teach patients different and exciting produce color combinations to turn ordinary snacks and meals into extraordinary snacks and meals. For example, cantaloupe and blueberries mixed in yogurt for breakfast; red and green apple slices for a snack; green kiwi, red radishes, and yellow corn in a green spinach salad for lunch; or roasted green brussels sprouts with white potatoes as a dinner side dish.

- Advise patients to learn how to identify, select, and prepare brightly colored produce such as kale and swiss chard by using the Internet or books such as the *Field Guide to Produce* by Aliza Green (Philadelphia, PA: Quirk Books; 2004).

Eat More Vegetarian Meals

Vegetarians and semi-vegetarians tend to have lower BMIs than omnivores. In a 2005 study of 55,459 people, the prevalence of overweight and obesity (BMI > 25) was 40% in omnivores vs 29% in vegetarians and semi-vegetarians (55).

The following counseling suggestions may help Fruitless Feasters incorporate more vegetarian-style meals:

- Suggest that patients aim for 1 to 2 meatless meals per week to start.

- Encourage patients to order a meatless meal at a restaurant; for example, a veggie burger or vegetable and black bean fajitas.

- Educate patients about vegetarian foods to purchase from the grocery store. Examples include vegetarian burgers instead of standard beef burgers to cook on the grill, meatless crumbles for tacos and spaghetti sauce, vegetarian chili to put on a potato or eat with a whole grain roll, canned beans such as low-fat refried beans for quick burritos, or drained and rinsed canned garbanzo, kidney, or black beans to toss on salads or into pitas.

If patients find that increasing fruits and vegetables causes them uncomfortable gas or bloating, have them try a digestive enzyme such as Bean-O (GlaxoSmithKline Consumer Healthcare, http://us.gsk.com) with their meal to aid in the digestion of complex plant sugars. It is also a good idea to ask patients to increase fiber *gradually*, in conjunction with increasing fluid intake, to decrease bloating.

Questions Clinicians Ask During Counseling Sessions

Following are potential questions to help the clinician and patient decide which of the four strategies or combination of strategies will best target the patient's needs. With practice, these strategies will lead the patient to more healthful eating habits.

- "What prevents you from eating more fruits and/or vegetables?"

- "How often do you buy fruits and vegetables at the grocery store?"

- "What types of fruits and vegetables do you usually buy?"

- "What fruits and vegetables do you like?"

- "What seasonings do you usually put on fruits and vegetables?"

- "What is your favorite way to cook vegetables?"

- "Have you ever tried a vegetarian meal? What was it?"

- "Which of the four strategies sound most useful to start practicing?"

- "Which strategies stand out as being something you have wanted to change?"

Case Study

M is a 45-year-old male, 6′0″, who weighs 238 pounds with a BMI of 32.3. He is a self-defined "steak and potatoes" kind of guy. He didn't grow up eating many vegetables, so now he rarely eats them. Because he lives alone, if he does buy them, they tend to go bad in his refrigerator and end up being a waste of money.

> **Clinician:** "M, as you probably realize, eating more fruits and vegetables is really important for overall health and for weight loss. The Fruitless Feaster is your most dominant eating pattern. Can I give you some tips?"

> **M:** "I guess so, but there is no way I am eating broccoli!"

> **Clinician:** "We don't have to start with the 'B' word. What fruits and vegetables do you like?"

> **M:** "I actually don't really think I like many fruits and vegetables. I didn't grow up eating them and I don't eat them much now. I think that if I had to choose, I like vegetables more than fruits, but they take too much time to prepare."

> **Clinician:** "Okay. Let's start by gradually increasing your knowledge about how to buy and prepare vegetables. We will take it one or two vegetables at a time, and I suggest that you stock up on frozen and pre-cut versions to make this as convenient as possible. Have you ever had a vegetable at a restaurant or friend's house that you remember liking?"

> **M:** "I've had asparagus at a steak house that was good. I also know I like buttered green beans."

> **Clinician:** "Okay, let's start there. Stock up on fresh asparagus and frozen green beans and maybe some frozen cauliflower, too. You can grill the asparagus while you are grilling your chicken or fish, and I will also make a note on your handout to remind you to purchase some lemon pepper, which you can use on the asparagus for flavor. The frozen green beans can be microwaved for about 5 minutes and sprinkled with some slivered almonds on top. That will give them a nutty taste. I'd like you to try this at least once or twice this week."

> **M:** "Okay, The seasonings and nuts make this more appealing. I'll give it a try, but no promises."

The Steady Snacker

Description

Steady Snackers mindlessly snack throughout the day, whether hungry or not. Just the sight or smell of food or even a food commercial can trigger their compulsion to eat. This type of snacking is unplanned as Steady Snackers are often unaware of the extra food they've tasted while preparing a meal, cleaning the kitchen, sitting at a meeting, attending a social event, or standing in the checkout line.

The Problem

Excess snacking may lead to weight gain and obesity. In a 2005 cross-sectional, descriptive study of 4,259 subjects, obese individuals were significantly more frequent snackers than the reference nonobese group (mean of 5.9 eating episodes per day vs a mean of 5.3). In this study, as the number of snacks per day increased, so did the total number of daily calories. For example, obese men who snacked three or more times during the day ate a mean of 830 more kcal (30% more) than those who did not snack as often (56).

Common snack foods tend to have more calories and fewer nutrients than main meal foods. The NPD Group, a market research company, has found that the most popular snacks among adults include high-calorie and/or low-nutrient options such as gum, chocolate candy, potato chips, mints, ice cream, cookies, and tortilla chips (57). Ovaskainen and colleagues collected 48-hour diet recalls of over 2,000 participants. They found 19% of the men and 24% of the women tended to have a snack-dominated meal pattern and these snackers tended to consume more calories and fewer nutrients than those participants who primarily ate main meals (58).

The goal is to have the Steady Snacker have healthful, planned, and portion-controlled snacks and fewer unhealthful, mindless, and unmeasured foods. Snacks can be part of a healthful diet, as demonstrated by the members of the National Weight Control Registry, who have successfully lost 70 pounds or more and have kept it off for 5 years or more. On average, these individuals eat 4 to 5 times per day (59).

Strategies for the Steady Snacker

The following strategies may help Steady Snackers succeed at weight loss and maintenance:

• Keep a snacking log

• Pre-plan snacks—when and what

• Stock up on healthy choices

• Tame what triggers too much snacking

Counseling Suggestions for Patient Strategies

Keep a Snacking Log

It's hard to take control of a habit if you're not fully aware of the extent of that habit. Self-observation and self-monitoring can help Steady Snackers become more aware of their snacking habit. For a discussion of self-monitoring, see Chapter 1.

The following counseling suggestions may help Steady Snackers keep a snacking log:

- Ask patients to keep a daily food log to become more mindful of what they are eating. The food log will help patients identify where, what, and why snacking is occurring throughout the day (60). (A food and activity food log form is available on the CD-ROM.)

- Advise patients to record on their food log why they ate each snack; for example: hunger, boredom, it was just there, anxiety, happiness, sadness, craving from a TV commercial, etc.

- Help patients use food labels, calorie books, and Web sites to find out how many calories they are eating each day. Patients need education about how to use these resources to accurately estimate calories. Research by Wansink and Chandon found that overweight participants underestimated by 125 to more than 350 kcal per meal (61).

- Focus only on snack calories with your patients. Patients often have difficulty looking up the calories in everything they are eating, so a compromise is to just keep a record of the calories in their snacks.

- Ask patients to record and total up their daily snack calories on their food log. It will become obvious that what seems like just a few innocent bites here or there amounts to a hefty sum at the end of the day, and that this type of snacking may sabotage weight-loss efforts.

There are several books available that help consumers determine the calories in foods, including fast-food items. One is *Calorie, Fat, & Carbohydrate Counter*—a pocket-sized resource that patients can use to look up calories in their favorite snack foods (62). Calorie information is also available for free on the Internet (eg, http://www.calorieking.com).

Pre-plan Snacks—When and What

Most Steady Snackers have a difficult time accounting for all of the snacks that they grab throughout the day. It is hard to keep track because it is a couple of almonds here, a hunk of cheese there, a handful of chips, raisins, and candy in the afternoon, and a couple of bites while making dinner.

The following counseling suggestions may help Steady Snackers pre-plan snacks—when and what:

- Review patients' daily schedules from the time they get up until the time they go to bed and discuss the most realistic times to add one to two preplanned snacks each day.

- Make a structured snack plan with your patients, which includes *when* they will snack and *what* they will snack on. Wing et al found that participants who receive highly structured eating plans are more likely to lose weight than participants who did not receive specific plans about when and what to eat (17 pounds vs 26.5 pounds in 6 months) (63).

- Brainstorm with patients for snack ideas that are appropriate for their preferences and lifestyle. For example, if your patient who likes salty snacks plans to have a snack at 3:00 PM and is not near a refrigerator or microwave, suggest snacks such as soynuts, a pre-portioned serving of almonds, turkey or soy jerky, or whole grain crackers with low-fat cheese.

- Advise patients to eat snacks from a plate or bowl instead of large containers or packages.

Stock Up on Healthy Choices

Snacking doesn't have to amount to excessive calories. According to data from four consecutive National Health and Nutrition Examination Surveys (NHANES) from 1971 to 2002, Americans are not snacking more frequently, but the types and portions of the snacks have substantially increased (64).

Nielsen et al found that from 1977 to 1996 Americans increased their energy intake from snacks, especially salty snacks and soft drinks, by 150 calories per day (65).

Healthful snacks, as a general rule, should be 100 to 200 kcal each for individuals who are following a calorie-restricted diet. See Box 4.9 for nutrition guidelines (66).

The following counseling suggestions may help Steady Snackers stock up on more healthful alternatives:

- Help patients develop a list of healthy snacks that are portion-controlled and suit their taste preferences.

- Suggest that patients purchase portion-controlled bags of baked chips, whole grain crackers, or whole grain cookies, or advise patients to preportion snacks in plastic sandwich bags (this is less expensive than buying snack-sized packages).

- Ask patients what types of foods they currently snack on and find more healthful versions. For example, if patients enjoy potato chips, suggest they try portion-controlled packs of popcorn for a similar salty crunch with more fiber and less fat.

- Remind patients that everyone in the household should be encouraged to eat healthful snacks. Often patients can feel pressure from children or spouses to purchase unhealthful snacks, but in time the whole household may learn to enjoy more healthful versions of their favorites.

- Encourage patients to have a wide variety of healthful snacks available. If patients get bored of the same one or two snacks, they may resort to old unhealthful snack choices. For healthful snack ideas, see Table 4.6.

Tame What Triggers Too Much Snacking

Certain emotions, situations, places, activities, and foods can trigger patients to snack. Watching television, stress, and lack of sleep are three of the most common snacking triggers.

The following counseling suggestions may help Steady Snackers take control of their snacking triggers:

- Ask patients to include their triggers for eating in their food log. For example, a snack may be triggered by frustration or boredom at work; reading the mail in the kitchen; passing by the office cafeteria; or hearing, smelling, or seeing someone else eat. (A one-day food and activity log is available on the CD-ROM.)

- Review patients' food logs and corresponding triggers and make an alternative plan for when those snacking triggers occur in the future. For example, if patients tend to snack when the kids nap, explore alternate activities such as reading a book or magazine, doing an exercise video, solving a sudoku puzzle, or calling a friend.

Box 4.9 ✦ Nutrition Guidelines for Healthy Snacks

Healthy snacks should meet most of these criteria per 100 kcal:
- > 2.5 g protein
- < 3 g fat
- > 1.4 g fiber
- < 120 mg sodium
- > 230 mg potassium
- > 60 mg calcium

Source: Data are from reference 63.

Table 4.6 ✦ Healthy Snack Ideas for Patient Taste Preferences

Crunchy-Salty	Crunchy-Sweet	Smooth-Salty	Smooth-Sweet
Celery with 1–2 tablespoons peanut butter	Apple with 1 tablespoon peanut butter	String cheese	8 oz low-fat yogurt
Soycrisps or soynuts	Whole-grain granola bar	4 oz low-fat cottage cheese	Banana
Almonds	100-calorie pack of kettlecorn-style popcorn	15 slices of turkey pepperoni	Fruit cup in its own juice
100-calorie bag of microwave popcorn	Portioned chocolate bar	Low-sodium vegetable juice	100% frozen fruit bar
Carrots dipped in 2 tablespoons low-fat ranch dressing	3/4 cup high-fiber cereal	6 rinsed black olives (rinsing removes 60% of sodium)	High-fiber muffin tops
High-fiber crackers with 2 tablespoons hummus	Pear with low-fat spreadable cheese wedge		8 oz low-fat chocolate milk

- Encourage patients to limit television to 2 hours or less each day. Adults who watch more than 2 hours of television per day eat more total calories from unhealthful snacks (such as pizza and soda) than adults who watch less than 1 hour of television per day (67).

- Advise patients to find de-stressing activities such as deep breathing, playing with a stress ball, taking a bath, or going for a walk. Stress has been shown to cause people to not only eat more but also to shift to higher-fat food choices. In one study, 34 female college students were seated in a room with bowls of chocolate candy, peanuts, chips and grapes. Half of the women were given a stressful, unsolvable puzzle and the other half were given an easy, nonstressful puzzle. The stressed women ate fewer grapes but 17% more chocolate candy than the nonstressed women (68).

- Advise patients to get about 7 hours of sleep per night. Less than 7 hours of sleep per night is associated with hormonal changes (such as decreased leptin levels and increased ghrelin levels), which increase appetite. Sivak estimates that for each hour of inactive wakefulness (such as watching TV at night instead of going to bed), an additional 147 snack calories are eaten (69). Of the 68,183 women monitored from 1986 to 2002 in the Nurses' Health Study, women who slept 7 to 8 hours per night had the lowest risk of major weight gain (33 pounds or more), whereas women who slept 5 hours or less per night were 32% more likely to gain a large amount of weight (70).

Questions Clinicians Ask During Counseling Sessions

Following are potential questions to help the clinician and the patient decide which of the four strategies or combination of strategies will best target the patient's needs. With practice, these strategies will lead your patient to more healthful eating habits.

- "What situations trigger you to snack?"
- "What times of day or night does mindless snacking occur most frequently?"
- "What types of foods lead you to mindless snacking?"
- "What places does your mindless eating commonly occur?"
- "What activities are you doing when you are snacking?"
- "What are your common emotional triggers for snacking?"

- "What are your favorite snack foods (crunchy, smooth, salty, sweet)?"
- "Which strategies most interest you to start using?"
- "Which strategies do you think will be most effective in changing your snacking habit?"

Case Study

M is a 31-year-old female, 5′5″, who weighs 210 pounds with a BMI of 35.0. She is a stay-at-home mom with a 3-year-old son and a 5-year-old daughter. Each day she prepares three meals for her children, such as macaroni and cheese, chicken nuggets, or sloppy joes. As M cleans up, she will nibble on the food that her kids don't finish. While the kids are napping or playing, she will often find herself grabbing nuts from the nut dish or popping sweets from the candy dish in her mouth. At night, she'll taste her husband's late-night dinner as she keeps him company.

> **Clinician:** "M, we both agree that steady snacking is where most of the extra calories are coming from. What situations trigger you to snack?"

> **M:** "I think most of the time I am snacking because I am just around the food. My worst trigger is probably eating off of my kids' plates; I guess I can stop that by just throwing that leftover food where it belongs —in the garbage! But that's hard."

> **Clinician:** "Of the four strategies we use to get control of snacking, what do you think about starting to record the foods you eat, with particular focus on recording your snacks and their calories? If you keep a written diary of everything you put in your mouth, it will take you from mindless to mindful eating—that is, being more aware of everything you eat. And by counting the calories, you will get a better handle on how many extra calories you are consuming without noticing."

> **M:** "Okay. I can do that. Kind of like detective work."

> **Clinician:** "I would also like to give you a list of healthy snacks to restock your house and help you determine the one to two times each day you can pre-plan a snack. What time do you feel like you most need or want a snack?"

> **M:** "I most need a planned snack in the afternoon when my kids are taking a nap. Right now I just snack all afternoon; having a set time will help me stay mindful. I definitely can get rid of the unhealthy snacks and replace them with less-tempting treats since my husband would prefer we have healthier things available like more fruit and low-fat yogurt."

> **Clinician:** "Sounds like you plan to make quite a few changes. On a scale of 1 to 10, how likely is it that you can make each of the changes you selected?"

> **M:** "They are all very doable. I'd give myself an 8 for being likely to change my snacks to healthier ones and stop eating off my kids' plates. On the other hand, I only feel like a 5 when I rate my confidence that I can write down my snacks with calories—but I sure will give it a try."

> **Clinician:** "What do you need to do to raise your confidence score above 5 for writing down your snacks and calories?"

> **M:** "Well—if I carried a little notebook around and had a convenient calorie-counting book to use, that would help a lot."

> **Clinician:** "Good ideas. Any notebook will work. *Calorie King* is a great calorie counting book to use. Bring your notebook with you to our next appointment so we can review your snacking habit and choices."

The Hearty Portioner

Description

Hearty Portioners eat too much food too fast and don't know when to stop. They often eat past their point of fullness and have no idea what constitutes a healthful portion. They are often members of the "clean your plate club," and because of this many suffer from indigestion and feeling sluggish after eating. Hearty Portioners stop eating either when they are uncomfortably full or there isn't any more food on their plate.

The Problem

The rise in obesity rates over the past 30 years is in large part due to the increasing portion size of most foods (71,72). Our patients are served large portions at restaurants, they over-serve themselves at home, and they buy food in increasingly larger sized packages. For example, between 1977 and 1996 the average size of salty snacks increased from 132 calories (1 oz) to 225 calories (1.6 oz) (71). When our patients are provided with larger portions, they eat more. For example, Ledikwe et al found that when a 12-inch sandwich is served, women eat 31% more calories and men 56% more calories than when a smaller sandwich is served (72). Fast eating can cause our patients to eat more. One researcher suggests that eating quickly can cause people to eat 70 calories more per meal or more than 200 calories a day compared with people who take their time while eating (13).

The goal is to help Hearty Portioners reduce their total daily calories by teaching them how to decrease portion size of high-calorie foods, select lower-calorie foods, and become more aware of healthful portion sizes. Most patients *know* that eating less will cause weight loss, but they have difficulty *doing* it and think they'll have to deprive themselves and go hungry. The four Hearty Portioner strategies focus on teaching people tricks, skills, and tips to actually increase eating enjoyment by slowing down the pace of eating and eating fewer calories in a society with ever-expanding portion sizes.

Strategies for Hearty Portioners

The following strategies may help Hearty Portioners succeed at weight loss and maintenance:

- Slow down your eating
- Eat more food for fewer calories
- Know serving sizes
- Avoid portion traps

Slow Down Your Eating

Hearty Portioners eat so quickly that their mind and body can't signal them to stop eating until it is too late and they are over stuffed. The gut sends hormones to the brain to signal fullness. Liu et al found it takes at least 10 minutes for the brain of healthy-weight individuals to respond to fullness and it may take obese people 20 minutes (73).

The following counseling suggestions may help Hearty Portioners slow down their eating:

- Advise patients to take at least 30 minutes to eat a meal.
- Have patients practice slow eating. This allows them to make each bite a conscious one and puts pleasure and enjoyment back into mealtime. As noted earlier, according to Melanson, eating slowly reduces intake by 70 calories per meal, which can translate to more than 200 calories per day (13). When patients slow their speed of eating, they are able to recognize more subtle signs of fullness and stop before their plate is clean.

- Teach patients to slow their pace of eating by using strategies such as putting their fork down between bites, chewing food thoroughly before swallowing, or scooping less food on each fork or spoonful.

- Advise patients to stop "preloading," the practice of filling up a fork or spoon in anticipation of your next bite before you are done chewing the previous bite.

- Encourage patients to eat without distraction. One study found that even a slight distraction, such as hearing a book on tape in the background, increased portion size at the meal by about 70 calories (74). A good recommendation is to suggest that patients eat without watching the TV, driving, reading the newspaper, or responding to e-mails.

Eat More Food for Fewer Calories

Eating big portions of food does not always have to lead to weight gain because many foods are low in calories even in large amounts. Low–energy-dense foods are foods that have a low number of calories per gram. As defined by Ello-Martin et al, foods with low energy density have less than 0.8 kcal/g, medium-density foods have less than 1.1 kcal/g, and high-density foods have more than 1.3 kcal/g (75).

The following counseling suggestions may help Hearty Portioners eat more food for fewer calories:

- Teach patients to eat more low–energy-dense foods such as vegetables, fruits, and broth soups at mealtimes. Pioneering research by Rolls et al found that consuming foods with a high water content (low energy density) decreases intake at a meal by at least 100 kcal (76).

- Encourage patients to eat low–energy-dense foods *before* a meal. Eating soup or a salad before a meal can decrease calories eaten at the meal. Rolls et al reported that 3 cups of salad made with low-fat salad dressing and low-fat cheese (100 calories total for salad) decreased calories at the meal by 12% (77).

- Teach patients the 25:25:50 rule. Twenty-five percent of the plate is their favorite whole grain or starchy food such as potatoes (about 1 cup or less), 25% is a lean protein such as chicken or fish (about the size of a deck of cards), and 50% or more of their plate is filled with produce. This visual image (Figure 4.1) is an easy way to teach patients to apply the principles of low energy density.

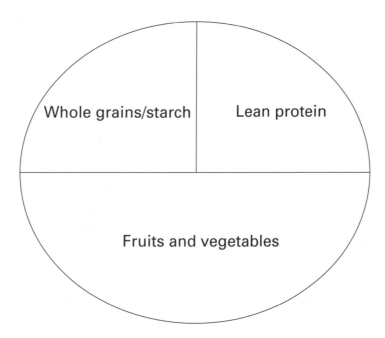

Figure 4.1 Plate with low energy-density.

Know Serving Sizes

Most patients have a difficult time knowing a healthful portion of food. Because large portions are usually served at restaurants or prepared at home, Hearty Portioners need help to recalibrate their eyes. Table 4.7 is a general guide to help patients estimate appropriate portion sizes (78).

The following counseling suggestions may help Hearty Portioners know serving sizes:

- Advise patients to eat with smaller utensils and downsize their plates and bowls. People rely on visual cues such as the size of a bowl, plate, or utensil to help gauge portions. In a study by Wansink et al, participants ate 31% more when using a large bowl instead of a smaller one and 14.5% more when using a large spoon rather than the small version (79).

- Teach patients to read food labels accurately. Hearty Portioners likely need help understanding food labels, especially when interpreting serving size. Rothman et al investigated patient comprehension of food labels and found patients had at least 30% error when interpreting labels (80). Teach them to look at *serving size* first.

- Ask patients to purchase pre-portioned items that are sold in small single-serving packages. A 2006 study found participants ate more chocolate candies out of a large container than a small container (81).

- Encourage patients to eat portion-controlled, low-calorie frozen meals once or twice a day. These entrees help patients visualize a perfect portion of pasta, stir fry, or fish. Remind them to add vegetables or a side salad until they feel full.

- Ask patients to invest in measuring cups and spoons and a digital food scale. When patients measure and weigh food, they can retrain their sense of portion size.

Table 4.7 ✦ Portion Size Estimation Table

Food	One Serving Looks Like
1 cup flake cereal	Fist
1 pancake	Compact disc
1/2 cup cooked rice, pasta, potato	1/2 baseball
1 slice of bread	CD cover
1 piece of cornbread	Bar of soap
1.5 ounce cheese	4 stacked dice or 1.5 slices
1/2 cup of ice cream	1/2 baseball
1 teaspoon margarine or butter	1 dice-sized cube
1 cup of salad	1 baseball
1 baked potato	Fist
1/2 cup fresh fruit	1/2 baseball
1/4 cup raisins	1 large egg
3 oz meat	Deck of cards
3 oz fish	Checkbook
2 tablespoons of peanut butter	Ping-pong ball

Source: Adapted from National Heart, Lung, and Blood Institute. Serving size card. http://hp2010.nhlbihin.net/portion/servingcard7.pdf. Accessed September 23, 2007.

- Instruct patients to visit the National Heart, Lung, and Blood Institute (NHLBI) portion distortion quiz (http://hp2010.nhlbihin.net/portion/keep.htm).

- Encourage patients take the portion challenge: Instruct your patients to measure and weigh everything they eat for 7 days. After the 7-day challenge they will have developed skills to better estimate portion size. This challenge should be done periodically because the American food environment tends to untrain this skill over time.

Avoid Portion Traps

Big portions of foods served at restaurants and buffet style celebrations pose some of the biggest challenges to Hearty Portioners. However, if they plan ahead and put some key strategies in place, they'll be better prepared and able to not succumb to these traps.

The following counseling suggestions may help Hearty Portioners overcome portion traps:

- Have patients keep a log of meals and snacks when portions are especially large and where they have a hard time controlling how much they eat, such as buffets, family-style meals, two-for-one deals at restaurants and grocery stores, baskets of bread and chips at the table, or lunch on the business account. A log will help them identify situations and settings that are especially difficult.

- Plan alternative actions for each situation or setting that lends itself to overeating. For example, if family-style meals are the portion problem, suggest that patients keep the food in the kitchen instead of on the table while eating, or, if the bread basket is too tempting to just have one piece, instruct your patient to take one and send the rest back with the waiter.

- Teach your patient to think twice about "meal deals" to make sure the combo special or supersize offering isn't a portion trap in disguise. If a "good deal" saves you money at the point of purchase but will be a drain on your health down the road from the extra fat and calories, then in the long run it may cost you extra money on medications, doctor visits, and time off from work. See Box 4.10 (82).

- Encourage patients to limit alcohol before meals. Alcohol can be a portion trap because it has been shown to stimulate appetite. Caton et al gave 12 nondieting male participants alcohol before a meal. Participants who drank the equivalent of 2.5 glasses of wine before a meal ate 200 calories more of the meal than participants who only had 0.5 glass of wine (83).

Questions Clinicians Ask During Counseling Sessions

Following are potential questions to help the clinician and patient decide which of the four strategies or combination of strategies will best target the patient's needs. With practice, these strategies will lead the patient to more healthful eating habits.

- "Why do you think you eat portions that are larger than you need?"

- "What triggers you to stop eating?"

Box 4.10 ✦ The True Costs of Upsizing Meals

It isn't a good deal to upsize a restaurant meal in the long run. The upfront dollar amount of a typical upsize is an additional $0.36, but factoring in other costs such as health care, gasoline, and other hidden costs, it is estimated that the meal is an additional $7.72!

Source: Data are from reference 79.

- "Do you consider yourself a slow, medium, or fast eater? Does it depend on the situation?"
- "Do you tend to go back for second helpings?"
- "Do you have a difficult time with portions in certain situations, such as buffets and family-style meals?"
- "Do you ever feel a signal to stop eating before you get stuffed?"
- "What would you consider the most filling foods you eat?"
- "Which strategies are you most confident you can start using immediately?"
- "Which of the four portioning strategies do you find the easiest? Hardest?"

Case Study

M is a 42-year-old man, 5′11″, who weighs 281 pounds with a BMI of 39.2. M is a financial planner who almost always stops for three meals a day, but doesn't have time to snack. He is usually very hungry when he sits down to a meal and tends to eat fast. M loves all types of food, but his favorite is Mexican food and he usually orders two baskets of chips to start.

Clinician: "M, you are definitely a Hearty Portioner and you agree that eating large amounts is a pattern that you would like to change. What's the biggest concern you have about your portion sizes?"

M: "I am extremely hungry when I sit down to eat, but I don't think I have trouble getting full. I do think, however, I have trouble getting *over*full. Most of the time I finish everything on my plate and feel stuffed after almost all of my meals. It's that Thanksgiving feeling three times a day!"

Clinician: "There are several strategies that can help. The most important is to slow down, I call it 'Pace and Pay Attention.'"

M: "I agree that I need to pay more attention when I am eating. I am rushing and don't really even know what my food tastes like after the first couple of bites. It is hard for me to slow down."

Clinician: "That's probably the most important thing you can do to get control. Here are some ideas—chew your food more slowly, don't talk when you're chewing, don't grab for the next bite until you swallowed the food in your mouth, take some water between bites, and pace yourself to the slowest eater at the table."

M (laughing): "I know who the slowest eater is—my wife. She'll get a real kick out of that idea."

Clinician: "Another useful strategy is to keep a log to identify portion-trap situations, such as ordering two baskets of tortilla chips before your meal."

M: "What do you mean by a log?"

Clinician: "A diary. You would keep a record of what you are eating, the portion size, and your level of fullness. Scale your fullness from 1 to 5, where 5 is absolutely stuffed. You want to stop eating when you get to a 3 or 4."

M: "That's a good idea. I'll slow down and remind myself to rate my fullness. I could circle the times when I feel over stuffed (a level 5) and try to get those down."

Clinician: "Okay, I will look at your logs next visit. Another idea you could try before the next time I see you is to use smaller plates. Using smaller plates and putting less on your plate to begin with will help you eat less."

M: "Okay, I am a 'clean plate club' member so if I put less on my plate and clean it, at least I won't be eating as much."

Clinician: "Take this Hearty Portioner handout and tell your wife that she is now going to be your speed gauge. Maybe you can ask her to help you find some small plates to use. I look forward to seeing you next time to review your logs and see how you do rating your fullness."

The Swing Eater

Description

Swing Eaters try to eat a strict diet of "good" foods but then they fall off the "wagon" and overeat the "bad" foods. Their diet swings from one extreme to the other, leaving Swing Eaters never feeling satisfied. They deprive themselves of the foods they really want while in social situations and end up eating those "bad" foods in private, which leaves them feeling guilty. Their vocabulary consists of good foods and bad foods, cheating and not cheating, restricting and overindulging.

The Problem

It is estimated that 46% of women and 33% of men are dieting at any one time (84). Dieting can involve practicing unhealthful habits. In one study, 714 women and 229 men in a community-based weight gain prevention program completed surveys about their weight control practices annually for 3 years. Twenty-two percent of women and 17% of men report using at least one unhealthful dieting behavior over the past year, including smoking, using laxatives or diet pills, or skipping breakfast (85).

Swing Eaters tend to be rigid in what foods they are "allowed" to eat and which foods are "forbidden." Fletcher et al found that this type of strict dieting increases cravings for forbidden foods and leads to overeating. It is a vicious cycle of restricting favorite foods and then overindulging in them. Strict dieting will increase dieters' guilt, anxiety, and depression (86). Dieters also tend to have lower body satisfaction as well as lower quality of life than nondieters (87).

The goal for the Swing Eater is to stop the strict all-or-nothing dieting. Swing Eaters need to practice enjoying their favorite (once forbidden) foods in moderation to stop the deprivation-overindulge cycle. According to the American Dietetic Association, if consumed in moderation in the appropriate portion size, all foods can fit into a healthful diet (88).

Strategies for Swing Eaters

The following strategies may help Swing Eaters succeed at weight loss and maintenance:

- Embrace all foods
- Add fiber and healthy fats for more eating pleasure
- Enjoy once off-limit foods in smaller portions
- Socialize and enjoy

Embrace All Foods

The American diet industry tends to teach patients all-or-nothing eating habits. Diets typically have a list of foods that are permitted and a list of foods that are off-limits. Patients have learned that to lose weight, they should restrict the quantity and frequency of certain "bad" or "feared" foods. In a 2004 study, dieters had 10 times the number of "feared" foods than nondieters and twice the feelings of guilt about foods they thought were high in fat. (89).

The following counseling suggestions may help the Swing Eater embrace all foods:

- Remind patients to embrace all foods and erase the "good" and "bad" list in their heads.

- Have patients list foods they consider "cheat" foods; then ask them to incorporate a moderate amount in their diet. For example, if they feel like pasta is a cheat food, ask them to prepare 1/2 cup (dry) whole wheat pasta (which equals 1 cup cooked pasta) at dinnertime.

- Educate patients that all calories count and no single food causes weight gain; rather, it's the individual's pattern of eating and accumulation of calories over time that matter most.

- Have patients keep a food log and record when they feel as if they "cheated." (A food and activity log is available on the CD-ROM and can be used to log food intake and feelings.) Use this information to start a discussion about "cheating" and how to view food choices and eating situations differently.

Add Fiber and Healthy Fats for More Eating Pleasure

Swing Eater patients have likely been restrictive with certain foods and portion sizes and, in turn, are dissatisfied with most of their meals and snacks. This dissatisfaction later leads to overindulging because they are hungry and seek enjoyment from tasty food. Gerstein et al have concluded that the most satisfying meals and snacks are those that make us physically full (satiety) while also tasting good (palatability). Meals and snacks need to be a blend of fiber-rich foods for satiety plus fat for increased palatability (90). All fats are a mix of saturated (not "heart smart") and unsaturated (heart-healthy) fatty acids. Solid fats such as butter and sticks of margarine contain more saturated fats and *trans* fats than do liquid fats such as olive, peanut, sesame, grapeseed, or canola oil.

The following counseling suggestions may help Swing Eaters improve their eating pleasure by adding fat and fiber to their meals:

- Encourage patients to include high-fiber foods at each meal and snack, such as whole grain crackers, breads, and cereals; fruits; vegetables; and beans.

- Remind patients that fat should be eaten in moderation because gram-for-gram fat has more than double the calories of protein or carbohydrate. (Fats have 9 kcal/g, carbohydrates and protein have 4 kcal/g, and alcohol has 7 kcal/g.)

- Educate patients about healthful types of fats. Healthful fats include those that are liquid at room temperature such as olive, peanut, sesame, grapeseed, and canola oil. Healthful fats can also be found in certain foods such as avocados, olives, nuts, and seeds.

- Teach patients the recommended amount of healthful oils that can be added in cooking and at the table per day. See Table 4.8.

- Educate patients about how to make their meals and snacks have satiety from fiber and palatability from fat. See Table 4.9.

Enjoy Once–Off-Limit Foods in Smaller Portions

Swing Eaters often tell themselves they should completely avoid certain foods such as cookies, chocolate, chips, cake, candy, pizza, and ice cream. In one study of 60 college-age women, those who restricted a forbidden food ate twice as much of the restricted food when allowed than women who were not restricted eaters (91). Restricting certain foods also results in increased desire to eat the food. Polivy et al found participants who deprived themselves of a food had stronger cravings for the food than those who allowed themselves to eat the food (92).

The following counseling suggestions may help Swing Eaters moderate once–off-limit foods:

- Remind patients not to get discouraged if they overeat an "off-limit" food once in a while. Your patients are accustomed to eating large quantities of their "off-limit" foods, and they will need to practice to moderate their intake of their favorite treats and formerly forbidden foods.

- Help patients moderate eating by advising them to purchase items in portion-controlled amounts. For example, they will be less likely to overeat chips if they are in a 100-calorie pack.

- Teach patients to savor every bite and make their treats special. For example, instead of just quickly eating an individual pack of cookies standing in the kitchen, patients can put the cookies on a small, pretty plate and brew a cup of tea.

- Help patients develop a mantra, such as, "I can enjoy these foods in moderation and they will not cause me to gain weight." Explain that they can use this mantra if feelings of guilt pop into their head. (For more information about cognitive restructuring techniques, see Chapter 1.)

- Educate patients that moderate amounts (about 200 calories) of their "cheat" foods are part of a healthful and balanced diet. The USDA categorizes fats, sugars, and alcohol as *discretionary calories* and advises Americans to consume these foods in moderation. The recommendation for discretionary calories is 195 kcal per day for a person on a 1,800-calorie diet (93).

Table 4.8 ✦ Recommended Amount of Added Oils[a] Per Day

	1600 kcal/d	1800 kcal/d	2000 kcal/d
Oil, g	22	24	27
Oil, tsp[b]	5	5	6

[a]Oil includes liquid oils and *trans* fat–free margarine.
[b]Recommendations in teaspoons are approximations based on 4.5 g of fat per teaspoon of oil.

Source: Adapted from the USDA Dietary Guidelines (4).

Table 4.9 ✦ Making Meals More Palatable

	Before Adding Satisfaction	After Adding Satisfaction
Breakfast	Bowl of plain oatmeal	Bowl of oatmeal with 2 tablespoons of almonds (fat) and berries (fiber)
Lunch	Chicken breast on top of salad, no dressing	Chicken breast on salad topped with 1 tablespoon low-fat dressing (fat) and 1 tablespoon of pine nuts (fat) with high-fiber crackers (fiber)
Dinner	Turkey burger wrapped in lettuce leaf, no bun	Turkey burger on a whole-grain bun (fiber) with 1/4 avocado (fat) and tomatoes (fiber)
Snack	Rice cakes	Apple (fiber) with 1 tablespoon peanut butter (fat)

Socialize and Enjoy

Most Swing Eaters have two eating styles—a public eater and a private eater. Many overweight individuals are self-conscious about eating because of perceived social pressures and may suppress intake when eating with someone. Krantz first confirmed that overweight subjects purchased less food when they were with someone vs when they were alone (94). Patients usually reserve their public eating to the most healthful "good" foods and indulge in "bad" foods when they are alone.

The following counseling suggestions may help Swing Eaters socialize and enjoy eating:

- Teach patients to eat and enjoy once-forbidden food with others. This will help them bridge their two eating styles into one and take back a healthful relationship with food. For example, if they are not likely to eat pizza with their friends because they feel self-conscious, suggest that they practice eating one piece of pizza and a salad.

- Have your patient ask themselves what they really feel like eating the next time they are at a social event and order it. This may be difficult for some patients because Swing Eaters rarely listen to what they "want" to eat and typically just order what they "should" eat.

- Remind Swing Eaters to savor and enjoy every bite and give themselves permission to eat as little or as much as they need to feel satisfied without feeling overstuffed. This will help them decrease the urge to overindulge when they are alone.

- Have patients do an activity called "Safe Places, Safe Portions." If they want to eat a food that they have difficulty portioning, suggest that they go to a safe place and order a safe portion. For example, instead of buying a large container of ice cream for their home (where they may overeat alone), they can go to a local ice cream shop and enjoy a small scoop.

Questions Clinicians Ask During Counseling Sessions

The following questions may help the clinician and patient decide which of the four strategies or combination of strategies will best target the patient's needs. With practice, these strategies will lead the patient to more healthful eating habits.

- "Why do you restrict yourself from eating certain things?"

- "Do you consider some foods 'good' and some foods 'bad,' and if so which foods fit into each group?"

- "What foods make you feel as if you 'cheated'?"

- "When and where do you find yourself overeating most often?"

- "Think about the foods that do you not allow yourself to enjoy—which would you like to start eating with less guilt?"

- "If you didn't have to worry about your weight and could eat what you wanted, what would be your favorite foods or most satisfying meals?"

- "Which strategies can you see yourself using successfully?"

- "All four strategies can be helpful, but which do you want to start trying now?"

Case Study

P is a 55-year-old woman, 5′5″, who weighs 247 pounds with a BMI of 41.1. She owns nearly every diet book ever written. She probably knows more about the glycemic index, counting calories, and calculating points than most health professionals. She makes clear distinctions between which foods are "good" and which foods are "bad." She knows to order fish and vegetables at dinner with her friends and avoid the chocolate cake dessert altogether. However, when she gets home, she often feels deprived and may have a couple of spoonfuls of ice cream. Then she feels guilty that she has had the ice cream and figures that she has ruined her healthy day. At this point, she will finish the rest of the ice cream before bed. She tells herself she will return to healthy eating tomorrow.

> **Clinician:** "P, your profile suggests you are a Swing Eater; that is, your eating in public is very different than your eating in private. Tell me about a situation when you restricted yourself and what happened afterward."
>
> **P:** "Oh, that's an easy question. I go out to dinner almost every Saturday night and typically don't feel satisfied when I leave. No matter what restaurant I'm at, I almost always get the fish. No matter how good the bread or the dessert looks, I will not eat them because I know those are fatty foods and my friends know I am on a diet. My friends can't believe my willpower, but what they don't know—and I feel guilty even talking about this—is that on my way home I often stop at the corner store for a pint of my favorite ice cream, usually chocolate."
>
> **Clinician:** "We need to get you out of this vicious cycle and help you develop a healthy and enjoyable relationship with food again. Next time you are in a restaurant, how do you feel about ordering what you have a taste for and giving yourself permission to eat as little or as much as you want to feel satisfied without feeling stuffed?"
>
> **P:** "That would be a change for me. A few of the restaurants I go to on Saturday have delicious desserts that I would love to have. My friends always split them, but I never have even a bite. Maybe if I started having dessert with them I would feel less like going to get ice cream later. I could try it this week."
>
> **Clinician:** "Great idea. And let's also work on another strategy, 'Embrace All Foods.' Try to remind yourself that this is not 'cheating' but rather this is an important step toward a healthy relationship with food. Take your time with the dessert and really appreciate and enjoy it. Years of dieting have taught you to think of dessert as a 'bad' thing, but actually splitting dessert with friends is healthy, fun, and can be part of a balanced diet. Try to practice not letting feelings of guilt ruin the taste and experience!"
>
> **P:** "But I could see myself still going home and eating cookies or ice cream because it has been such a habit for such a long time."
>
> **Clinician:** "It's good that you are thinking ahead; that really shows you are ready to make changes. We can practice the strategy of enjoying once–off-limit foods in smaller portions. It's important to get rid of the ice cream and cookies in your house. However, if you really want ice cream after you split dessert with your friends, what do you think about ordering a dish of ice cream there or go to an ice cream shop for just one scoop?"

P: "I like that. I still feel like I can have ice cream and cookies so I am not anxious about getting it out of my house, but I can eat them in situations when I will be less likely to overeat. I can give it a try."

Clinician: "I look forward to seeing you next time to talk about how much you enjoyed the dessert with your friends, your attitude toward 'cheating,' and your ice cream– and cookie-free home. Next time we may have you start a list of all the foods you have considered 'cheat' foods and begin incorporating them one at a time."

P: "I like that idea, I will start that list for our next visit right away."

Summing Up the Eating Domain

In this chapter, you have learned how to target the different barriers patients have to eating a low-calorie, healthful diet. Whether your patients skip meals, feast on most of their calories in the evening, dine out excessively, skimp on fruits and vegetables, snack all through the day, indulge on supersized portions, or swing from deprivation to overindulging, you are now equipped to develop a plan that meets their individualized needs. By using the Lifestyle Patterns Approach, you can help each of your patients better understand their unique eating "personality," which can be a combination of a few different eating patterns. With the right counseling strategies, you can help patients start where they are at, prioritize which pattern(s) to work on first, help them make healthful realistic changes to their diet, and target different patterns as needs arise. In the next chapter, you will learn how to help overweight patients in the domain of exercise.

References

1. National Heart, Lung, and Blood Institute and North American Association for the Study of Obesity. Practical Guide on the Identification, Evaluation, and Treatment of Overweight and Obesity in Adults. Bethesda, MD: National Institutes of Health; 2000. NIH publication number 00-4084.

2. International Food Information Council Foundation. International Food Information Council (IFIC) Foundation 2007 Food and Health Survey: Consumer Attitudes Toward Food, Nutrition and Health. http://www.ific.org/research/upload-/2007Survey-FINAL.pdf. Accessed September 23, 2007.

3. Institute of Medicine Website. http://www.iom.edu/CMS/3788/4576/4340.aspx. Accessed September 23, 3007.

4. US Department of Agriculture. *Dietary Guidelines for Americans*, 2005. http://www.health.gov/dietaryguidelines/dga2005/document/default.htm. Accessed December 10, 2007.

5. Mela DJ. Determinants of food choice:relationships with obesity and weight control. *Obes Res*. 2001;9(Suppl):249S-255S.

6. Farshchi HR, Taylor MA, Macdonald IA. Beneficial metabolic effects of regular meal frequency on dietary thermogenesis, insulin sensitivity, and fasting lipid profiles in healthy obese women. *Am J Clin Nutr*. 2005;81:16-24.

7. Wing RR, Phelan S. Long-term weight loss maintenance. *Am J Clin Nutr*. 2005;82(Suppl):222S-225S.

8. Kerver JM, Yang EJ, Obayashi S, Bianchi L, Song WO. Meal and snack patterns are associated with dietary intake of energy and nutrients in US adults. *J Am Diet Assoc*. 2006;106:46-53.

9. Kruger J, Blanck HM, Gillespie C. Dietary and physical activity behaviors among adults successful at weight loss maintenance. *Int J Behav Nutr Phys Activ*. 2006;3:17-27.

10. Stroebele N, De Casdtro JM. Effect of ambience on food intake and food choices. *Nutrition*. 2004;20:821-838.

11. Hetherington MM, Anderson AS, Norton GN, Newson L. Situational effects on meal intake: a comparison of eating alone and eating with others. *Physiol Behav*. 2006;88:498-505.

12. Barkeling B, Linne Y, Melin E, Rooth P. Vision and eating behavior in obese subjects. *Obes Res*. 2003;11:130-134.

13. Andrade A, Minaker T, Melanson K. Eating rate and satiation. *Obesity*. 2006;14(Suppl):A6-A7.

14. Craighead L. *The Appetite Awareness Workbook*. Oakland, CA: New Harbinger Publications; 2006.

15. Drapeau V, King N, Hetherington M, Doucet E, Blundell J, Tremblay A. Appetite sensations and satiety quotient: predictors of energy intake and weight loss [published online ahead of print October 11, 2006]. *Appetite.* 2007;48:159-166.

16. Ello-Martin JA, Ledikwe JH, Rolls BJ. The influence of food portion size and energy density on energy intake: implications for weight management. *Am J Clin Nutr.* 2005;82(1 Suppl):236S-241S.

17. Otten JJ, Hellwig JP, Meyers CD, eds. *Dietary Reference Intakes: The Essential Guide to Nutrient requirements.* Washington, DC: National Academies Press;2006.

18. USDA National Nutrient Database for Standard Reference. http://www.nal.usda.gov/fnic/foodcomp/search/. Accessed December 10, 2007.

19. Position of the American Dietetic Association:health implications of dietary fiber. *J Am Diet Assoc.* 2002;102:993-1000.

20. Morse SA, Ciechanowski PS, Katon WJ, Hirsch IB. Isn't this just bedtime snacking? The potential adverse effects of night eating symptoms on treatment adherence and outcomes in patients with diabetes. *Diabetes Care.* 2006;29:1800-1804.

21. Gluck ME, Geliebter A, Satov T. Night eating syndrome is associated with depression, low self-esteem, reduced daytime hunger, and less weight loss in obese outpatients. *Obes Res.* 2001;9:264-267.

22. Vander Wal JS, Waller SM, Klurfeld DM, McBurney MI, Dhurandhar NV. Night eating syndrome: evaluation of two screening instruments. *Eat Behav.* 2005;6:63-73.

23. Ceru-Bjork C, Andersson I, Rossner S. Night eating and nocturnal eating: two different or similar syndromes among obese patients? *Int J Obes Relat Metab Disord.* 2001;25:365-372.

24. Cho SC, Dietrich M, CJP Brown, Clark CA, Block G. The effect of breakfast type on total daily energy intake and body mass index. *J Am Coll Nutr.* 2003;22:296-302.

25. Keim NL, Van Loan MD, Horn WF, Barbieri TF, Mayclin PL. Weight loss is greater with consumption of large morning meals and fat-free mass is preserved with large evening meals in women on a controlled weight reduction regimen. *J Nutr.* 1997;127:75-82.

26. Wansink B, Painter JE, Lee YK. The office candy dish: proximity's influence on estimated and actual consumption. *Int J Obes* (Lond). 2006;30:871-875.

27. Waller SM, Vander Wal JS, Klurfeld DM, McBurney MI, Cho S, Bijlani S, Dhurandhar NV. Evening ready to eat cereal consumption contributes to weight management. *J Am Coll Nutr.* 2004;23:316-321.

28. Wardle J. Conditioning processes and cue exposure in the modification of excessive eating. *Addict Behav.* 1990;15:387-393.

29. Pawlow LA, O'Neil PM, Malcolm RJ. Night eating syndrome: effect of brief relaxation training on stress, mood, hunger, and eating patterns. *Int J Obes Relat Metab Disord.* 2003;27:970-978.

30. Guthrie JF, Lin BH, Frazao E. Role of food prepared away from home in the American diet, 1977-78 versus 1994-96: changes and consequences. *J Nutr Educ Behav.* 2002;34:140-150.

31. Bowman SA, Vinyard B. Fast food consumption of US adults: impact on energy and nutrient intakes and overweight status. *J Am Coll Nutr.* 2004;23:163-168.

32. Kant AK, Graubard BI. Eating out in America, 1987-2000: trends and nutritional correlates. *Prev Med.* 2004;38:243-249.

33. Of Interest to You: Who carries out their meals and why. *J Am Diet Assoc.* 1998;98:820.

34. Diliberti N, Bordi PL, Conklin MT, Roe LS, Rolls BJ. Increased portion size leads to increased intake in a restaurant meal. *Obes Res.* 2004;12:562-568.

35. Young LR, Nestle M. Expanding portion sizes in the US marketplace: implications for nutrition counseling. *J Am Diet Assoc.* 2003;103:231-234.

36. Patterson RE, Kristal A, Rodabough R, Caan B, Lillington L, Mossaavar-Rahmani Y, Simon, MS, Snetselaar L, Van Horn L. Changes in food sources of dietary fat in response to an intensive low-fat dietary intervention: early results from the Women's Health Initiative. *J Am Diet Assoc.* 2003;103:454-460.

37. Duffey KJ, Popkin BM. Shifts in patterns and consumption of beverages between 1965 and 2002. *Obesity.* 2007;15:2739-2747.

38. Mootan MG, Osborn M. Availability of nutrition information from chain restaurants in the United States. *Am J Prev Med.* 2006;30:266-267.

39. Krukowski RA, Harvey-Berino J, Kolodinsky J, Narsana RT, DeSisto TP. Consumers may not use or understand calorie labeling in restaurants. *J Am Diet Assoc.* 2006;106:917-920.

40. Rothman RL, Housam R, Weiss H, Davis D, Gregory R, Gerbretsadik T, Shintani A, Elasy TA. Patient understanding of food labels: the role of literacy and numeracy. *Am J Prev Med.* 2006;31:391-398.

41. Stein K. Healthful fast foods not part of healthful revenue. *J Am Diet Assoc.* 2006;106:344-345.

42. Rolls BJ, Ello-Maetin JA, Tohill BX. What can intervention studies tell us about the relationship between fruit and vegetable consumption and weight management? *Nutr Rev.* 2004;62:1-17.

43. Van Duyn MAS, Pivonka E. Overview of the health benefits of fruit and vegetable consumption for the dietetics professional: selected literature. *J Am Diet Assoc.* 2000;100:1511-1521.

44. US Department of Agriculture. MyPyramid Web site. http://www.mypyramid.gov. Accessed September 23, 2007.

45. Shintani TT, Hughes CK, Beckhan S, O'Connor HK. Obesity and cardiovascular risk intervention through the ad libitum feeding of traditional Hawaiian diet. *Am J Clin Nutr.* 1991;53(6 Suppl):1647S-1651S.

46. International Food and Information Council Web site. Consumer-tested Messages and Tips: An Overview. http://www.ific.org/tools/tips.cfm. Accessed September 23, 2007.

47. John JH, Ziebland S. Reported barriers to eating more fruit and vegetables before and after participation in a randomized controlled study. *Health Educ Res.* 2004;19:165-174.

48. Reinaerts E, de Nooijer J, Candel M, de Vries N. Explaining school children's fruit and vegetable consumption: the contributions of availability, accessibility, exposure, parental consumption, and habit in addition to psychosocial factors. Appetite. 2007;48:248-258.

49. US Food and Drug Administration. Center for Food Safety and Applied Nutrition. A Food Labeling Guide—Appendix A: Definitions of Nutrient Content Claims. http://www.cfsan.fda.gov/~dms/flg-6a.html. Accessed September 23, 2007.

50. Brown BJ, Hermann JR. Cooking class increase fruit and vegetable intake and food safety behaviors in youth and adults. *J Nutr Educ Behav.* 2005;37:104-105.

51. Wansink B, Lee K. Cooking habits provide a key to 5 a day success. *J Am Diet Assoc.* 2004;104:1648-1650.

52. Zhao L, Kirkmeyer SV, Tepper BJ. A paper screening test to assess genetic taste sensitivity to PROP. *Physiol Behav.* 2003;78:625-633.

53. Guenther PM, Dodd KW, Reedy J, Krebs-Smith SM. Most Americans eat much less than recommended amounts of fruits and vegetables. *J Am Diet Assoc.* 2006;106:1371-1379.

54. Herber D, Bowerman S. Applying science to changing dietary patterns. *J Nutr.* 2001;131(Suppl):3078S-3081S.

55. Newby PK, Tucker KL, Wolk A. Risk of overweight and obesity among semivegetarians, lactovegetarians, and vegan women. *Am J Clin Nutr.* 2005;81:1267-1274.

56. Forslund HB, Torgerson JS, Sjostrom L, Lindroos AK. Snacking frequency in relation to energy intake and food choices in obese men and women compared to a reference population. *Int J Obes.* 2005;29:711-719.

57. NPD Group. Fruit is #1 Snack Food Consumed by Kids (press release). June 16, 2005. http://www.npd.com/press/releases/press_050616a.html. Accessed September 23, 2007.

58. Ovaskainen ML, Reinivuo H, Tapanainen H, Hannila ML, Korhonen T, Pakkala H. Snacks as an element of energy intake and food consumption. *Eur J Clin Nutr.* 2006;60:494-501.

59. Wing RR, Hill JO. Successful weight loss maintenance. *Annu Rev Nutr.* 2001;21:323-341.

60. Boutelle KN, Kirschenbaum DS. Further support for consistent self-monitoring as a vital component of successful weight control. *Obes Res.* 1998;6:219-224.

61. Wansink B, Chandon P. Meal size, not body size, explain errors in estimating the calorie content of meals. *Ann Intern Med.* 2006;145:326-332.

62. Borushek, Allan. The *Calorie King: Calorie, Fat and Carbohydrate Counter.* Costa Mesa, CA: Family Health Publications; 2007.

63. Wing RR, Jeffert RW, Burton LR, Thorson C, Nissinoff KS, Baxter JE. Food provision vs structured meal plans in the behavioral treatment of obesity. *Int J Obes Relat Metab Disord.* 1996;20:56-62.

64. Kant AK, Graubard BI. Secular trends in patterns of self-reported food consumption of adult Americans: NHANES 1971-1975 to NHANES 1999-2002. *Am J Clin Nutr.* 2006;84:1215-1223.

65. Nielsen SJ, Siega-Riz AM, Popkin BM. Trends in energy intake in US between 1977 and 1996: similar shifts seen across age groups. *Obes Res.* 2002;10:370-378.

66. Anderson JW, Patterson K. Snack foods:comparing nutrition values of excellent choices and junk foods. *J Am Coll Nutr.* 2005;24:155-157.

67. Bowman SA. Television viewing characteristics of adults: correlations to eating practices and overweight and health status. *Prev Chron Dis* [serial online]. 2006;3(2).http://www.cdc.gov/pcd/issues/2006/apr/05_0139.htm. Accessed September 28, 2007.

68. Zellner DA, Loaiza S, Gonzalez Z, Pita J, Morales J, Pecora D, Wolf A. Food selection changes under stress. *Physiol Behav.* 2006;87:789-793.

69. Sivak M. Sleeping more as a way to lose weight. *Obes Rev.* 2006;7:295-296.

70. Patel SR, Malhotra A, White DP, Gottlieb DJ, Hu FB. Association between reduced sleep and weight gain in women. *Am J Epidemiol.* 2006;164:947-954.

71. Nielsen SJ, Popkin BM. Patterns and trends in food portions sizes, 1977-1998. *JAMA.* 2003;289:450-453.

72. Ledikwe JH, Ello-Martin JA, Rolls BJ. Portion size and the obesity epidemic. *J Nutr.* 2005;135:905-909.

73. Liu Y, Goa JH, Liu HL, Fox P. The temporal response of the brain after eating revealed by functional MRI. *Nature.* 2000;405:1058-1062.

74. Bellisle F, Dalix AM. Cognitive restraint can be offset by distraction, leading to increased meal intake in women. *Am J Clin Nutr.* 2001;74:197-200.

75. Ello-Martin JA, Ledikwe JH, Rolls BJ. The influence of food portion size and energy density on energy intake: implications for weight management. *Am J Clin Nutr.* 2005;82(1 Suppl):236S-241S.

76. Rolls BJ, Bell EA, Thorwart ML. Water incorporated into a food but not served with a food decreases energy intake in lean women. *Am J Clin Nutr.* 1999;70:448-455.

77. Rolls BJ, Roe LS, Meengs JS. Salad and satiety: energy density and portion size of a first course salad affect energy intake at lunch. *J Am Diet Assoc.* 2004;104:1570-1576.

78. National Heart, Lung, and Blood Institute. Serving size card. http://hp2010.nhlbihin.net/portion/servingcard7.pdf. Accessed September 23, 2007.

79. Wansink B, van Ittersum K, Painter JE. Ice cream illusions: bowls, spoons, and self-served portion size. *Am J Prev Med.* 2006;31:240-243.

80. Rothman RL, Housam R, Weiss H, Davis D, Gregory R, Gebretsadik T, Shintani A, Elasy TZ. Patient understanding of food labels. *Am J Prev Med.* 2006;31:391-398.

81. Geier AB, Rozin P, Doros G. Unit Bias: a new heuristic that helps explain the effect of portion size on food intake. *Psychol Sci.* 2006;17:521-525.

82. Close RN, Schoeller DA. The financial reality of overeating. *J Am Coll Nutr.* 2006;25:203-209.

83. Canton SJ, Ball M, Ahern A, Hetherington MM. Dose-dependent effects of alcohol on appetite and food intake. *Physiol Behav.* 2004;81:51-58.

84. Bish CL, Blanck HM, Serdula MK, Marcus M, Kohl III HW, Khan LK. Diet and physical activity behaviors among Americans trying to lose weight: 2000 Behavioral Risk Factor Surveillance System. *Obes Res.* 2005;13:596-607.

85. Neumark-Sztainer D, Sherwood NE, French SA, Jeffery RW. Weight control behaviors among adult men and women:cause for concern? *Obes Res.* 1999;7:179-188.

86. Fletcher BC, Pine KJ, Woodbridge Z, Nash A. How visual images of chocolate affect the craving and guilt of female dieters. *Appetite.* 2007;48:211-217.

87. Burns CM, Tijhuis MA, Seidell JC. The relationship between quality of life and perceived body weight and dieting history in Dutch men and women. *Int J Obes Relat Metab Disord.* 2001;25:1386-1392.

88. Position of the American Dietetic Association:total diet approach to communicating food and nutrition information. *J Am Diet Assoc.* 2002;102:100-108.

89. Gonzalez VMM, Vitousek KM. Feared food in dieting and non-dieting young women: a preliminary validation of the Food Phobia Survey. *Appetite.* 2004;43:155-173.

90. Gerstein DE, Woodward-Lopez G, Evans AE, Kelsey K, Drewnowski A. Clarifying concepts about macronutrients' effect on satiation and satiety. *J Am Diet Assoc.* 2004;104:1151-1153.

91. Stirling LJ, Yeaomans MR. Effect of exposure to a forbidden food on eating in restrained and unrestrained women. *Int J Eat Disord.* 2004;35:59-68.

92. Polivy J, Coleman J, Herman CP. The effect of deprivation on food cravings and eating behavior in restrained and unrestrained eaters. *Int J Eat Disord.* 2005;38:301-309.

93. US Department of Agriculture. MyPyramid Web site. Inside the pyramid: discretionary calories. http://www.mypyramid.gov/pyramid/discretionary_calories.html. Accessed September 23, 2007.

94. Krantz DS. A naturalistic study of social influences on meal size among moderately obese and nonobese subjects. *Psychosom Med.* 1979;41:19-27.

Chapter 5

✦ ✦ ✦

Counseling for Exercise Lifestyle Patterns

Physical Activity: An Integral Component of Lifestyle Modification

Although we use the terms *exercise* and *physical activity* interchangeably, *physical activity* is the broader term denoting any body movement produced by skeletal muscle resulting in energy expenditure, and *exercise* is physical activity that is planned or structured (1). Both physical activity and exercise done with moderate intensity can improve or maintain one or more of the components of physical fitness, such as cardiorespiratory endurance (aerobic fitness), muscular strength, muscular endurance, flexibility, and body composition (1).

Combining dietary modification and exercise is the most effective approach for weight loss (2-4) and, perhaps most importantly, maintaining an exercise regimen seems to be one of the best predictors of long-term weight maintenance (5,6). Yet, despite the importance of using physical activity as part of a weight-loss program, only about half of individuals trying to lose weight reported using exercise and, even among those, only slightly more than half met the minimal recommendations for physical activity (7). These findings are consistent with the US population at large. According to the 2003 Behavioral Risk Factor Surveillance System (BRFSS), the majority of US adults do not engage in physical activity at the minimum recommended level of at least 30 minutes per day, 5 or more days per week (8).

Physical Activity Recommendations

For healthy adults, the new recommendations to prevent chronic disease, recently updated by the American College of Sports Medicine and the American Heart Association, include the following (9):

- Do moderate intense cardio 30 minutes per day, 5 days per week *or* do vigorously intense cardio 20 minutes per day, 3 days per week

And

- Do 8 to 10 strength-training exercises with 8 to 12 repetitions of each exercise, twice per week

Note that *moderate-intensity physical activity* is defined here to mean you're working hard enough to increase your heart rate and break a sweat, yet still able to carry on a conversation—which can be done with brisk walking. Also, the 30 minutes of physical activity can be accumulated throughout the day, with 10 minutes being the minimum length of each bout of physical activity (9). Recommendations specific to overweight and obese adults include (10): engaging in approximately 60 minutes of moderate to vigorous activity on most days of the week to help manage body weight, and at least 60 to 90 minutes daily of moderate-intensity physical activity to sustain weight loss.

Clearly, there is a gap between the exercise recommendations for our patients wanting to lose weight and what our patients are actually doing in terms of exercise to lose weight. To help our patients meet these recommendations, behavior modification strategies are needed to target desired changes in exercise behavior (11).

Physical Activity General Counseling Tips

The concept of accumulating lifestyle physical activities vs having to exercise in a gym has made it easier for clinicians to counsel overweight patients in the exercise domain. Also, the Lifestyle Patterns Approach gives clinicians new tools to help them feel comfortable counseling patients about getting started with a physical activity program, moving their bodies more, and progressing their program safely and effectively. Physical activity recommendations should be based on each patient's needs, initial ability to perform physical activity, and interest level (12). Physical activity programs should start slow and increase in intensity and duration, recognize each person's barriers to becoming active, and suit each person's lifestyle (13). Outlining when clinicians need to refer patients to a certified fitness professional or consult with their health care provider is an important and integral part of this program.

Most adults do not need to see their health care provider before starting a moderate-intensity physical activity program (14). However, a patient with a medical history of any underlying cardiovascular risk factors (eg, hypertension, cigarette smoking, family history), functional or musculoskeletal limitations, or medications that may affect the patient's participation in an exercise program (eg, hypertension or diabetes medications) warrants a physician's clearance to design a safe and effective program. A cardiac stress test is recommended for patients with known cardiovascular or pulmonary disease or one or more signs or symptoms suggestive of cardiovascular and pulmonary disease, including chest, neck, or jaw pain that may be due to ischemia; shortness of breath at rest or with mild exertion; or unusual fatigue or shortness of breath with usual activities (15). If your patient intends to engage in vigorous physical activity (activity intense enough to represent a substantial cardiorespiratory challenge), a stress test is recommended if the patient meets any of the criteria mentioned previously *or* if he/she meets age criteria (men ≥ 40 years of age; women ≥ 50 years of age) (15). Bottom line—when in doubt, refer the patient to see his or her physician.

According to the National Institutes of Health Consensus Development Panel on Physical Activity and Cardiovascular Health (16), the following attitudinal factors regarding physical activity are associated with adoption of an active lifestyle:

- Perceives a net benefit

- Chooses an enjoyable activity

- Feels safe doing the activity

- Can easily access the activity on a regular basis

- Can fit the activity into the daily schedule

- Feels that the activity does not generate financial or social costs that he or she is unwilling to bear

- Experiences a minimum of negative consequences such as injury, loss of time, negative peer pressure, and problems with self-identity

- Is able to successfully address issues of competing time demands
- Recognizes the need to balance the use of labor-saving devices (eg, power lawnmower, automobile) and sedentary activities (eg, watching TV, using computer) with activities that involve a higher level of physical exertion

Exercise Lifestyle Patterns

As explained in Chapter 2, our program has identified seven exercise lifestyle patterns:

- Couch Champion
- Uneasy Participant
- Fresh Starter
- All-or-Nothing Doer
- Set-Routine Repeater
- Tender Bender
- Rain Check Athlete

The discussion format of the seven exercise lifestyle patterns that follows includes:

- A description of each exercise pattern.
- A discussion with supportive research of why each pattern is a problem.
- The four strategies to help patients reshape the problem pattern into a more healthful one (highlights of this information are included on the corresponding patient-teaching handout).
- Questions about the pattern that clinicians can ask during counseling.
- Pattern-specific case studies. Please keep in mind that the case scenarios that follow each pattern should be viewed as excerpts taken from a longer counseling process. The primary intent of the case studies is to demonstrate dialogue and phraseology that are consistent with the particular pattern.

The Couch Champion

Description

Couch Champions don't like to exercise. When younger, many weren't involved in sports and gym was their least favorite class. As they got older, they settled right into an inactive lifestyle in which most of their leisure time is spent doing sedentary activities like working on the computer, reading, watching television, or relaxing on the couch. Given a choice of taking a walk or reading and relaxing—the relaxing activity always wins out.

The Problem

The intertwined epidemics of sedentary lifestyle and obesity have led to an increase in chronic disease, impaired physical functioning, and reduced quality of life (17). Technological changes over the last few decades have resulted in a decrease in both work-related and household-related physical activity (18). Sedentary leisure "screen-time" activities like computer use and television viewing have been consistently associated with greater risk of obesity (18,19). One statewide walking survey revealed that obese individuals walked approximately 2,000 fewer steps per day than normal-weight individuals (20).

Strategies for Couch Champions

The following strategies may help Couch Champions succeed at weight loss and maintenance:

- See benefits
- Move more
- Count steps
- Buddy up

See Benefits

For Couch Champions, barriers to exercise, such as sweating or lack of comfort while exercising, typically overshadow everything else. As discussed in Chapter 1, if patients better understand the positive effects of making changes in their behavior, they may be more likely to do so. Counseling should include helping patients better understand and pay attention to the many short- and long-term benefits of engaging in a physical activity program (14).

Couch Champions typically complain of low energy. Moderate exercise has been shown to regulate mood by enhancing energy (21). In one study in which 18 volunteers (nonsedentary) were asked to eat a candy bar or walk briskly for 10 minutes, Thayer found that walking was associated with significantly higher self-rated energy and lower tension (lasting for 2 hours) compared with eating the candy bar (22).

The following counseling suggestions may help Couch Champions see benefits:

- Explain the many benefits of engaging in more physical activity, such as improved cardiorespiratory fitness; blood pressure and blood glucose control; enhanced mood and self-esteem; and a reduction in cardiovascular disease, cancer risk, and osteoporosis, among others (16,23).

- Help patients understand how being more active can boost their energy level.

- Help patients understand that when they come home from work feeling tired and having low energy, that this is a great time to take a walk and get an energy boost.

- Have patients rate their energy level after a walk by asking themselves, "Is my energy level less, the same, or increased after walking?" In time, patients will see the connection more clearly and use exercise as a strategy to boost their energy level.

- Encourage patients to make a list of all of the positive consequences they can look forward to experiencing when they start building more activity into their daily routine.

- Discuss that they don't need to sweat or feel uncomfortable to engage in and benefit from a physically active lifestyle.

Move More

Lifestyle physical activity, defined as the "accumulation of unstructured activities of daily living according to individual preference and convenience" (24), may be more successful than structured exercise programs in motivating sedentary overweight individuals to move their bodies more and become physically active on a regular basis (24). All lifestyle physical activity is beneficial, including walking during the course of your normal day's routine, taking the stairs instead of the elevator, vacuuming, gardening, yard work, occupational tasks, playing sports with your kids, walking your dog, etc (25). Different than planned exercise, engaging in lifestyle activities has many benefits that can be attractive to individuals new to exercise, such as convenience (doesn't require travel to and from a facility), low cost (no expensive equipment required), and flexibility (can be done at home, away from home, while at work, or on vacation) (13).

The following counseling suggestions may help Couch Champions move more:

- Introduce the concept of physical activity (vs planned exercise)—that increasing all physical activity counts toward improving health and boosting weight loss.

- Share ways to sneak more physical activity into one's daily routine by following the tips in Box 5.1.

- Have patients commit to walking even just 5 to 10 minutes to start, with a longer-term goal of accumulating a minimum of 30 minutes of walking each day (60 minutes for the maximum weight-loss benefit). See Table 5.1 (26).

- Review patients' daily schedules and give them ideas about how to most easily achieve this goal; for some people, it will be easiest to break up the walking into three 10-minute sessions (eg, by parking car farther away from work and walking 10 minutes from car to the office, taking a 10-minute walk after lunch, and walking 10 minutes back to the car), but for other people it may be easier to do it all in one session (a 30-minute walk after work).

Count Steps

Measuring steps taken by wearing a pedometer or step counter is an inexpensive, simple way to increase physical activity (27). A pedometer can serve as a step-tracking tool, an activity feedback device, and as a physical reminder to increase activity (28). A qualitative study of 13 inactive or irregularly active women showed that wearing a pedometer motivated individuals to increase their physical activity, set goals, and be more accountable when asked to submit their step logs (29). In a study of 56 previously sedentary overweight/obese adults, setting a 10,000-step-per-day goal has been shown to improve weight loss (30). In one study, the women who were told to walk 10,000 steps per day walked more than women

---

Box 5.1 ✦ Move More Tips

- Take the stairs instead of the elevator.
- Walk up and down the escalator.
- Park your car farther away from your destination.
- Get off the bus or train one stop earlier and walk.
- Have a walking meeting with a coworker.
- Walk to coworker's office instead of e-mailing.
- Add a walk to your lunch hour.
- Use work break time for walking time.
- Pace while talking on the phone (using a cell phone or cordless phone).
- Take a walk while waiting at the airport or for an appointment.
- Walk to the store or to mail letters.
- Walk once around the mall before you shop.
- When unloading groceries from your car, carry one bag at a time into the house.
- Walk longer when taking your baby out in the stroller.
- Walk your child to and from school.
- Take your dog on more frequent and longer walks.
- Hide your television remote control.
- Work in your garden (mowing, raking, weeding, digging, etc).
- Shovel snow.
- Wash your own car.
- Do your own housework (scrubbing, mopping, dusting, polishing, etc).
- When carrying laundry upstairs, make several trips instead of one.

Table 5.1 ✦ All Activities Count—But Some Count More!

Activity	Energy Expenditure (kcal/30 min)	
	150-lb Person	220-lb Person
Sleeping	31	45
Reclining and reading	34	50
Sitting, playing with children	85	125
Vacuuming	119	175
Very brisk walking (4.0 MPH)	170	250
Biking, moderate effort	273	400
Running at 9 minutes/mile	374	550

who were instructed to take a brisk, 30-minute walk (31). Thirty-four participants in another pedometer program used 11 primary "lifestyle activity" strategies to increase daily physical activity. The top six strategies used were walking to a meeting or work-related task (64.7%), walking after (50%) or before (35.3%) work, walking to a destination or store (29.4%), parking farther away (50%), and using the stairs rather than the elevator (23.5%) (32). Of note, obese individuals used the "parking farther" strategy significantly more than overweight individuals.

The following counseling suggestions may help Couch Champions count steps:

- Encourage patients to wear a pedometer daily as a way to motivate more activity, measure and mark progress, and improve goal-setting.

- Instruct patients about how to use a pedometer (see Box 5.2 [33-35]).

- Personalize step goals based on the patient's baseline values, health goals, and lifestyle (28).

- Encourage patients to bring the pedometer step logs to future appointments so they can be reviewed.

Buddy Up

Having social support in the form of a spouse (36), family member or friend (37), work colleague (38), or even a dog (39) has been shown to encourage exercise and/or help people achieve their walking goals. Steptoe et al found that patients who reported greater support for lifestyle change from family and friends tended to engage in more physical activity when evaluated at 4 months (40). Social support can give Couch Champions the accountability they need to follow through with their walking or exercise program. People also may find it more fun to do an activity with someone else vs going it alone.

The following counseling suggestions may help Couch Champions buddy up:

- Ask patients to take an inventory of the supportive people in their life—at work, at home, and in their social life—who can be their walking buddy, tennis or bowling friend, or exercise partner. Pet dogs can also count as companions for walking or jogging.

- Explain to patients that using a personal trainer is another way to increase accountability and motivation and suggest buddying up with a professional who can meet the patient at home or in the park.

- Have patients develop a specific plan for buddying up that includes who they will buddy up with, what type of activity they will do together, when and where they will do the activity, and for how long.

Box 5.2 ✦ Tips for Using a Pedometer

- Purchase a pedometer that counts steps, not miles. Many sporting goods stores carry accurate pedometers for under $30.00.
- Clip the pedometer to your waistband in line with the front midline of the thigh. If you are wearing clothing that lacks a waistband or belt, you can attach the pedometer to undergarments or a bra (clip in the front and center). People with large stomachs can place the pedometer on the side of the hip (34).
- Calibrate your pedometer to check accuracy by setting your pedometer on zero, then counting while you walk 100 steps. You should see that it registers between 90 and 110 steps. If so, your pedometer is working fine; if not, you may need to adjust its placement by moving it closer to or farther from your belly button and then checking it again. If it's still not working correctly, you may want to return it and try another brand.
- Use your pedometer for 3 days to calculate your average baseline daily activity (35). You can put it on in the morning and wear it all day until you go to bed. Take it off for bathing (or swimming).
- Record your baseline daily steps taken in an activity log or in an online exercise tracker.
- Set a goal week to week to increase your daily steps taken by 250 to 500. So the first week, you'll be taking on average 500 extra daily steps; the second week, an additional 500 extra daily steps—and so on. The key is to build at a pace that's challenging to your body but not too hard to keep up on a daily basis. Set a long-term goal to achieve at least 10,000 steps (or approximately 3 to 5 miles depending on stride length) per day. This may take anywhere from weeks to months to achieve depending on your starting point.
- As you progress in your walking program, it's important to pay attention to the pace of your walking. To build cardiorespiratory fitness, you need to be walking at a brisk pace, not strolling.
- Continue to record your daily steps taken week to week.
- Though pedometer use is recommended as a specific strategy for Couch Champions, it can be helpful for anyone interested in self-monitoring physical activity.

Note to the Health Care Provider: A food and activity log can be printed from the CD-ROM. Online exercise trackers are listed in Appendix F.

Questions Clinicians Ask During Counseling Sessions

Following are potential questions to help the clinician and patient decide which of the four strategies or combination of strategies will best target the patient's needs. With practice, these strategies will lead the patient to become more physically active.

- "Why do you think you lead a fairly sedentary lifestyle?"
- "What are your thoughts and attitudes about being more physically active?"
- "How do you think you might benefit from becoming more physically active?"
- "What are the barriers that make it hard for you to be more active?"
- "Where and when can you build more activity into your daily routine?"
- "Are there people in your life whom you could see buddying up with for exercise?"
- "Of the four strategies, which ones are you most confident you can adopt?"
- "Have you been successful at using any of these strategies in the past?"

Case Study

R is a 40-year-old woman, 5′3″, who weighs 231 pounds with a BMI of 41. Although R's life is hectic, most of her activities are inactive, such as sitting at the computer, watching television, driving carpools for her three children, or collapsing at night onto the couch. R knows she needs to exercise but hates the thought of joining a health club because, frankly, she hates the thought of exercising.

> **Clinician:** "R, One of the primary strategies to burn more calories is to be as physically active as you can be. I know you have a very busy life with a lot of responsibilities, but 'busy' doesn't necessarily mean the same thing as being physically active. We need to help you find ways to sneak in physical activities throughout the day."

> **R:** "I'm not opposed to being more physically active but I certainly don't see myself joining a gym. My husband exercises three times a week. He has the discipline to do that—I don't!"

> **Clinician:** "Knowing that your predominant exercise pattern is a Couch Champion, the last thing I would recommend you do is to put on a leotard and join a gym. That's not you. What you want to do is move your body throughout the day—in the course of everyday life. Here are some options to choose from. For every hour that you are on the computer, you could get up and walk for 10 minutes, preferably outside in your neighborhood. You could also park your car farther away from your office. Or, since your husband likes to exercise, you could ask him to take a brisk walk with you after dinner."

> **R:** "I like the idea of parking my car farther away because my parking lot is huge and I usually end up wasting time looking for the closest parking space. I would also look forward to taking after-dinner walks with my husband. I think he would like it too."

> **Clinician:** "Another strategy that a lot of my patients use is to deliberately walk around while they watch their kid's sports games. Are any of your kids in team sports?"

> **R:** "Yep. Two of them are—my daughter is on a softball team and my son plays soccer. Now that you mention it, I do see a few of the parents pacing the sidelines throughout the game."

> **Clinician:** "Great. Is this something you would be willing to try also? You see, the point is that all activity counts. If you can work up to accumulating or sneaking in 30 minutes or more of brisk walking on most days of the week, this would be a great way to start off."

> **R:** "Yes, I could probably get in at least 20 minutes of walking during the games. You know, physical activity was never explained to me that way. I'm going to give this a try."

The Uneasy Participant

Description

Uneasy Participants are not comfortable exercising around others, which keeps them out of the gym. They compare themselves to others and think people will stare and see how out of shape they are. They are self-conscious about exercising in a group, are embarrassed about their body size, and fear further embarrassment if they sweat a lot or have trouble getting up from the floor.

The Problem

Feeling too fat to exercise is a common barrier among the overweight, particularly for women (41). Additionally, obese adults commonly experience weight-based stigmatization, which is associated with body image disturbance (42). Thus, it is not surprising that Haimovitz et al found that women often avoid situations that further increase their body dissatisfaction (43). In contrast to these observations, people who are physically active are more satisfied with their body shape (44).

Strategies for Uneasy Participants

The following strategies may help Uneasy Participants succeed at weight loss and maintenance:

- Dress the part
- Work out at home
- Sneak in walks
- Be mindful when moving

Dress the Part

During exercise, people feel more comfortable and confident when they wear loose-fitting clothing that permits easy movements (45). Uneasy Participants are relieved to realize that tight, body-hugging spandex does not have to be the recommended exercise attire.

The following counseling suggestions may help Uneasy Participants dress the part:

- Encourage patients to choose comfortable, loose-fitting exercise clothes in a moisture-wicking synthetic fabric that will absorb sweat and keep them cool.
- Inform patients about potential online resources for purchasing active women's wear in larger sizes, such as Junonia (http://www.junonia.com) or Just My Size (http://www.jms.com).
- Instruct women about the importance of having a good-fitting sports bra.
- Ask patients when they last bought a pair of gym shoes. If all they have is an old pair of gym shoes, instruct them about the importance of having a good pair of athletic shoes that matches the type of activity they'll be doing.
- Encourage patients to buy athletic shoes that feel comfortable, where the width and length are ample, and the shoe accommodates their arch type (46). Running shoes offer the most cushion, support, and flexibility, so let patients know that salespeople may recommend running shoes for their walking program.

Work Out at Home

Exercising in the comfort, safety, and privacy of their own homes makes sense for Uneasy Participants. In a study of approximately 350 sedentary men and women ages 50 to 65 years old, King et al found that a home-based program was as effective in improving fitness as was a group-based program (47). Perri et al also identified the benefits of a home-based exercise program in a study of obese women, ages 40 to 60 years (48). During the second 6 months of this program, subjects in the home-based program rated higher in exercise participation and treatment adherence than participants in the group program. At 15 months, the home program participants had significantly greater weight loss than those in the group program. These studies indicate that the convenience, flexibility, and time-saving nature of exercising at home can help to improve compliance.

The following counseling suggestions may help Uneasy Participants work out at home:

- Encourage patients to make a list of their different home exercise options, such as powerhouse cleaning (multitasking their house cleaning with continuous movement and breaking a sweat); home exercise videos/DVDs; home aerobic equipment such as a treadmill, exercise bike, or elliptical machine; or using resistance-training free weights, bands, or machines.

- Inform patients about potential online resources for purchasing home exercise videos/DVDs, such as Collage Video (http://www.collagevideo.com), Video Fitness (http://www.videofitness.com), or Exercise TV (http://www.exercisetv.tv). Among others, exercise options include aerobics, toning, dance, yoga, pilates, core strengthening, resistance training, stability ball, kickboxing, and chair exercises.

- Help patients devise a specific home exercise plan that includes the type of exercise, when, where, how, for how long, and how often this plan will be carried out. See Total Physical Fitness Program Components in Table 5.2 (10,12,15,23,49,50).

Sneak in Walks

When taking a walk, one's appearance (concern about perspiring in nice clothes, ruining hair, uncomfortable shoes) and the surroundings (lack of time, having to carry things, lack of sidewalks, or unsafe neighborhoods) are important factors that can help or hinder one's physical activity program (51). Encouraging Uneasy Participants to plan ahead and consider these factors by bringing athletic shoes to work or wearing more comfortable clothing can go a long way to helping them build more physical activity into their day. Our experience has shown us that once Uneasy Participants become accustomed to being more active at home, they become more open to suggestions to step "outside" of their home and start building more activity into their daily lifestyle through "inconspicuous" activities like home gardening, walking the dog, walking children to and from school, taking walks with a friend around a shopping

Table 5.2 ✦ Total Physical Fitness Program Components

	Aerobics	Resistance Training	Flexibility
What is it?	Any physical activity that uses large muscle groups and causes your body to use more oxygen than it would while resting	Activities that use repeated movements against low or moderate resistance	Ability to move a joint through its complete range of motion
How does it help you?	Burns calories, builds cardiorespiratory fitness, and reduces health risks	Builds, tones, and maintains muscular strength, improves function and ability to perform activities of daily living	Improves joint range of motion and function, and enhances muscle performance
Where is it done?	Home, neighborhood, health club	Can be done with free weights, machines or resistance bands at home, health club, or while away traveling	Anywhere. Any stretching exercises, including yoga, tai chi and pilates movements
How often is it recommended?	≥ 30 minutes of moderate-intensity activity on most days per week 60–90 minutes of daily moderate-intensity physical activity for long-term weight loss maintenance	2–3 nonconsecutive days per week	A minimum of 2–3 days per week
Special considerations	Patients with (or at risk for) cardiopulmonary disease or other significant medical conditions should have physician clearance	Patients with (or at risk for) cardiopulmonary disease or muscular-skeletal disorders should have physician clearance	Precede stretching with a warm-up to increase muscle temperature

Source: Data are from references 10, 12, 15, 23, 49, and 50.

mall, walking with work colleagues during lunch breaks, or walking with family members in their neighborhood. All of these lifestyle activities allow Uneasy Participants to subtly increase their activity level while gaining confidence and comfort.

The following counseling suggestions may help Uneasy Participants sneak in walks:

- Encourage patients to explore the inconspicuous ways they can increase their activity level, such as integrating more activity into their normal day's routine or joining a gender-based workout facility like Curves or Women's Workout World (for women) or Cuts Fitness for Men or the Blitz (for men).

- Discuss ways patients can sneak more physical activity into their daily routine by following the Move More suggestions in Box 5.1 (page 99).

- Encourage patients to plan ahead by bringing athletic shoes to work or wearing more comfortable clothing to encourage more activity.

- Encourage patients to consider buddying up with a friend, work colleague, family member, or dog to increase their comfort level while walking.

- Discuss setting a goal to accumulate a minimum of 30 minutes of moving their body each day as a way to supplement their home exercise program (60 minutes for the maximal weight-loss benefits).

Be Mindful While Moving

Another strategy for Uneasy Participants is to focus less on their external state (how they look when exercising) and more on their internal condition (how they feel when exercising). This relationship between mind and body fitness helps people feel one with their bodies and can help reduce stress (52). The goal is to help Uneasy Participants progress from feeling anxious at the thought of exercise to looking at exercise as a way to increase mindfulness and inner peace. Uneasy Participants can accomplish this by either engaging in a mind/body type exercise like yoga, pilates, or tai chi, or paying attention during exercise to their body in motion, such as the repetitive rhythms of their breath or moving feet. These strategies can work to increase a sense of mindfulness and relaxation during exercise. Research on mind/body exercise programs such as yoga and tai chi shows that they have significant mental and physical value (53).

The following counseling suggestions may help Uneasy Participants be mindful while moving:

- Encourage patients to be more mindful when exercising by focusing their thoughts and feelings on their active body—the rhythm of their breathing and the repetitive movements of their feet—and to repeat a word that elicits relaxation such as the word *calm.*

- Discuss with patients that if during exercise they find themselves thinking about all the things they should be doing or other stressful topics, they need to acknowledge those thoughts but quickly refocus on being more mindful and in the moment.

- Explore with patients their interest level in trying mind/body type exercises like yoga, tai chi, or pilates, either in a class or through a home video/DVD.

Questions Clinicians Ask During Counseling Sessions

The following questions may help the clinician and the patient decide which of the four strategies or combination of strategies will best target the patient's needs. With practice, these strategies will lead the patient to more healthful habits and increased physical activity.

- "What are the reasons you're not comfortable exercising in a group setting?"

- "Have you tried exercising in a group setting before?" "What was your experience?"

- "What types of clothes do you feel comfortable wearing for exercise?" "Do you have a good pair of athletic shoes?"

- "How do you feel about exercising at home?"

- "Do you have any experience exercising at home?"

- "What are the barriers to exercising at home?"

- "Could you see building more activity into your daily routine by walking more?"

- "Would you feel more comfortable walking in your own neighborhood or somewhere where nobody knows you?"

- "Do you have any experiences or feelings regarding trying a mind/body type exercise like yoga, pilates, or tai chi?"

- "Do you understand what it means to be more mindful when exercising?"

- "Of the four strategies, which ones are you most confident you can adopt?"

- "Have you been successful at using any of these strategies in the past?"

Case Study

J is a 33-year-old woman, 5′6″, who weighs 229 pounds with a BMI of 37. J is single and works as a legal secretary. She played sports in high school (that was long before she gained all the extra weight), but has become very self-conscious about her body over the past 10 years. She is uncomfortable exercising in front of others and as a result hasn't been as physically active as she would like.

Clinician: "J, your dominant exercise pattern is called the Uneasy Participant. That means that you are not comfortable exercising in front of others. If this sounds accurate to you, our game plan will be to find ways to get you moving that are within your comfort zone."

J: "That certainly sounds like me. I actually have had a membership to a health club but haven't used it for over 5 years."

Clinician: "Have you ever exercised in your apartment?"

J: "No, not really. I do own a stepper but I don't use it."

Clinician: "Do you have any exercise tapes or DVDs?"

J: "No."

Clinician: "What do you think about purchasing an exercise DVD for your home? 'Walk Away the Pounds' is one of the most popular programs. That way you can get in a great workout at home and don't have to worry about anybody else. Does this interest you?"

J: "That sounds good. I've actually heard of that program. What do you think about yoga? My health club has yoga classes but I'm too embarrassed to go."

Clinician: "Yoga is great for many things—stretching, relaxation, and strengthening certain muscle groups. Maybe you'd be interested in picking up a yoga tape as well for your home?"

J: "That's a good idea too. I like this plan."

The Fresh Starter

Description

Fresh Starters don't know how to start an exercise program. They may be uncomfortable being around exercise machines or weights because they don't know how to use them. They've never really exercised but are willing to learn as long as they get the proper instructions.

The Problem

People who are inactive can improve their health by engaging in moderate-intensity activities on a regular basis (54). Being new to exercise, Fresh Starters often have low confidence in their abilities to undertake an exercise program. Lack of confidence or low self-efficacy is one of the personal barriers to becoming more physically active (55). Marcus et al studied stages of change for exercise behavior and found that employees who had no experience with exercise (in contrast with those who exercised regularly) had little confidence in their ability to exercise (56).

Strategies for Fresh Starters

The following strategies may help Fresh Starters succeed at weight loss and maintenance:

- Increase your confidence
- Plan aerobic exercise
- Build muscle
- Improve flexibility

Counseling Suggestions for Patient Strategies

Increase Your Confidence

Because Fresh Starters have little to no experience with exercise, they also have little to no confidence in their ability to carry out an exercise program. Helping Fresh Starters increase their confidence level is the first step to helping them take control. In a press release, Paul Estabrooks, coauthor of *The Psychology of Physical Activity,* says that "confidence can be developed by having small successes with exercise, seeing others like yourself exercise, or by having those close to you support a decision to exercise" (57).

The following counseling suggestions may help Fresh Starters raise confidence:

- Give patients an overview of the three components of a total physical fitness program that includes aerobics (walking, jogging, biking, swimming, etc), resistance training (lifting weights), and flexibility (stretching). See Table 5.2 (page 104) for more information on a total physical fitness program.

- Advise patients to choose the easiest activity to start with to help increase their feelings of success and boost their confidence: a Lifestyle Activities walking program (aerobics).

- Help patients set small goals—even just 5 to 10 minutes to start—and work up to accumulating a minimum of 30 minutes of moving their body during the course of their normal day's routine (60 minutes for the maximum weight-loss benefits). See Box 5.1 (page 99) for Move More Tips.

- Encourage patients to ask for support from family members at home for their participation in a walking program.

Plan Aerobic Exercise

Aerobic activity is defined as any physical activity that uses large muscle groups and causes one's body to use more oxygen than it would while resting (49). Aerobic fitness is achieved when the intensity of the activity is at a moderate level or more and practiced for at least 30 minutes during the course of the day on 3 to 5 days per week (23). Common examples include walking briskly, cycling, swimming, or active household work, such as cleaning the house and manually mowing the lawn. In contrast to aerobic fitness, physical fitness relates to the ability of an individual to perform the physical activity and depends on agility, balance, coordination, speed, power, and reaction time (15). In a 1-year diet and exercise weight-loss study involving 201 sedentary women, Jakicic et al found that subjects who engaged in at least moderate-intensity activity for 40 minutes, 5 days per week lost weight and improved cardiorespiratory fitness (58).

The following counseling suggestions may help Fresh Starters plan aerobic exercise:

- Educate patients about how they can integrate aerobics into their daily routine through a Lifestyle Activities brisk walking program or through a more structured exercise program.

- Explain to patients about the basics of how to start aerobics using the FITTE (Frequency, Intensity, Time, Type, Enjoyment) Principle (see Box 5.3) (59-61).

- Discuss with patients the importance of proper hydration and nutrition before and after workouts. See Box 5.4 (61).

- Encourage patients to track their aerobic progress by logging their aerobics daily on an activity log or in an online activity tracker; ask them to bring logs to future appointments to discuss with the clinician. (A food and activity log is available on the CD-ROM.)

Box 5.3 ✦ Tips on Using the FITTE Principle

Frequency
- *Frequency* refers to the number of times you engage in moderate-intensity aerobics each week.
- Aim for five times of aerobic physical activity per week.
- If you can only find the time to do planned aerobics once per week in the beginning, at least that's a start. But you'll need to increase the frequency if you want to see results.
- The focus should be on developing an exercise habit that is realistic and sustainable.

Intensity[a]
- *Intensity* refers to the vigor or pace of your aerobics activity. If you want to build fitness, you need to exercise at a level that is challenging to your heart, lungs, and entire body.
- A good way to gauge that level of intensity is to use scale from 0 to 10 to rate the effort or strain you are experiencing while doing aerobics. Let 0 = how you feel at rest and 10 = how you feel if you were working as hard as possible. You want to work at an exertion rating of 6 or 7; at this pace, you'd feel like you were walking quickly to catch a train or bus that is about to leave the station.
- Remember to warm-up before and cool-down after exercise to decrease your chances of injury. Simply march in place or ride an exercise bike for a few minutes to warm muscles; then begin your workout by building your pace slowly. Taper your pace at the end of the workout so your heartbeat returns to normal and then end by stretching your warm muscles.

continued

Box 5.3 ✦ (continued)

Time
- *Time* refers to the duration of your walking or other exercise.
- "The minimum goal is to accumulate 30 minutes of aerobics on the days that you exercise. Multiple short bouts or one 30-minute session produces the same benefits" (60).
- For better weight-loss results, gradually progress to 60 minutes of daily activity. The total number of calories burned is determined by how long you exercise (duration) and how hard you exercise (intensity).

Type
- *Type* refers to the kind or mode of activity you choose.
- Many people start with brisk or power walking, but you may want to try other aerobic activities from time to time to keep your mind and body challenged and motivated.
- Other aerobic activities include such things as using aerobics videos at home, hiking, dancing, tennis, swimming, jumping rope, or using cardio machines such as a treadmill, exercise bike, elliptical trainer, or stair climber/stair stepper.

Enjoyment
- *Enjoyment* refers to doing exercises that you find fun.
- If you get bored with walking on a treadmill, try walking outdoors (or vice versa).
- Seek activities and exercise partners that help you look forward to your workouts.

---

[a]McInnis et al recommend: "To avoid injuries and promote compliance especially in those new to exercise, start at a low to moderate intensity (a 5 on the perceived exertion scale [of zero (easiest) to 10 (hardest)]) and gradually progress over weeks or months to a more challenging intensity" (59).

Source: Data are from references 59 and 60.

Box 5.4 ✦ Tips on Workout Nutrition and Hydration

- Drink a small glass of juice or eat a piece of fruit to boost energy before a morning workout.
- Eat a breakfast that includes whole grains and fruit.
- Eat small frequent meals and snacks during the day to maintain your blood glucose level.
- Eat a light healthy snack 1 hour before your noon or after-work workout.
- Stay hydrated before, during, and after your workout.
- Limit caffeine.
- It may take some time experimenting to identify your best workout nutrition and hydration plan.

Source: Adapted from reference 61 with permission from the American Council on Exercise.

Build Muscle

Building muscle through resistance training is an important component of a total exercise program for anyone who wants to lose weight. Resistance exercise increases muscle strength and endurance and maintains or increases muscle mass (10). Resistance exercise helps to maintain resting metabolic rate (RMR) and improve an individual's ability to become more physically active (62). Rather than leading to actual weight loss, the main benefits that people reap from a resistance-training program are the favorable changes in body composition such as a decrease in the percentage of body fat and being able to sustain fat-free mass (63). The firming and toning effects on the muscles can also affect one's appearance. Another advantage to resistance training, discussed in a review article about physical activity as treatment and prevention of obesity, is improved ability to perform activities of daily living (50).

Fresh Starters may not have experience lifting weights. Accordingly, the following counseling suggestions may help them build muscle:

- Teach patients the basics of starting a safe resistance-training program. See Box 5.5 (64,65).

- Explain the benefits of getting skilled instruction on safe techniques either from a skilled fitness professional, a class instructor, a home video/DVD, or a book.

- Have patients develop a resistance-training program plan including where, when, for how long, and how often. (See Table 5.2, page 104.)

Improve Flexibility

Improving flexibility is an important component of physical fitness. Good flexibility has been shown to improve joint range of motion and function and enhance muscle performance (66). Flexibility allows people to carry out their activities of daily living, reaching for things above their head or bending down to pick things up off of the floor. Joint range of motion can be increased by a single 15- to 30-second stretch for each muscle group per day (66). Yoga, tai chi, and pilates movements may also be used to improve flexibility (15).

Box 5.5 ✦ Resistance-Training Program Tips

- In general, if you're new to resistance training and not well coordinated, it's a good idea to start with resistance exercise machines for the first 10 to 12 weeks of your program because machines may require less coordination than free weights or resistance bands (64).
- With all methods (free weights, resistance bands or machines), be sure to get instruction on proper technique from a qualified trainer or an exercise video/DVD or book.
- "One set of 8-12 repetitions, working the muscle to the point of fatigue, is usually sufficient. Breathe normally throughout the exercise. Lower the resistance with a slow, controlled cadence throughout the full range of motion. Lifting the weight to a count of 2 and lowering to a count of 3 or 4 is effective. When you are able to perform 12 repetitions of an exercise correctly, increase the amount of resistance by 5% to 10% to continue safe progress" (65).
- Pay attention to your posture while you train. In a proper sitting posture, your feet are planted firmly on floor (short people may have to rest feet on stool), your neck and shoulders are relaxed, your head is up and looking forward, and your abdominal muscles are tightened. In a proper standing pose, your feet are shoulder-width apart with your toes pointing forward, your knees are relaxed and never locked, your neck and shoulders are relaxed, your head is up and looking forward, your abdominal muscles are tightened, and your buttocks are tucked under to avoid arching your back. Work out in front of a mirror so you can check your form periodically. Stop if you feel pain!
- Carry your water bottle and hydrate between routines.
- If you decide that a home routine using free weights, resistance bands, or multipurpose weight machines best fits your schedule, check out stores in your area that sell exercise equipment. Ask the equipment vendors whether they will send out a free personal trainer if you buy their equipment.
- If you decide to join a fitness club to take advantage of the many weight machines available, ask whether personal trainers are available to help you develop a safe program. Many clubs also offer free orientations to the weight room and a free hour with a personal trainer upon joining.

Stretching exercises have been shown to improve flexibility and strength in resistance-training programs (67). Controversy exists about the benefits of stretching before aerobics. Warming up one's muscles (eg, marching in place or walking on a treadmill) was found to have the best postexercise effects, such as reduced stiffness, when compared with stretching and massage (68). Warming up was also found to improve aerobic performance (69).

The following counseling suggestions may help Fresh Starters improve flexibility:

- Discuss with patients the benefits of engaging in a regular stretching program: to release tension, increase range of motion, maintain flexibility, and feel good. See Box 5.6 for Stretching Dos and Don'ts (15).

- Talk with patients about their interest in using a stretching book or a stretching, yoga, pilates, or tai chi video/DVD; other options could include signing up for a class or using a personal trainer to guide their stretching program.

Questions Clinicians Ask During Counseling Sessions

The following questions may help the clinician and the patient decide which of the four strategies or combination of strategies will best target the patient's needs. With practice, these strategies will lead the patient to more healthful habits and increased physical activity.

- "What do you know about starting an exercise program?"

- "Do you have any experience with doing aerobics, resistance training, or flexibility/stretching exercises?"

- "Can you identify any barriers to starting an exercise program?"

- "Given the proper instruction and support, what exercises are you most interested in starting?"

- "Of the four strategies, which ones are you most confident you can adopt?"

- "Have you been successful at using any of these strategies in the past?"

Box 5.6 ✦ Stretching Dos and Don'ts

- Before stretching, *do* warm up by marching in place or walking on a treadmill for a few minutes. *Don't* stretch cold muscles.
- *Do* stretch major muscle groups that have reduced range of motion.
- *Do* a stretching routine at least 2 or 3 times per week, ideally 5 to 7 days per week (15).
- *Do* breathe naturally while stretching.
- *Do* hold stretches to a point of gentle tension for 15 to 30 seconds. Repeat each stretch 2 to 4 times (15).
- *Don't* bounce.
- *Don't* overstretch to the point of pain. Stretches that require moderate joint flexibility may not be appropriate for everyone (15).

Case Study

G is a 52-year-old woman, 5'5'', who weighs 162 pounds with a BMI of 27. G is a residential realtor, is married, and has three grown children who have moved away from home. She is active at work, showing houses almost every day. But because she was never in school athletics or participated in sports, G does not know the first thing about how to exercise properly.

Clinician: "G, do you think this is a good time to start an exercise program?"

G: "Yes, I do. The kids are out of the house and I have more flexibility in how I manage my time."

Clinician: "Do you have any experience with doing aerobics, resistance training, or flexibility/stretching exercises?"

G: "No I don't, and that's my biggest concern."

Clinician: "For a complete exercise program, all three components are important. Once you understand how to do them properly, you can exercise on your own or at a gym. The easiest component to start with is a planned aerobics program since you are already walking during the day."

G: "I sure am. I'm on my feet all day long, but I don't really know what aerobics is!"

Clinician: "For an aerobic workout, you want to walk at a moderately vigorous pace for at least 30 minutes a day. At that pace you feel winded but can still talk. It's a speed where you are walking very quickly, like you would to catch a bus that is about to pull away. Do you think you can do that?"

G: "Well, I certainly can't do that when I am with my customers. It's funny that you mentioned a bus. I take a bus every day to work. Instead of catching the bus at my normal stop, I could pretty easily walk for 30 minutes after work, and catch the bus farther down the line. And being at the end of the day, I don't have to worry about getting too sweaty."

Clinician: "That sounds like a great plan. We can discuss resistance training and stretching on your next visit. If you want to get a head start, pick up a weight-training or stretching DVD for beginners at your video store."

The All-or-Nothing Doer

Description

All-or-Nothing Doers are either "on" or "off" when it comes to exercise. They may be weekend warriors who, after a sedentary work week, spend hours pounding the pavement jogging or working out at the gym. Or maybe they join a health club and go faithfully 5 or 6 days per week for weeks on end, but then they're unable to follow through on this unrealistic plan, and so they completely stop going and instead find themselves spending all their nights on the couch.

The Problem

All-or-Nothing Doers who are overweight are at an increased risk of injury because of their inconsistent exercise. Higher-intensity exercise is associated with greater cardiovascular risk, orthopedic injury, and lower adherence than lower-intensity exercise (12). Exercising consistently has many benefits. Research indicates that regular, moderate activity is good for your heart and overall health (49).

Strategies for All-or-Nothing Doers

The following strategies may help All-or-Nothing Doers succeed at weight loss and maintenance:

- Tone it down
- Be consistent
- Enjoy building skills
- Prevent relapse

Tone It Down

Moderate-intensity activity, such as brisk walking for 30 minutes daily, has been shown to produce health benefits and weight loss. In a study of previously sedentary healthy adults, Dunn et al found that a lifestyle physical activity intervention is as effective as a structured exercise program for improving physical activity, cardiorespiratory fitness, and blood pressure (70). If All-or-Nothing Doers can moderate their exercise goals to include low- to moderate-intensity walking in addition to their vigorous planned exercise, they will have more exercise options available when needed.

The following counseling suggestions may help All-or-Nothing Doers tone it down:

- Help patients understand that when they don't have time for their full workout that they can still benefit by building more walking time into their day's routine by following the Move More Tips in Box 5.1 (page 99).
- Encourage patients to set a goal to accumulate at least 30 minutes of brisk walking on the days they don't do their normal workout (60 minutes for maximum weight loss benefits).
- Discuss with patients that tracking their daily activity in a log or an online exercise tracker can help motivate them to walk more. (The CD-ROM includes a food and activity log.)
- Review patients' schedule to help them determine when they can fit in more walking time.

Be Consistent

Focusing on exercise consistency is a new concept for All-or-Nothing Doers, who are used to being either "on" or "off" when it comes to exercise. In a study by Chambliss of factors that helped overweight, sedentary women lose weight and improve their cardiorespiratory fitness, a consistent duration of exercise (at least 150 minutes of walking per week) was more important than whether the exercise intensity was vigorous or not (71).

The following counseling suggestions may help All-or-Nothing Doers be consistent:

- Help patients understand that it's better to do a moderate exercise program consistently than to do an intense exercise program inconsistently.
- Discuss ideas for using prompts and reminders to help patients maintain a consistent exercise program. For example, patients may bring gym shoes to work so they can fit in brisk walking during break time or schedule 30 minutes of daily walking into their calendar for the days they can't get to the health club. Providing environmental cues or prompts for physical activity can be effective reminders and encourage patients to exercise (13).
- Ask patients to consider hiring a personal trainer for a few sessions to help develop a consistent exercise routine that fits their schedule. See Box 5.7 for Tips for Choosing a Personal Trainer (72).

Enjoy Building Skills

In one weight-reduction program study, intrinsic motivation factors, such as interest and enjoyment in the type of exercise, had the strongest correlation with weight-loss outcomes (73). Similarly, Ryan et al

---

Box 5.7 ✦ Tips for Choosing a Personal Trainer

- Check whether the trainer has been certified by a nationally recognized and accredited certifying organization, such as the Cooper Institute, American College of Sports Medicine (ACSM), American Council on Exercise (ACE), National Strength and Conditioning Association (NSCA), National Academy of Sports Medicine (NASM), National Federation of Professional Trainers (NFPT), National Council on Strength and Fitness (NCSF), or National Exercise Trainers Association (NETA).
- Ask the trainer about his or her education; for example, many qualified trainers have a bachelor's or master's degree in exercise physiology or exercise science.
- Ask the trainer for references and check them.
- Make sure the trainer carries professional liability insurance.
- Ask trainers about their experience, including how long they've practiced and the types of clients they train. Look for a trainer with experience in cases similar to yours. A trainer should ask about your medical history and make sure you have a release from your doctor if you are under a doctor's care.
- Ask trainers about rates, scheduling, and where they see clients.
- Decide whether the trainer you've met and investigated is someone you can work with.

Source: Data are from reference 72.

found better adherence to exercise when individuals reported more enjoyment (74). Learning new skills and exercise challenges, such as swimming, speed walking, ice skating, spinning classes, tennis, or racquetball, can help All-or-Nothing Doers escape their all-or-nothing rut by feeding their goal-oriented personality in new ways.

The following counseling suggestions may help All-or-Nothing Doers enjoy building skills:

- Ask patients to make a list of active leisure-time activities in or around their neighborhood that they would find enjoyable and could see getting involved in, such as bowling, kite flying, going apple picking, walking hiking trails, tennis, swimming, dancing, snowshoeing, race walking, bike riding, or golfing. Let them know the benefits of these activities. For example, Kobriger et al found that subjects who walked the golf course during a typical 18 holes of golf exceeded 10,000 steps (75).

- Suggest that patients create a specific plan (what, when, where, for how long, and how often) to try one new activity.

- Encourage patients to try new activities with a friend or buddy, which will increase accountability.

Prevent Relapse

Exercise relapse is a common occurrence for All-or-Nothing Doers. These individuals may stop exercising because of time constraints, stress, work deadlines, job change, illness, or injury. People who drift away from their exercise program should be taught how to deal with relapse and become active again (15). Identifying the factors that lead to program relapse is key to helping All-or-Nothing Doers be successful.

The following counseling suggestions may help All-or-Nothing Doers prevent relapse:

- Encourage patients to better understand their "on" and "off" exercise triggers by having them circle and discuss the answers that apply to the following two statements:
  - ▸ "My triggers for stopping exercise are time, injury, illness, work demands, stress, family responsibilities, travel, or other."
  - ▸ "My triggers for starting exercise are weight loss, to feel better, health reasons, or other."

- Help patients develop an action plan to reduce their top one or two exercise-stop triggers. For example, if injury prevents them from exercising, they might need to scale down the exercise intensity level and add warm-ups and cool-downs and a regular stretching program to their routine. If time is a problem, review their calendar with them and help them develop a plan in which they can fit in regular lifestyle activities instead of taking the time to go to the health club. If their workload is a problem, encourage them to ask for help either at work or at home so they can free some time for exercise. If stress is a problem and patients say that low moods derail their program, encourage them to discuss their moods with their personal physician.

- Encourage patients to track their daily exercise and use a system of rewards as a way to acknowledge their continued achievements (15). See the Sample Rewards for Exercise Compliance in Box 5.8.

Questions Clinicians Ask During Counseling Sessions

The following questions may help the clinician and the patient decide which of the four strategies or combination of strategies will best target the patient's needs. With practice, these strategies will lead patients to more healthful habits and increased physical activity.

- "Why do you think that you start and stop your exercise program?"
- "What causes you to stop exercising?"
- "How are you feeling when your exercise program is 'on'?"
- "How do you feel about moderating your current exercise program?"
- "What are the barriers to carrying out a consistent exercise program?"
- "Are you willing to build more activity into your daily routine?"
- "Which of the four strategies sound most useful to start practicing?"
- "Which strategies stand out as being something you have wanted to change?"

Box 5.8 ✦ Sample Rewards for Exercise Compliance

- Enjoy a day out with a friend.
- Have a spa day.
- Have a special outing in a park.
- Attend a sporting event.
- Get a massage.
- Purchase a new outfit.
- Buy some flowers.
- Take a trip.

Case Study

A is a 33-year-old man, 6′2″, who weighs 262 pounds with a BMI of 33.7. A works for a technology consulting company that requires him to travel out of town bimonthly, typically for an entire week at a time. Although he enjoys physical activity and exercises on most days that he is home, A doesn't exercise when he is out of town. A recognizes this as a problem.

> **Clinician:** "A, you are an All-or-Nothing doer when it comes to exercise. I often see this pattern in people who have to work out of town, just like you."

> **A:** "I know and it's killing me. I really like to exercise. I just don't do it when I'm away. I get so caught up in my work that I'm exhausted by the end of the day and just collapse."

> **Clinician:** "What is your exercise routine when you're at home?"

> **A:** "I go to the gym at the end of the day, on my way home. I usually use the elliptical machine or stepper for 30 to 40 minutes, then use free weights for another 20 minutes. It's a complete set."

> **Clinician:** "That's a great workout. It sounds to me that you can develop an exercise routine when you're on the road, but it will have to be modified from the one you do at home. For one thing, you may find that exercising in the morning will work better for you because you're already in the hotel and you'll be refreshed. Second, you may not have the time to do your complete 60-minute workout routine because of your schedule for that day and the equipment in the hotel health club. What do you think?"

> **A:** "I hear you. That's always been difficult for me. I have this mindset that if I can't do my full program, it's not worth it."

> **Clinician:** "Moderation and flexibility are the keys here. A 30-minute workout is better than no workout at all! I know you're going out of town this week. What do you think you can do to fit in some exercise while out of town?"

> **A:** "I know all of the hotels I visit have fitness rooms. I guess I can get up earlier and try doing maybe just 30 minutes. That's really all I'll have time for."

> **Clinician:** "That will be a great start. Be sure to pack your exercise clothes. I'm going to ask you about it at our next session."

> **A:** "Okay, I'll try it."

The Set-Routine Repeater

Description

Set-Routine Repeaters are used to doing a fixed exercise routine, but that also keeps their weight fixed. They have been exercising at a safe and comfortable pace without advancing their exercise routine or challenging their body in new ways. This may be the person who faithfully jumps on the treadmill every Monday, Wednesday, and Friday and turns up the speed to 2.8 where she walks and talks on her cell phone for 30 minutes. Or it's someone who fits in his 40-minute workout on the elliptical two times per week at the health club, which allows him time to read his fitness magazine but without ever considering the need to increase the duration, frequency, or intensity of his workout; try other aerobic machines; or add a resistance-training component.

The Problem

A person's body adapts to doing the same type of exercise. With time, doing the same exercise will not produce the same benefits because the body becomes more efficient in doing that exercise (76). Jakicic et al found that the higher the total volume of physical activity, the greater the weight lost among overweight women (77).

Strategies for the Set-Routine Repeater

The following strategies may help Set-Routine Repeaters succeed at weight loss and maintenance:

- Change the pace
- Vary workout type
- Add weight lifting
- Try exercise tools

Change the Pace

Different intensities and types of exercise produce different benefits (10). Increasing the intensity, frequency, and duration of exercise is more tolerable when individuals are used to regular exercise and have already established a baseline level of fitness (14). This applies perfectly to Set-Routine Repeaters who aren't new to exercise. The FITTE Principle can help guide Set-Routine Repeaters to change the pace of their exercise routine. Interval training principles offer them another option as well (78).

The following counseling suggestions may help Set-Routine Repeaters change the pace:

- Instruct patients how to use the FITTE Principle (Box 5.3, pages 108–109) to design a plan to change the pace of their current exercise routine. For example, you might offer the following suggestions:

  - ▶ Change the "F" (frequency) of the workout by adding another workout session to their weekly plan.
  - ▶ Change the "I" (intensity) of the workout by (*a*) exercising at a 6 or 7 on an exertion scale from 0 (no effort) to 10 (working as hard as possible); (*b*) using the talk test (able to talk but only in broken up sentences due to breathlessness from exertion; or (*c*) using a heart rate monitor (see Box 5.9 for tips) (79).
  - ▶ Change the "T" (time) of their workout by, for example, increasing the length of the workout by 10%. If the patient is exercising for 40 minutes three times per week (or a total of 120 minutes workout time for the week), he or she would add another 12 minutes (or 10% of the total 120 minute workout time), yielding a new workout of 44 minutes three times per week.

- Discuss the concept of interval training as a means of increasing the pace of exercise. For example, the patient could alternate walking for 2 minutes with walking at a higher treadmill speed or running for 2 minutes. Interval training gives options to vary the intensity and duration of the work interval and the rest/recovery interval, as well as the number of repetitions of each interval (78). Interval training can be appropriate for individuals who are interested and have good coordination.

Vary Workout Type

Varying the type of aerobic exercise can increase adherence and enjoyment (80). Cross-training is one way to introduce new types of exercise to a workout routine and decrease chances of injury because muscles, bones, and joints will have less exposure to the same stresses of the same activity (81).

Box 5.9 ✦ Using a Heart Rate Monitor

A heart rate monitor is a tool that you can use to gauge the intensity of your workout. To figure out your target heart rate zone (which is the range your heart should be beating in during aerobic exercise), subtract your age from 220 and then multiply that number by 50% to get your lower target heart rate and then by 80% to get the upper level of your target heart rate. For example, if you are 40 years old, your target heart rate is between 90 and 144. New exercisers and people who are not fit can strive to be in the lower end of the zone, and those who are more fit can strive to be in the higher end of the zone.

These target heart rate guidelines are estimates for healthy people. People who have health problems or are taking medications that affect their heart rate should talk to their physician regarding their exercise intensity goals.

Source: Data are from reference 79.

To help Set-Routine Repeaters vary types of exercise, counselors should be prepared to suggest ideas for trying new activities. For example:

- If patients always jump onto the treadmill at the health club, encourage them to try other aerobic equipment such as the elliptical trainer, stair stepper, or exercise bike.

- If they always workout alone, encourage them to sign up for a class that interests them and sounds fun and challenging, such as kickboxing, step or dance aerobics, bosu ball class, or spinning.

- If patients always walk or run outside, assess their interest in signing up to be a part of a race-walking group or a community-based fitness run, which can give them a reason to set new workout goals (82).

- If patients always walk inside on a home treadmill, encourage them to try to shake up their routine a bit by walking on outdoor hiking trails, trying snowshoeing in winter, or just adding music to their workout.

- Encourage patients to find an exercise buddy who will try new activities with them to make these activities more fun.

Add Weight Lifting

As discussed for Fresh Starters, weight lifting (resistance training) has been shown to be an effective way to boost one's exercise program because it helps to maintain resting metabolic rate, improves one's strength and ability to do normal activities of daily living, and improve one's body composition (59). For Set-Routine Repeaters, another benefit of resistance training is that it helps fight exercise boredom by adding an entirely new component to the fitness routine.

The following counseling suggestions may help Set-Routine Repeaters add weight lifting:

- Review with patients the basics of starting a safe resistance-training program (see Box 5.5, page 110).

- Have patients develop a resistance-training program plan (twice per week if possible) including where, when, for how long, and how often. See Table 5.2 (page 104) for resistance-training information as part of a Total Physical Fitness Program.

- Explain the benefits of getting skilled instruction on safe resistance-training techniques from a skilled fitness professional, a class instructor, a home video/DVD, or a book.

Try Exercise Tools

Although tools are not necessary for an exercise program to be effective, trying a new exercise tool or gadget can make exercise more fun and challenging (82). The key is finding the right fitness gadget that's available for the patient's favorite activity.

The following counseling suggestions may help Set-Routine Repeaters try exercise tools:

- Discuss with patients their interest in trying an exercise gadget such as a heart rate monitor to help them increase the intensity of their workout and better monitor their fitness level. See Box 5.9 for tips on using a heart rate monitor (79).

- Talk with patients about their interest in other tools and gadgets, such as a pedometer to track their daily steps taken; an accelerometer to measure calories burned from physical movements; a GPS tracker to plan routes and measure run or walk distances; a stability or bosu ball to improve their core workout; or water gloves, weights, and shoes for water aerobics.

Questions Clinicians Ask During Counseling Sessions

The following questions may help the clinician and the patient decide which of the four strategies or combination of strategies will best target the patient's needs. With practice, these strategies will help the patient become more physically active.

- "Tell me about your current exercise routine and how long you've been doing it."
- "Are you bored by your routine?"
- "What is your interest in changing your current routine to a more challenging one?"
- "What other types of exercise interest you?"
- "What's your interest in starting a resistance-training program?"
- "Do you see any barriers that will make it hard for you to change the pace, try something new, or start a resistance-training program?"
- "Do you have any interest in taking classes, signing up for a fun walk or run, or buddying up with a friend?"
- "Do fitness gadgets such as a heart rate monitor or a pedometer interest you?"
- "Of the four strategies, which ones are you most confident you can adopt?"
- "Have you been successful at using any of these strategies in the past?"

Case Study

D is a 55-year-old woman, 5′3″, who weighs 183 pounds with a BMI of 32.5. D is frustrated that she is unable to lose any more weight despite following a calorie-controlled diet and exercising for the past 4 months. She is rather proud of her exercise routine because she does it faithfully and consistently— walking on the treadmill for 30 minutes at a pace of 3.5 miles per hour, three times per week. She knows it is exactly 30 minutes because she does it while watching her favorite television show.

> **Clinician:** "D, I think it is great that you are exercising, but it's time to change your exercise routine. By doing the same exercise and using the exact same muscles, they have become very efficient. You are not getting the most out of exercise. How hard do you think you are working? Are you short of breath or sweating?"

D: "Not really. I did feel like I was pushing at first but not any more."

Clinician: "There a few ways to pick up your exercise program. Since you use a treadmill at home and that's comfortable for you, let's use the FIT principle. That stands for frequency, intensity, and time. Changing any or all of these will make a difference in your exercise routine. For example, you can add one day per week; speed up your walking to get a more intensive workout, say up to 3.8 or 4.0 miles per hour; or walk longer, such as 40 minutes instead of 30 minutes."

D: "Isn't it funny? I never really thought of doing that. I've been so comfortable doing my own routine that I thought I was in good shape. I certainly can do that. Should I change everything you said?"

Clinician: "I'd recommend that you pick one, then advance from there. Which one would you like to start with?"

D: "I guess I can increase the speed. How do I know what's good for me?"

Clinician: "Use the talk test. You want to exercise to a point where you can still talk but not in complete sentences. You will have to take a breath after every few phrases."

D: "I'll give it a try."

Clinician: "The other activity I want to talk to you about is starting a weight-training program by using either free weights or resistance bands. Since you haven't done this before, it's important that you get proper instruction first. We can go over this on your next visit."

D: "That sounds good. Let's start with the FIT thing first though."

The Tender Bender

Description

Tender Benders have an established medical condition or injury that impairs their ability to exercise. For example, a Tender Bender may have bad knees or a foot condition, a sore back or shoulder, arthritis and achy joints, or a heart condition. What Tender Benders share is that they don't know how to adapt their exercise program to their particular condition or functional limitation, or they are uncertain which activities they can do safely.

The Problem

People with or recovering from health conditions often avoid physical activities because they're unsure of the exercise guidelines that pertain to their condition. Yet, engaging in physical activities can often help these individuals decrease their pain level as well as increase their energy, muscle strength, sense of balance, and coordination (83). Tender Benders need to understand how to modify their exercise program so it's safe for their condition.

Strategies for Tender Benders

The following strategies may help Tender Benders succeed at weight loss and maintenance:

- Set limits
- Make activity time short and sweet

- Adapt your program
- Seek expert advice

Set Limits

Tender Benders need to get medical clearance from their health care provider regarding what types of exercise they can and cannot do (83). Sometimes the specific exercise parameters will come from a physician specialist (such as an orthopedic surgeon, cardiologist, endocrinologist, neurologist, or podiatrist) or from a physical therapist who has been working with the patient. The bottom line is that patients need clear directions from health care professionals who know their medical condition.

The following counseling suggestions may help Tender Benders set limits:

- Make sure that patients consult with their health care professional and get clear directions about what they can and cannot do in terms of exercise; this includes getting a cardiac stress test if needed.

- Encourage patients to get information about the types of exercises and stretches they can do and if there are any precautions regarding exercising safely, such as "no twisting or jumping," "no exercising in the heat or humidity," "use ice on achy joints before and after working out," "take your arthritis medications on the days you exercise," or "stop and get help if you experience dizziness, shortness of breath, or chest pains."

- Discuss with patients their specific parameters for exercise.

Make Activity Time Short and Sweet

Because of the functional limitations of some Tender Benders, they initially may tolerate exercise better in short bouts. Accumulating short bouts of activity can be an effective strategy for boosting health and weight loss. Even in the absence of weight loss, chronic medical conditions such as hypertension, insulin resistance, elevated blood glucose levels, and dyslipidemia have been shown to improve as a result of enhanced physical activity in overweight or obese adults (59).

The following counseling suggestions may help Tender Benders make activity time short and sweet:

- Ensure that patients have a pair of supportive and good-fitting athletic shoes.

- Encourage patients to start small, adding whatever activities they're able to do, and then building from there. For example, they could begin by walking to mail a letter, taking their dog for a walk, or walking to their neighbor's house instead of driving. See Box 5.1 (page 99) for Move More Tips.

- Help patients set realistic activity goals that are safe for their condition.

- Encourage patients to consider wearing a pedometer daily to track their steps taken.

- Instruct patients to write down the number of steps taken daily on an activity log and record number of minutes of activity each day as a way to track progress and set new goals; encourage them to bring logs to discuss with the clinician at future appointments. (A food and activity log is available on the CD-ROM.)

- Explain to patients that increasing physical activity slowly in the beginning will not contribute dramatically to weight loss but it will help them increase their fitness level gradually so they can do much more activity later on.

Adapt Your Program

Alternative exercise regimens (such as pilates, tai chi, yoga, water aerobics, and even a chair aerobics class or home video/DVD) give Tender Benders exercise options that may better fit their needs and physical condition. People with arthritis, for example, may do well with exercise regimens that involve little impact on their joints, such as swimming, walking, or bicycling (84). Patients with heart disease or other stress-related conditions may follow the recommendations of Dean Ornish, MD, who prescribes yoga exercises and relaxation techniques to reverse symptoms of heart disease (85). Although some of these alternative exercise options may not burn a lot of calories, they do contribute to overall feelings of well-being.

The following counseling suggestions may help Tender Benders adapt their program:

- Encourage patients to try alternative activities that relax and challenge their bodies in new ways (eg, yoga, tai chi, pilates, water aerobics, fit-ball class).

- Have patients investigate classes in their community or alternative exercise videos/DVDs that interest them.

- Encourage patients to focus on the positive gains of being more active (eg, more energy, less stiffness, improved mood and sleep, better range of motion).

Seek Expert Advice

People who are trying to choose an exercise program while dealing with a health condition may benefit from working with a personal trainer, especially one who has experience working with clients with similar conditions (83). Tender Benders can get supervision in the form of one-on-one help, as part of a group, or as part of a rehabilitation or wellness facility program.

The following counseling suggestions may help Tender Benders seek expert advice:

- Explain to patients that they may want to consider getting expert advice from a professional if they want to keep advancing their exercise program.

- Discuss with patients their options, such as hiring a personal trainer or joining a medically based fitness program (eg, hospital wellness center, physical therapy, cardiac rehabilitation) where they can be instructed and monitored on safely progressing with their exercises. See Tips for Choosing a Personal Trainer in Box 5.7 (page 114).

Questions Clinicians Ask During Counseling Sessions

The following questions may help the clinician and the patient decide which of the four strategies or combination of strategies will best target the patient's needs. With practice, these strategies will help the patient develop a safe physical activity routine.

- "What are your exercise limitations?"
- "Have you gotten clearance from your doctor to exercise?"
- "Did your doctor tell you what exercise you can and cannot do?"
- "What do you see as barriers to adapting a program to meet your needs?"
- "Have you participated in a walking or alternative exercise program like water aerobics before? What was your experience?"
- "How do you feel about working with a fitness professional who can guide and supervise your program?"
- "Do you know of any supervised exercise programs in your area for people with your condition?"
- "Of the four strategies, which ones are you most confident you can adopt?"
- "Have you been successful at using any of these strategies in the past?"

Case Study

S is a 65-year-old woman, 5'5", who weighs 200 pounds with a BMI of 33.4. S has rheumatoid arthritis, which is moderately controlled with anti-inflammatory medication. Her physical activities have become progressively more limited in the past 5 years. Currently, she walks around her apartment but uses a motorized cart when she is out of the house for long periods of time.

Clinician: "S, it's going to be hard to get you moving around more due to your rheumatoid arthritis. Nonetheless, the more activity you can do, the healthier you will feel and the more calories you will be able to burn off."

S: "I know. It's really frustrating for me. I want to be more active, but my joints are so painful. I walk around my apartment as much as I can. It's safe there since I can sit down whenever I need to."

Clinician: "Have you ever done aqua-aerobics? Water takes the weight off of your joints and you can use the resistance of the water to move around."

S: "Yes, I did. It was part of my physical therapy a few years ago. But it has been about 3 years since I've been in therapy."

Clinician: "Is this something you would like to pursue?"

S: "Actually, my doctor has mentioned to me that this would be a good thing to try. Yes, I'm interested in finding out more."

Clinician: "You can either call your doctor for a referral back to PT, or you can call your local community center and see if there is a water aerobics class you can sign up for. Sometimes they call it *aquasize*."

S: "That's a good idea. It would also get me out of the house. I'll call."

The Rain Check Athlete

Description

Rain Check Athletes want to exercise but can't seem to find the time. They're busy people who feel frustrated because they know they need to exercise and even want to exercise, but competing demands always take priority, "forcing" them to take another rain check.

The Problem

Lack of time is one of the most common exercise barriers (10). Structured exercise is time-consuming and competes with the many responsibilities of daily life, especially considering travel time to and from an exercise facility (14). Because people who exercise regularly complain about time constraints as much as people who don't exercise, "perceived available time" may be the bigger issue rather than actual time limitations (15).

Strategies for Rain Check Athletes

The following strategies may help Rain Check Athletes succeed at weight loss and maintenance:

- Fit in walking
- Schedule activity in a date book

- Combine activity with other things
- Ask for help

Counseling Suggestions for Patient Strategies

Fit in Walking

Increasing lifestyle activities is the most time-efficient and convenient way to build more activity into one's daily routine. Walking can be done anywhere and at any time, which makes it an attractive form of exercise for busy people (15). Multiple short bouts of activity such as brisk walking for 10 minutes three times per day may better fit the busy schedule of a Rain Check Athlete.

The following counseling suggestions may help Rain Check Athletes fit in walking:

- Encourage patients to increase their activities of daily living by following the Move More Tips in Box 5.1 (page 99).

- Have patients commit to walking for 5 to 10 minutes to start, with a longer-term goal of accumulating a minimum of 30 minutes of moving their body each day (60 minutes for maximum weight-loss benefits).

- Discuss with patients how wearing a pedometer can help motivate them to walk more and track their progress. Advise them on selecting an appropriate model—accuracy of commercially tested pedometers exceeded 96% at speeds 3.0 miles per hour but decreased at slower walking speeds. This has implications for elderly patients who may do better with more sensitive (eg, piezoelectric) pedometers (33). See tips on using a pedometer in Box 5.2 (page 100).

- Review patients' daily schedules and give them ideas about how to most easily achieve this goal; for some people, it will be easiest to break up the walking into three 10-minute sessions (eg, by parking car farther away from work and walking 10 minutes from car to the office, taking a 10-minute walk after lunch, and walking 10 minutes back to the car), but for other people it may be easier to schedule a single daily session (ie, a 30-minute walk after work).

- Have patients write down a specific plan about when they will fit in 30 minutes of daily walking—both during their work week and on the weekend.

Schedule Activity in a Date Book

Cues or prompts for physical activity, such as writing in exercise dates on weekly schedules, can be effective reminders for regular physical activity (13). Also, the act of scheduling exercise just like scheduling their work appointments or family obligations can help Rain Check Athletes give higher priority to exercise.

The following counseling suggestions may help Rain Check Athletes schedule activity in date book:

- Encourage patients to use a "business-like" approach by scheduling "exercise meetings" into their weekly calendar.

- Go hour-by-hour through patients' weekly calendars to find the time they need to fit in regular exercise.

- Encourage patients to treat themselves like they would a client or family member by being accountable and not breaking their exercise appointments.

Combine Activity with Other Things

Busy people are often experts at multitasking—doing more than one activity or job at a time. This skill can be applied to exercise as well. For example, a person can work out on a home treadmill while watching a favorite television show, have a walking meeting with a coworker, or take a yoga class with a friend as a way to socialize and relieve stress.

The following counseling suggestions may help Rain Check Athletes combine activity with other things:

- Encourage patients to connect socially with people while exercising by having walking meetings with colleagues, signing up for an exercise class with a friend, or scheduling regular after-dinner walks with a family member.
- Encourage patients to multitask by combining exercise with watching a favorite television or news program or listening to music, a favorite book on tape, or a podcast.
- Have patients think about using exercise time as a way to de-stress by using that time to brainstorm solutions to work or family problems.

Ask for Help

Asking for help to free up time for exercise may lead to a longer-term solution for Rain Check Athletes. Are there people at work to whom they can delegate a job? Or, can family members contribute more at home? By asking the supportive people in their life for help, Rain Check Athletes can find time for their own self-care and exercise.

The following counseling suggestions may help Rain Check Athletes ask for help:

- Have patients discuss their time barriers at work and at home and think about possible ways to make more time for themselves.
- Encourage patients to talk to someone they trust about ways they can delegate more at home and work and lighten their load to make more time for exercise.
- Suggest that patients find out whether their workplace, place of worship, community, or health care provider offers weight-loss challenge groups, walking groups, or other "get healthy" group programs.
- Encourage patients to consider joining an online weight-loss community for more accountability.

Questions Clinicians Ask During Counseling Sessions

The following questions may help the clinician and the patient decide which of the four strategies or combination of strategies will best target the patient's needs. With practice, these strategies will lead the patient to a more physically active lifestyle.

- "How would you describe your time limitations when it comes to exercise?"
- "Do you have any experiences with exercise?"
- "How do you feel about exercise?"
- "How do you feel about fitting in more activity during the course of your normal day's routine?"
- "Have you ever thought of scheduling exercise like you do your work appointments?"
- "Have you thought of combining exercise with other activities, such as having a walking meeting with a colleague or unwinding after a busy day by taking a walk with your spouse?"
- "How do you feel about asking for help at work and at home to make more time to exercise?"
- "Of the four strategies, which ones are you most confident you can adopt?"
- "Have you been successful at using any of these strategies in the past?"

26. Ainsworth BE, Haskell WL, Whitt MC, Irwin ML, Swartz AM, Strath SJ, O'Brien WL, Bassett DR Jr, Schmitz KH, Emplaincourt PO, Jacobs DR Jr, Leon AS. Compendium of physical activities: an update of activity codes and MET intensities. *Med Sci Sports Exerc.* 2000;32(9 Suppl):S498-S516.

27. Rooney B, Smalley K, Larson J, Havens S. Is knowing enough? Increasing physical activity by wearing a pedometer. *WMJ.* 2003;102:31-36.

28. Taking steps toward increased physical activity: using pedometers to measure and motivate. *President's Council on Physical Fitness and Sports Research Digest.* 2002;3(17). http://www.fitness.gov/pcpfsdigestjune2002.pdf. Accessed December 12, 2007.

29. Heesch KC, Dinger MK, McClary KR, Rice KR. Experiences of women in a minimal contact pedometer-based interventions: a qualitative study. *Women Health.* 2005;41:97-116.

30. Schneider PL, Bassett DR Jr, Thompson DL, Pronk NP, Bielak KM. Effects of a 10,000 steps per day goal in overweight adults. *Am J Health Promot.* 2006;21:85-89.

31. Hultquist CN, Albright C, Thompson DL. Comparison of walking recommendations in previously inactive women. *Med Sci Sports Exerc.* 2005;37:676-683.

32. Croteau KA. Strategies used to increase lifestyle physical activity in a pedometer-based intervention. *J Allied Health.* 2004;33:278-281.

33. Melanson EL, Knoll JR, Bell ML, Donahoo WT, Hill JO, Nysse LJ, Lanningham-Foster L, Peters JC, Levine JA. Commercially available pedometers: considerations for accurate step counting. *Prev Med.* 2004;39:361-368.

34. Hill JO, Peters JC, Jortberg MS. *The Step Diet Book: Count Steps, Not Calories to Lose Weight and Keep It Off Forever.* New York, NY: Workman Publishing; 2004.

35. Tudor-Locke C, Burkett L, Reis JP, Ainsworth BE, Macera CA, Wilson DK. How many days of pedometer monitoring predict weekly physical activity in adults? *Prev Med.* 2005; 40:293-298.

36. Burke V, Giangiulio N, Gillam HF, Houghton S, Milligan RAK. Health promotion in couples adapting to a shared lifestyle. *Health Educ Res.* 1999;14:269-288.

37. Nies MA, Motyka CL. Factors contributing to women's ability to maintain a walking program. *J Holist Nurs.* 2006;24:7-14.

38. Blake SM, Caspersen CJ, Finnegan J, Crow RA, Mittlemark MB, Ringhofer KR. The shape up challenge: a community-based worksite exercise competition. *Am J Health Promot.* 1996;11:23-34.

39. Kushner RF, Blatner DJ, Jewell DE, Rudloff K. The PPET study: People and pets exercising together. *Obesity.* 2006;14:1762-1770.

40. Steptoe A, Rink E, Kerry S. Psychosocial predictors of change in physical activity in overweight sedentary adults following counseling in primary care. *Prev Med.* 2000;31:183-194.

41. Ball K, Crawford D, Owen N. Too fat to exercise? Obesity as a barrier to physical activity. *Aust N Z J Public Health.* 2000;25:331-333.

42. Friedman KE, Reichmann SK, Costanzo PR, Zelli A, Ashmore JA, Musante GJ. Weight stigmatization and ideological beliefs: relation to psychological functioning in obese adults. *Obes Res.* 2005;13:907-916.

43. Haimovitz D, Lansky LM, O'Reilly P. Fluctuations in body satisfaction across situations. *Int J Eat Disord.* 1993;13:77-84.

44. Jankauskiene R, Kardelis K, Pajaujiene S. Body weight satisfaction and weight loss attempts in fitness activity involved women. *J Sports Med Phys Fitness.* 2005;45:537-545.

45. The President's Council on Physical Fitness and Sports. Fitness Fundamentals: Guidelines for Personal Exercise Programs. http://www.fitness.gov/fitness.htm. Accessed September 28, 2007.

46. Walking Shoes: Features and Fit That Keep You Moving. http://www.mayoclinic.com/health/walking/HQ00885_D. Accessed September 28, 2007.

47. King AC, Haskell WL, Taylor CB, Kraemer HC, DeBusk RF. Group- vs home-based exercise training in healthy older men and women: a community-based clinical trial. *JAMA.* 1991;266:1535-1542.

48. Perri MG, Martin AD, Leermakers EA, Sears SF. Effects of group- versus home-based exercise in the treatment of obesity. *J Consult Clin Psychol.* 1997;65:278-285.

49. National Heart, Lung, and Blood Institute. Your Guide to Physical Activity and Your Heart. NIH publication no. 06-5714. June 2006. http://www.nhlbi.nih.gov/health/public/heart/obesity/phy_active.pdf. Accessed September 28, 2007.

50. Jakicic JM, Otto AD. Physical activity considerations for the treatment and prevention of obesity. *Am J Clin Nutr.* 2005;82(1 Suppl):226S-229S.

51. Dunton GF, Schneider M. Perceived barriers to walking for physical activity [published online ahead of print Sept 15, 2005]. *Prev Chronic Dis.* 2006;3:A116.

52. James S. Use movement to explore the connection between body and mind. WebMD Weight Loss Clinic. 2006. http://www.medicinenet.com/script/main/art.asp?subject=mind_and_body_fitness. Accessed September 28, 2007.

53. La Forge R. Mind-body fitness: encouraging prospects for primary and secondary prevention. *J Cardiovasc Nurs.* 1997;11:53-65.

54. Centers for Disease Control and Prevention. Physical Activity for Everyone: The Importance of Physical Activity. http://www.cdc.gov/nccdphp/dnpa/physical/importance/index.htm. Accessed September 28, 2007.

55. Centers for Disease Control and Prevention. Overcoming Barriers to Physical Activity. http://www.cdc.gov/nccdphp/dnpa/physical/life/overcome.htm. Accessed September 28, 2007.

56. Marcus BH, Selby VC, Niaura RS, Rossi JS. Self-efficacy and the stages of exercise behavior change. *Res Q Exerc Sport.* 1992;63:60-66.

57. Kansas State University Agricultural Experiment Station and Cooperative Extension Service. Self-confidence can help inspire motivation to exercise [press release]. June 21, 2002. http://www.oznet.ksu.edu/news/sty/2002/exercise_motivation062102.htm. Accessed September 28, 2007.

58. Jakicic JM, Marcus BH, Gallagher KI, Napolitano M, Lang W. Effect of exercise duration and intensity on weight loss in overweight, sedentary women: a randomized trial. *JAMA.* 2003;290:1323-1330.

59. McInnis KJ, Franklin BA, Rippe JM. Counseling for physical activity in overweight and obese patients. *Am Fam Physician.* 2003;67:1249-1256.

60. Jakicic JM, Wing RR, Butler BA, Robertson RJ. Prescribing exercise in multiple short bouts versus one continuous bout: effects on adherence, cardiorespiratory fitness, and weight loss in overweight women. *Int J Obes Relat Metab Disord.* 1995;19:893-901.

61. American Council on Exercise. Eat well to stay motivated and energized. Fit Facts from the American Council on Exercise. 2002. http://www.acefitness.org/fitfacts/pdfs/fitfacts/itemid_291.pdf. Accessed September 28, 2007.

62. Fletcher G, Trejo JF. Why and how to prescribe exercise: overcoming the barriers. *Cleve Clin J Med.* 2005;72:645-656.

63. Stiegler P, Cunliffe A. The role of diet and exercise for the maintenance of fat-free mass and resting metabolic rate during weight loss. *Sports Med.* 2006;36:239-262.

64. American Council on Exercise. The great debate: free weights vs. strength training equipment. Fit Facts from the American Council on Exercise. 2004. http://www.acefitness.org/fitfacts/pdfs/fitfacts/itemid_289.pdf Accessed September 28, 2007.

65. American Council on Exercise. Strength training 101. Fit Facts from the American Council on Exercise. 2001. http://www.acefitness.org/fitfacts/pdfs/fitfacts/itemid_82.pdf. Accessed September 28, 2007.

66. Quinn E. Stretching: what the research shows. About.com: Sports Medicine. 2006. http://sportsmedicine.about.com/cs/flexibility/a/aa022102a.htm. Accessed September 28, 2007.

67. Kokkonen J, Nelson AG, Tarawhiti T, Buckingham P, Glickman-Weiss E. Stretching combined with weight training improves strength more than weight training alone. *Med Sci Sports Exerc.* 2000;32(5 suppl): abstract 649.

68. Weerapong P, Hume PA, Kolt GS. Warm-up, stretching, and massage before exercise: effects on passive stiffness and delayed-onset muscle soreness. *Med Sci Sports Exerc.* 2004;36(5 suppl): abstract 134.

69. Janes A, Foster C, deKoning JJ, Lucia A, Esten P, Kernovek T, Pocari JP. Effect of warm-up on cycling time trial performance. *Med Sci Sports Exerc.* 2004;36(5 suppl):abstract 834.

70. Dunn AL, Marcus BH, Kampert JB, Garcia ME, Kohl III HW, Blair SN. Comparison of lifestyle and structured intervention to increase physical activity and cardiorespiratory fitness: a randomized trial. *JAMA.* 1999;281:327-334.

71. Chambliss HO. Exercise duration and intensity in a weight-loss program. *Clin J Sport Med.* 2005;15:113-115.

72. American Council on Exercise. How to choose a personal trainer. Fit Facts from the American Council on Exercise. 2001. http://www.acefitness.org/fitfacts/pdfs/fitfacts/itemid_19.pdf. Accessed September 28, 2007.

73. Teixeira PJ, Going SB, Houtkooper LB, Cussler EC, Metcalfe LL, Blew RM, Sardinha LB, Lohman TG. Exercise motivation, eating, and body image variables as predictors of weight control. *Med Sci Sports Exerc.* 2006;38:179-188.

74. Ryan RM, Frederick CM, Lepes D, Rubio N, Sheldon KM. Intrinsic motivation and exercise adherence. *Int J Sport Psychol.* 1997;28:335-354.

75. Kobriger SL, Smith J, Hollman JH, Smith AM. The contribution of golf to daily physical activity recommendations: how many steps does it take to complete a round of golf? *Mayo Clin Proc.* 2006;81:1041-1043.

76. King BJ. Age-less exercise. Alive.com Web site.http://www.alive.com/print_version.php?chosen_topic_id=366&site_id=1. Accessed September 26, 2007.

77. Jakicic JM. Winters C, Lang W, Wing RR. Effects of intermittent exercise and use of home exercise equipment on adherence, weight loss and fitness in overweight women: a randomized trail. *JAMA*. 1999;282:1554-1560.

78. American Council on Exercise. Interval training. Fit Facts from the American Council on Exercise. http://www.acefitness.org/fitfacts/pdfs/fitfacts/itemid_87.pdf. Accessed September 28, 2007.

79. American Council on Exercise. Monitoring exercise intensity using heart rate. Fit Facts from the American Council on Exercise. 2001. http://www.acefitness.org/fitfacts/pdfs/fitfacts/itemid_38.pdf Accessed September 28, 2007.

80. Glaros NM, Janelle CM. Varying the mode of cardiovascular exercise to increase adherence. *J Sport Behav*. 2001;24:42-62.

81. American Council on Exercise. Cross training for fun and fitness. Fit Facts from the American Council on Exercise. 2001. http://www.acefitness.org/fitfacts/pdfs/fitfacts/itemid_27.pdf. Accessed September 28, 2007.

82. American Council on Exercise. Battling boredom. Fit Facts from the American Council on Exercise. 2001. http://www.acefitness.org/fitfacts/pdfs/fitfacts/itemid_18.pdf. Accessed September 28, 2007.

83. American Council on Exercise. Exercising with a health challenge. Fit Facts from the American Council on Exercise. 2001. http://www.acefitness.org/fitfacts/pdfs/fitfacts/itemid_92.pdf. Accessed September 28, 2007.

84. American Council on Exercise. Exercise and arthritis. Fit Facts from the American Council on Exercise. 2001. http://www.acefitness.org/fitfacts/pdfs/fitfacts/itemid_22.pdf.Accessed September 28, 2007.

85. American Council on Exercise. Is yoga for you? Fit Facts from the American Council on Exercise. 2001. http://www.acefitness.org/fitfacts/pdfs/fitfacts/itemid_70.pdf. Accessed September 28, 2007.

Chapter 6

◆ ◆ ◆

Counseling for Coping Lifestyle Patterns

Coping: The Missing Piece in the Lifestyle Modification Puzzle

Coping and stress management are generally recognized as important factors for weight loss and weight maintenance (1,2). Furthermore, Drapkin et al have found that individual differences in coping styles can account for the variance in long-term weight loss (3). However, despite the importance of coping, many clinicians are unfamiliar with the concepts and methods of coping and, more importantly, how to help patients attain more healthful coping styles and skills. In our work, we have found that the coping lifestyle dimension often "trumps" the other two lifestyle dimensions (eating and exercise) in predicting weight-loss outcomes. In practice, patients may know how to eat healthfully and engage in more physical activity, but the stresses of life and their coping skills often determine success or failure. This notion is illustrated in Figure 6.1.

Based on the theory of behavioral economics, there is a direct relationship between the level of perceived stress and how health decisions are made (4). For example, when food stimuli and hunger are controlled and emotions are calm, individuals are more likely to make rational decisions about food choices (moderate eating) and feel motivated. In contrast, when food stimuli and hunger are uncontrolled and emotions are tense, individuals make more irrational decisions about what to eat (disordered eating) and feel less motivated. Therefore, when stress is combined with a permissive environment, individuals will often make poor decisions about their health. The goal is to help patients identify their stressors and teach them constructive coping skills. Before we address the seven coping lifestyle patterns, it is important to briefly review the general topic of stress and coping.

Stress and Coping

Stress is an accepted part of life. Stressful life events, minor or major, have been related to both physical and mental health (5). How one responds to stress, or copes, depends on previous life stressors and various personality traits. Coping is defined as the thoughts and behaviors that people use to manage the internal (mental or emotional) and external (physical) demands of situations that are judged as stressful (6). It's the individual's perception of the situation that is important in determining stress—whereas one person will view a tight work deadline as stressful, another will view it as challenging and exciting. Given that the situation is considered stressful, individuals use a range of coping styles to manage the

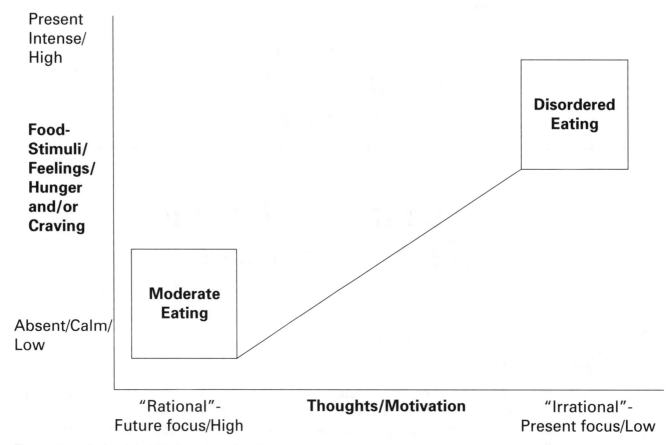

Figure 6.1   Behavioral economics of eating. Adapted with permission from Dr. Brad Saks.

stress. The style of coping that individuals display distinguishes one person from another. Some deal with stress by using avoidance coping (eg, tried to reduce tension by eating more to avoid thinking about the problem) while others use active behavioral coping (eg, talked with a friend, tried to learn more about the situation) (6). The objective for the clinician is to identify what coping mechanism(s) are used by the patient, and help the patient acquire more effective coping skills when necessary.

Coping Styles and Flexibility

The term *coping styles* refers to the range of behaviors that are observed when a person is distressed. They are often unique to the individual and occur with regularity and predictability (7). Common examples include:

- Impulsivity—responds to situation based on immediate needs and thoughts
- Withdrawal or escapist—avoids dealing directly with the situation
- Active cognitive—thinks about several alternatives on how to handle the situation
- Active behavioral—talks with a friend and seeks social support

A person's ability to modify his or her coping according to situational demands is referred to as *coping flexibility*. This is a positive trait that allows the individual to develop more effective responses to life stressors. These responses include adjusting goals or priorities to cope with changing circumstances, setting limits, seeking social support, or asking for advice or counseling (8). It is coping flexibility, per se, rather than the use of specific coping responses, that best predicts successful adaptation to stressful circumstances (9).

Perhaps one of the most effective coping methods, particularly for a dieter, is called *anticipatory coping*, which refers to efforts to deal with an event that is certain to occur in the near future (eg, attending a buffet party or visiting in-laws). This future-oriented coping allows people to manage stressful situations in advance.

As you will see for each of the coping lifestyle patterns in the following sections, the clinician is prompted to help patients to develop positive coping skills and behaviors that include anticipatory and/or flexible coping skills when indicated. Although these types of behavioral and cognitive psychological interventions may be new skills for many clinicians, they have been shown to enhance weight loss in overweight and obese individuals (10). As you review this chapter on counseling patients about coping skills, keep in mind that some may need additional help from a mental health professional (see Box 6.1 for referral guidelines).

The discussion format of the seven coping lifestyle patterns that follows includes:

- A description of each coping pattern.
- A discussion of why each pattern is a problem, with supportive research.
- The four strategies to help patients reshape the problem pattern into a more healthful one (highlights of this information are included in the corresponding patient education handout).
- Questions about this pattern that clinicians can ask during counseling.
- Pattern-specific case studies. Please keep in mind that the case scenarios that follow each pattern should be viewed as excerpts taken from a longer counseling process. The primary intent of the case studies is to demonstrate dialogue and phraseology that are consistent with the particular pattern.

Coping Lifestyle Patterns

As explained in Chapter 2, there are seven coping lifestyle patterns:

- Emotional Eater
- Self-Scrutinizer
- Persistent Procrastinator
- People Pleaser
- Fast Pacer
- Doubtful Dieter
- Overreaching Achiever

Box 6.1 ✦ Reasons to Consider Referring Patients to a Mental Health Professional

Consider referring patients to a mental health professional if the patient:
- Has symptoms consistent with binge eating (see Box 6.2).
- Has severe body-image distortions (see Box 6.4).
- Demonstrates a global sense of low self-esteem.
- Scored very high on several of the maladaptive coping patterns in the Lifestyle Patterns Quiz.
- Exhibits signs of severe depression and or suicidal thoughts.

Note: This list was developed with the assistance of the Clinical Health Psychologists at the Wellness Institute.

The Emotional Eater

Description

Instead of eating when hungry, Emotional Eaters turn to food for comfort when they're lonely, anxious, stressed, or depressed. Food is their trusted friend who never talks back. Food is always there when they need it, but the truth is that food only makes them feel better temporarily because it never really solves their problems.

The Problem

According to Thayer, about one third of us resort to eating as a way to make us feel better and improve our mood. Overeating for emotional reasons, he argues, is more common in women than in men; is most often associated with negative moods like depression, anxiety, anger, boredom, and loneliness; and is one of the most important causes of overweight (11). In his ongoing research, Thayer has found that people in bad moods often have low energy and tension and turn to food to get an energy boost and feel better right away. Food does help to increase their energy level, but only for a short while—studies have found that one's mood sinks soon after eating a sugary snack (11).

Some studies also suggest that stress eaters gravitate toward sweet, high-fat foods and energy-dense meals (12). In physiological studies, individuals with higher stress-induced cortisol reactivity tend to consume more food and more sweet food items than low-reactor individuals, suggesting that cortisol reactivity may be a marker for vulnerability to stress-induced eating (13).

Controlling emotional eating is an important treatment strategy. Blair et al found that individuals who reported an improvement in their emotional eating behaviors were more successful losing weight than individuals who continued to have high levels of emotional eating (14). Emotional eating can negatively affect long-term weight maintenance as well. One study of weight management in women reported that 70% of participants who had relapsed after losing weight ate unconsciously in response to emotions (15).

Note that the Emotional Eater described here is different than someone with binge eating disorder (BED), an eating disorder that is listed in the *Diagnostic and Statistical Manual of Mental Health Disorders* of the American Psychiatric Association (16). See Box 6.2 for information about BED (16,17).

Strategies for Emotional Eaters

The following strategies may help Emotional Eaters succeed at weight loss and maintenance:

- Track your feelings
- Know your triggers

Box 6.2 ✦ Could Your Patient Have Binge Eating Disorder?

There are two characteristics of emotional eating that should raise concern for binge eating disorder (BED) as defined in the *Diagnostic and Statistical Manual of Mental Health Disorders* (16):

- When the patient eats a large amount of food (defined as an amount that is definitely larger than most people would eat in a similar period of time under similar circumstances) in a short period of time (usually within a 2-hour period) for at least 2 days per week for 6 months, and
- When eating is associated with a feeling of being out of control during the episode (a feeling that one cannot stop eating or control what or how much one is eating) and feeling very distressed (17).

If you suspect BED in your patient, referral to a mental health professional with experience in this area is indicated.

- Cope without food
- De-stress

Track Your Feelings

Tracking the feelings, emotions, and situations that lead to emotional eating is the first step toward taking control. Each person has different triggers for his or her emotional eating behaviors. Thayer (11) discusses how some moods predictably lead to emotional eating whereas other moods are less obvious but just as important to understand. Self-awareness is key to helping Emotional Eaters better understand their moods that cause them to overeat.

The following counseling suggestions may help Emotional Eaters track their feelings:

- Have patients keep an ABC (antecedents, behavior, consequences) food and mood behavior chain diary for at least a few days (or longer if needed) by drawing three columns labeled A, B, and C on a blank piece of paper. The ABC model is a key tool used in behavioral weight control (18).

- Explain to patients how to complete the diary (see Table 6.1 for an example): A (antecedents) is for the trigger situations and emotions that come before eating, B is for the behavior of eating (specifying what the patient ate and how much), and C (consequences) is for the feelings and attitudes that occur after eating. If patients have trouble completing the diary, they can ask themselves the following questions: "How much of my eating is emotionally related, expressed either in percent or number of eating occasions per week?" and "What are my typical triggers for emotional eating?"

- Encourage patients to bring a completed ABC diary to their next visit so you can review it together.

Know Your Triggers

Patients need to learn to monitor their mood state and notice emotional-eating trigger situations as soon as possible (19). The previously described ABC tracking exercise is an excellent way to help patients make the connection between their mood and food. However, some patients may already have enough self-awareness to make their own connections without having to do the actual self-monitoring exercise.

The following counseling suggestions may help Emotional Eaters know their triggers:

- Ask patients whether they already can identify the situations and emotions that cause them to eat emotionally.

- If necessary, help patients analyze their ABC food/mood diary and identify their trigger situations and emotions.

- Encourage patients to write down their trigger situations and emotions.

Cope Without Food

Emotional Eaters can improve their mood with distracting or pleasurable nonfood activities, such as taking a walk, calling a friend, listening to music, or taking a relaxing bath (19). The best general way to

Table 6.1 ✦ Sample ABC Food/Mood Behavior Chain Diary

Antecedents	Behavior	Consequences
Got yelled at by boss; feeling stressed	Grabbed candy bar and Coke from vending machine	Felt better at first, but left work still feeling stressed
Home alone on a Saturday night; feeling lonely	Ate 1/2 bag of cookies and 1/2 bag of chips	Good taste helped improve my mood initially, but then feelings of guilt set in.

change a bad mood is through a combination of relaxation, stress management, cognitive, and exercise strategies (20). By learning new ways to better manage their moods, Emotional Eaters can help themselves eat less (11). In one study, participants who were able to think of coping responses that could help them in high-risk overeating situations, such as tension at work or an argument with a spouse, lost more weight than those who were unable to think of coping responses (3).

The following counseling suggestions may help Emotional Eaters cope without food:

- Discuss with patients the importance of learning to "mood surf," or delay an immediate response to their moods (eg, eating) as a way to not amplify the mood or make it worse (19). In mood surfing, the patient is asked to "ride out" the emotion or desire to eat in a similar way that a surfer would ride out a wave. Waves build to a crescendo, then slowly pass—that is the normal course of events. In contrast, Emotional Eaters often feel that the wave of emotion (or desire to eat) will build to a tsunami unless they interrupt it by eating. Ask the patient to observe and feel the emotion. Chances are the emotion or trigger to eat will slowly diminish.

- Encourage patients to develop an emotional eating action plan with specific nonfood action steps they can take the next time they experience their emotional eating triggers. See Box 6.3 for an example.

- Remind patients that exercise is still the most effective mood-regulating behavior (20).

- Ask patients to write their plan on an index card and carry it with them so the next time their trigger emotions occur, they can refer to this plan.

- Remind patients that even if they catch themselves in the midst of their emotional eating, it's never too late to push away from the food and initiate their emotional eating action plan.

De-stress

Whereas the first three strategies help Emotional Eaters lessen their emotional eating episodes and find nonfood ways to cope, this last strategy focuses on longer-term solutions. Many stress management techniques are available. Mind/body techniques such as progressive muscle relaxation, deep breathing exercises, meditation, visualization, yoga, and tai chi all involve practice before their benefits can be seen and valued (11). Pawlow and Jones found that a brief progressive relaxation training exercise led participants to report increased levels of relaxation as well as a lower heart rate and less anxiety, perceived stress, and salivary cortisol level than control subjects (21). One study of patients with disorders such as

---

Box 6.3 ✦ Sample Emotional Eating Action Plan

When Feeling Lonely:
- Call a friend.
- Log on to an Internet chat group.
- Write a letter to someone.
- Go to the health club.

When Feeling Stress at Work:
- Take slow, deep breaths.
- Talk it out with someone I trust.
- Take a walk outside.
- Journal my thoughts.

obesity and hypertension found that a short-term yoga-based lifestyle and stress-management program significantly reduced participants' anxiety level scores within 10 days (22). Massage, stretching, and exercise are additional options to help Emotional Eaters de-stress and better cope with their feelings. Some Emotional Eaters, such as those who have clinical depression or BED, may benefit from a referral to a professional therapist who deals with the psychological aspects of weight management and eating.

The following counseling suggestions may help Emotional Eaters de-stress:

- Ask patients about their interest in trying some of the listed stress-management techniques. Encourage them to check in their community for classes or investigate stress management–related videos/DVDs or books.

- Remind patients to use humor to release stress; for example, they can seek out friends who make them laugh or see funny movies.

- Encourage patients to keep a journal or log of their stress level before and after they try stress management techniques. Thayer recommends that people rank their stress on a 7-point scale (from 0 = no stress to 7 = lots of stress), and analyze how changes in their stress level are related to different activities (11). Evaluating how exercise or deep breathing helps decrease stress levels can reinforce the benefit of these techniques.

- If appropriate, discuss with patients options for more help from therapists who deal with stress-related eating issues. If patients want/need more help, refer them either back to the primary physician or to a therapist.

Questions Clinicians Ask During Counseling Sessions

The following questions may help clinicians and the patient decide which of the four strategies or combination of strategies will best target the patient's needs. With practice, these strategies will lead the patient to more healthful habits and improved coping skills.

- "What are the situations and triggers that cause you to eat?"
- "How do you usually react to these triggers?"
- "Have you ever tried some nonfood ways to cope with these triggers?"
- "Has anything helped you in the past?"
- "Do you see any barriers that would prevent you from following a new and healthier emotional eating action plan?"
- "Have you ever tried any stress-management techniques or classes, or read any books on this topic?"
- "Does exercise ever help you to de-stress?"
- "Have you ever considered seeing a professional therapist to help you with your emotional eating?"
- "Of the four strategies, which ones are you most confident you can adopt?"
- "Have you been successful at using any of these strategies in the past?"

Case Study

G is a 46-year-old woman, 5'3", who weighs 177 pounds with a BMI of 31.4. G is married with two daughters, ages 14 and 12. She had worked full-time before having her children and now spends her time doing carpools, going to her daughters' sports events, and taking care of the household. She is fairly knowledgeable about diet and nutrition, having attended several commercial weight-management programs in the past, and she tries to be as physically active as time allows. G desperately wants to lose weight but has been unsuccessful.

Clinician: "When I see patients who know what to do regarding diet and physical activity but who are not successful in losing weight, the answer is usually found in the coping patterns profile. In other words, when 'life' gets in the way, it's hard to follow a diet and exercise plan. In your case, your dominant coping pattern is Emotional Eater. Do you see yourself as an Emotional Eater?"

G: "Yes, I do."

Clinician: "What do you think triggers your emotional eating?"

G: "I'm not really sure. I think everything."

Clinician: "How much of your unplanned eating is emotionally driven?"

G: "Oh, probably all of it, but I'm not sure. It's hard to separate out my rushing from one game or practice to another from emotional eating. I don't know. I feel tense a lot."

Clinician: "I presume that you have kept, or have been asked to keep, a food journal in the past with some of the commercial weight-loss programs you have done. Have you ever recorded the events or feelings that trigger eating?"

G: "I have kept a diary many times. It always helps when I do it. But I only recorded my foods and the calories or Weight Watcher points."

Clinician: "Good. What I want you to do this week is to keep a food diary with four columns. The first column is for the time and place that you ate; the second is where you write down what and how much you ate; in the third column you should rank how hungry you were (0 = not hungry, 4 = very hungry) when you started eating; and the fourth column is a space for noting other reasons for eating, including your emotions or activities. Keeping this record will help you uncover the times when emotions are the primary trigger to your eating. I think you will find it very interesting and eventually therapeutic."

G: "I'm sure I will. I'll try to do it the best I can."

Clinician: "Good. Remember to bring this log to your next visit so we can look at it together. See if you can identify any particular stress patterns during the week. We'll want to focus on those."

The Self-Scrutinizer

Description

Self-Scrutinizers are their own worst enemy because they frequently engage in negative self talk. They feel ashamed of their bodies, which impairs their feelings of self-worth. Self-Scrutinizers think their self-worth is related to their weight on the scale or the image in the mirror, not who they are as a person or what they've accomplished in life. They have trouble separating their body image from their self-esteem, which affects their relationships, social skills, and day-to-day decision-making.

The Problem

In a society where "thin is in," it's not surprising that body dissatisfaction is common among those who are overweight or obese. The discrepancy between "ideal" and "real" often leads to further distortion of body size, fixation on physical appearance, and avoidance of social situations (23). The body parts that most commonly cause dissatisfaction are the waist or abdomen, thighs, lower body, and buttocks (23). Body image dissatisfaction is associated with low self-esteem and reported depressive symptoms (19). Body image dissatisfaction is related more to one's perception than to the degree of obesity (19,24). Interestingly, body image distortion may be less of a problem among minority women, who often have heavier weight ideals and better body image satisfaction compared with their white counterparts (24). Extreme body image dissatisfaction in the form of a clinical disorder called body dysmorphic disorder (BDD) occurs in a small percentage of obese women. See Box 6.4 for a description of BDD (19).

Kiernan and colleagues found that participants with negative body images were less successful in a weight-loss program than those participants with more positive body images (25). Among participants dissatisfied with their bodies, 26% were successful (defined as a loss of 2 BMI units in 1 year) vs 63% of the participants who were satisfied with their bodies (25). Bacon et al compared a weight-management program that emphasized improved body acceptance and body image with a program that focused on diet only. The former program had a lower dropout rate (8% vs 41%) and its participants exhibited more long-term healthful behavior changes (26). Body image concerns can also be a major obstacle to weight maintenance because body dissatisfaction at the end of a weight-loss program seems to be a good predictor of weight regain (23). Of note, Stewart and colleagues found that strict dieters had more dissatisfaction with their body shape and size, as measured on the body shape questionnaire, than did those who were more flexible with their diet (27). In this study, patients with a history of engaging in rigid dieting reported symptoms of mood disturbances and dissatisfaction with body image (27).

Strategies for Self-Scrutinizers

The following strategies may help Self-Scrutinizers succeed at weight loss and maintenance:

- Be real about body image
- Stop body-checking
- Think positive thoughts
- Enjoy your body

Box 6.4 ✦ Body Dysmorphic Disorder

Individuals with body dysmorphic disorder (BDD) are preoccupied with minor or made-up appearance imperfections that cause substantial distress at work, at home, and in their social life (19). If you suspect BDD in your patient, referral to a qualified therapist is indicated.

Be Real About Body Image

For some Self-Scrutinizers, the measurements around their waist or hips or how much they weigh take on more importance than what they do for a living or their personal values. It can become a vicious cycle whereby one's poor body image leads to poor self-image, low self-esteem, and feelings of unworthiness. People have to like themselves enough to want to improve their health. Subsequently, poor self-esteem can be a roadblock to any healthful lifestyle program (28). Breaking this cycle can begin with helping patients be more realistic about their body image. It's important that patients understand the differences between the terms *physical appearance* (an objective term that signifies what someone looks like) and *body image* (a subjective term that denotes one's views of one's own body) (19). Being dissatisfied with some aspects of appearance is common, but when this dissatisfaction interferes with one's self-image and self-worth or prevents one from socializing, then this needs to be addressed in counseling (19).

The following counseling suggestions may help Self-Scrutinizers be real about body image:

- Have patients list their life accomplishments that they're most proud of and help them realize that these are separate from their body image or the readings on the bathroom scale. (See Box 6.5.)

- Encourage patients to think about how their bodies have many facets beyond appearance, such as being strong, being able to hug their children, being able to give birth, their ability to give and receive sexual pleasure, etc (29).

- Encourage patients to do an exercise created by Thomas Cash, a pioneer in the psychology of physical appearance (30). To help people challenge body-image assumptions that cause them distress, Cash asks them to refute the assumption, "My appearance is responsible for much of what has happened to me in life." He also has them write down what they would like to believe. Clinicians can use this exercise to help patients think about their body image in a more realistic perspective.

Stop Body-Checking

Body-checking refers to the practice of pinching skinfolds or scrutinizing parts of one's own body, such as hips, thighs, or buttocks, in the mirror. Cooper et al have found that body-checking maintains one's negative body image as it creates a preoccupation with scrutinizing oneself (19).

The following counseling suggestions may help Self-Scrutinizers stop body-checking:

- Encourage patients to decrease their focus on specific areas of their body (eg, hips or buttocks) when looking at themselves in a mirror and begin viewing their body as a whole instead of in parts (31).

- Discuss with patients the importance of not pinching skinfolds to measure fatness because the pinching reinforces their negative body image.

- Discuss "normal mirror behaviors" with patients and assure them that it's okay to look briefly at their whole body in the mirror to see that they, along with their clothes, look presentable (19).

Box 6.5 ✦ Body Image Teaching Point

Patients and clinicians need to understand that improving the patient's body image does not take the place of weight loss; rather, it is to be done in combination with weight loss.

Data are from reference 19.

Think Positive Thoughts

Recurrent self-critical comments about appearance such as "I am fat" or "I look awful" only promote a negative body image (19). By helping patients change their self-talk from negative to positive, clinicians help them improve their body image. As discussed in Chapter 1, this cognitive-behavioral technique is called cognitive restructuring.

The following counseling suggestions may help Self-Scrutinizers think positive thoughts:

- Ask patients to keep a log of their thoughts and feelings about their body and decrease the negative language they use. Self-critical comments just perpetuate an individual's poor body image (19). For example, discourage patients from using words such as *too big*, *gross*, or *fat* when they describe or think about their body/body parts (31). Instead, encourage patients to use more factual words and phrases with specific information, not generalizations. (For example, instead of saying "I look like a fat slob," restructure those thoughts to more positive ones such as "My weight is 175 pounds. I am dressed neatly but wish I could wear more stylish clothes.")

- Have patients think about the negative words they sometimes use and how these are words they would never use to describe a friend's body; the goal should be to treat themselves as respectfully as they treat their friends.

- Inform patients about *The Body Image Workbook* (30), a resource that's appropriate for many individuals seeking to improve their body image. This book is not appropriate for individuals with eating disorders, major depression, or BDD (32).

Enjoy Your Body

Being more confident socially, socializing more, buying new clothes, and forming relationships are important goals for individuals with body image dissatisfaction (19). Positive body image experiences help patients accept and even enjoy their bodies (19). One cognitive approach is to help patients take steps to feel better about their own bodies (29).

The following counseling suggestions may help Self-Scrutinizers enjoy their bodies:

- Help patients take note of positive body image experiences, such as getting a new hairstyle, buying new makeup, participating in sports like walking or swimming, or buying nice clothes (19).

- As a way to create new positive body image experiences, encourage patients to think about activities they used to enjoy but have abandoned (19).

- Encourage patients to explore a range of activities that will help them better enjoy their body, such as engaging in exercise, enjoying intimacy with their mate, listening to a relaxation tape, taking a yoga class, relaxing in a hot bath as a way to unwind, treating themselves to a manicure and pedicure, or wearing new perfume.

Questions Clinicians Ask During Counseling Sessions

The following questions may help the clinician and the patient decide which of the four strategies or combination of strategies will best target the patient's needs. With practice, these strategies will lead the patient to more healthful habits and improved coping skills.

- "How do you feel about your body?"
- "Can you describe how you feel when you look in the mirror?"

- "How has you body image affected your day-to-day functioning?"
- "Do you engage in self-criticism and negative self-talk as it relates to your body image?"
- "What kinds of things do you say to yourself?"
- "What situations cause you to be self-critical?"
- "Have you done anything to feel better about your body?"
- "Do you have positive body experiences that you enjoy such as going to a spa or getting your hair done or buying a new outfit?"
- "Of the four strategies, which ones are you most confident you can adopt?"
- "Have you been successful at using any of these strategies in the past?"

Case Study

A is a 28-year-old woman, 5′9″, who weighs 189 pounds with a BMI of 28. A had already lost 8% of her body weight on her own before she made a counseling appointment to seek further guidance. She eats a healthful diet that includes all of the food groups and exercises at least four days a week. Yet despite this effort, she is very unhappy with her body shape. She wants to have smaller hips and is determined to work as hard as she can to achieve this goal. However, she doesn't know what else to do.

> **Clinician:** "A, first of all, I want to congratulate you on losing 8% of your body weight already. That is really great. And your diet looks pretty healthy regarding food choices. I would like to review your portion sizes as a potential strategy to reduce calories a bit more. Before we talk about that, I want to review your coping patterns profile. One pattern in particular, the Self-Scrutinizer, is very high. This pattern is associated with dissatisfaction with body weight or body shape. What do you think about that?"

> **A:** "I don't like my hips. Never did. They're too big."

> **Clinician:** "A, our body shape is determined, in part, by our genes. That's biological. It is very difficult to shape and mold our body like a craftsman would shape and mold a clay vase. There is nothing standing in your way to be as healthy as you can be by diet and exercise, but you may not control the final size and shape of your hips."

> **A (becoming teary eyed):** "I'm listening."

> **Clinician:** "I have an exercise I want you to do this week. I want you to make two lists. One list is all of the accomplishments you have achieved in your life which you are proud of—personal and professional. List them all. Now, in the second list, list all of the goals that you have not achieved yet—they're on your 'to do' list. After you have finished your lists, put a star next to the items on both lists that are directly related to the size of your hips; that is, add stars where your level of success in achieving the accomplishments is either hindered or helped by the size of your hips. Do you understand what I want you to do?"

> **A:** "Yes. I think so."

> **Clinician:** "This is an exercise that I have my patients do that helps them put their body image and self-image in better perspective. We can talk about your lists next week."

The Persistent Procrastinator

Description

Persistent Procrastinators know the importance of losing weight and want to do so, but they somehow never seem to make it happen. Procrastinators may be anxious about starting a program and failing again, or they may feel overwhelmed and not know how to begin. They're tired of saying they'll get to it next week, when next week never seems to come.

The Problem

Chronic procrastination (defined as the "voluntary delay of an action despite expecting to be worse off for the delay") is on the rise, increasing from 5% of Americans in 1978 to 26% in 2007 (33). In a comprehensive analysis of procrastination, Steel found that procrastinators have less confidence in themselves and are less sure that they can actually complete a task; this applies to tasks people don't like to do, such as starting a diet and exercise program or filing taxes (33). As Marano has noted, procrastinators turn "delay into a lifestyle," which can undermine their ability to achieve goals and, in its most severe form, can lead to anxiety and depression (34).

Procrastination should not simply be attributed to laziness or idleness. Instead, it involves the voluntary choice of one behavior or activity (eg, watching television or reading) over one that is likely to be more beneficial for health and weight loss (eg, running on the treadmill). In this example, the individual is favoring an activity that is more pleasant in the short-term even if it is detrimental in the long-term. Researchers (33) have found several reasons for this seemingly irrational behavior. They include (*a*) task aversion (the individual finds the activity so aversive that he or she will do anything to avoid it); (*b*) low self-efficacy (the individual avoids the activity because he or she lacks the confidence to accomplish it); (*c*) lack of immediate reward (the individual's decisions are driven more by impulsiveness than long-range planning because he or she tends to get easily bored); and (*d*) distractibility (the individual has low organizational and self-regulatory skills). Therefore, treatment for Persistent Procrastinators is directed toward the underlying causes.

Strategies for Persistent Procrastinators

The following strategies may help Persistent Procrastinators succeed at weight loss and maintenance:

- List pros and cons
- Set mini-goals
- Prompt yourself
- Use rewards

List Pros and Cons

When procrastinators feel overwhelmed with the "task" of trying to lose weight, their motivation level may become uncertain. Clinicians need to address the motivation issue head-on by encouraging patients to list all of the pros and cons of following through with the program that they can identify (19). See the examples in Tables 6.2 and 6.3. Clinicians can use these lists to foster discussions about the patients' efforts needed to eat more healthfully and become more active. Once a patient's reasons for procrastinating are better understood, the clinician can help them devise a better plan.

Table 6.2 ✦ Sample Pros and Cons Lists for Healthful Eating

Pros	Cons
Lose weight	Will have to cook more
Look better	May cost more money because I'll be eating less fast-food
Good for my heart	I may get flack from my friends who love to eat lots of food

Table 6.3 ✦ Sample Pros and Cons Lists for Exercise

Pros	Cons
Get fit	Will take time away from my work
Have more energy	May cost money if I have to join a health club or buy home exercise equipment
I'm following my doctor's recommendations; this is good for my blood glucose	I'm not comfortable exercising around others

The following counseling suggestions may help Persistent Procrastinators list pros and cons:

- Ask patients which behavior(s) they want to address: eating and/ or physical activity.

- If patients wish to address eating issues, encourage them to fill out a table of pros and cons of eating more healthfully.

- Discuss with patients ways to address their reasons for procrastinating (eg, if patient is procrastinating to avoid an unpleasant task, show them easy ways to make healthful eating more pleasant; or, if distractions are a problem, help them focus and follow through with specific tasks).

- Discuss with patients simple ways to make modifications so that the cons are less of a concern (eg, for a patient's concern that she'll have to cook more, you can give her ideas for quick, healthful meals on the run that take little preparation time).

- If patients wish to discuss physical activity issues, help them address why they procrastinate when it comes to exercise and have them complete a table of the pros and cons of becoming more active.

- Discuss with patients simple ways to make modifications so that the "becoming active" cons are less of a concern (eg, if a patient expresses concern about the cost of joining a health club, you can discuss how walking is a less expensive way to become more active).

Set Mini-Goals

To Persistent Procrastinators, changing one's lifestyle to lose weight and improve health is a lofty goal without immediate benefits, and the lack of an immediate reward can quickly diminish a procrastinator's motivation. Because many Persistent Procrastinators are impulsive, they need to know how doing a task will help them today vs some time down the road. Breaking a large goal into easier-to-follow step-by-step tasks will help Persistent Procrastinators succeed (34).

The following counseling suggestions may help Persistent Procrastinators set mini-goals:

- Explain to patients the concept of setting mini-goals as a way to help focus their weight-loss program and motivate them to follow through and not put off specific tasks.

- Help patients set mini-goals that are appropriate for their eating and exercise lifestyle patterns and that they feel are doable (eg, if the patient is a Meal Skipper, instead of setting a general goal to eat healthier, set a mini-goal to eat breakfast daily, or if the client is a Couch Champion, instead of setting a general goal to become more active, set a mini-goal to walk for 20 minutes daily to start).

- Help patients decrease any barriers they anticipate to following through with their mini-goals (eg, if patient's wife does the grocery shopping for the family, he'll need to ask her to shop for a high-fiber cereal, nonfat milk, and fresh berries, or if patient doesn't own a good pair of athletic shoes, she'll need to buy a pair before she gets started).

- Encourage patients to think about the immediate benefits that they'll experience when following these mini-goals. For example, eating breakfast and daily walking will give them an energy boost (immediate benefit) in addition to helping them manage their weight better (longer-term benefit).

Prompt Yourself

A common trait of Persistent Procrastinators is that they are easily distracted by things going on in their environment. Distractions such as e-mail, Internet chat rooms, and cell phones can make it hard for Persistent Procrastinators to curb their impulsiveness and follow through with their healthful lifestyle mini-goals (35). Environmental cues and prompts have been successful in reminding people to engage in physical activity and exercise (36). Reminder prompts can also be applied to helping individuals comply with diet-related mini-goals.

The following counseling suggestions may help Persistent Procrastinators prompt themselves:

- Encourage patients to use reminder prompts whenever possible to help them follow through with their mini-goals. (See examples in Box 6.6.)

- Discuss with patients how buddying-up for exercise or getting an online diet buddy may encourage more accountability because buddies can remind each other to follow through.

- Have patients think about small things they can do to limit their distractions, such as turning off their cell phones when exercising or avoiding e-mails when eating lunch at work.

Use Rewards

Contingency management, which involves strategies that attempt to change behavior by modifying its consequences, and self-reward are effective behavioral weight-management techniques (36). Paying attention to small successes along the way to long-term weight loss will help Persistent Procrastinators

---

Box 6.6 ◆ Sample Reminder Prompts for Procrastinators

- Keep fresh fruit basket on counter.
- Leave water bottle on desk at work.
- Have preprinted grocery list on counter with healthy options you can circle week to week.
- Keep take-out menus handy with healthy options circled.
- Toss meal-replacement bars in purse or briefcase.
- Keep healthy recipes to try on counter.
- Lay out gym clothes the night before.
- Place stretching mat and exercise book in bedroom.
- Use personal digital assistant (PDA) for exercise reminders.
- Write exercise times in business calendar.

appreciate their accomplishments, feel more confident, and boost motivation. Clinicians sometimes need to point out these small successes to patients if they don't notice them on their own.

The following counseling suggestions may help Persistent Procrastinators use rewards:

- Encourage patients to pay attention to the small successes they're experiencing week to week, such as eating more fruits and vegetables, downsizing their fast-food meals, or taking the stairs at work instead of the elevator.

- Discuss with patients their interest in keeping a success journal as a way to reinforce how far they've come.

- Have patients develop a list of healthful ways to reward themselves as they meet certain weight goals. See Box 6.7 for sample rewards.

Questions Clinicians Ask During Counseling Sessions

The following questions may help the clinician and the patient decide which of the four strategies or combination of strategies will best target the patient's needs. With practice, these strategies will lead the patient to more healthful habits and improved coping skills.

- "Why do you think you procrastinate?"
- "Are you a procrastinator in most things you do, or is it just when it comes to diet and physical activity?"
- "What often distracts you from doing what you want to do?"
- "Has anything helped you overcome your procrastination?"
- "Of the four strategies, which ones are you most confident you can adopt?"
- "Have you been successful at using any of these strategies in the past?"

Case Study

G is a 32-year-old single man, 6'1", who weighs 265 pounds with a BMI of 35. G works for an electronics store and lives alone. He has been concerned about his escalating weight since finishing college and has tried several diets on his own without success. Typically, he followed the diets for a few weeks then stopped them for unspecified reasons. He hasn't previously sought professional help for his weight, even though his doctor suggested it several times over the past 2 years.

> **Clinician:** "G, there is a lot we need to go over regarding your diet and physical activity. Your diet and exercise patterns profile will be quite useful as a starting point. But there is one coping pattern I want to go over as well. Your dominant coping pattern is

---

Box 6.7 ✦ Sample Rewards for Procrastinators

- Do a fun activity with a friend.
- Take a vacation.
- Pamper yourself with a spa day.
- Have a romantic night out with your spouse.
- Attend a special sporting event.
- Enjoy a concert.

Persistent Procrastinator. As the name implies, individuals who score high in this pattern tend to put off doing things—that is, wait for another day. Does this sound like this is your personality?"

G: "Yes, that's me. Always has been. Even in school, I would wait until the very end to get my work done. It used to drive my parents crazy."

Clinician: "Is that how you have been approaching your weight as well?"

G: "I guess so, although I hadn't thought about it that way."

Clinician: "What is it about weight control that makes you procrastinate?"

G: "I don't know. I guess I get so frustrated trying to lose weight that I just put it off. And the chart says I should weigh under 190 pounds for my height—that's 75 pounds less than where I am now!"

Clinician: "What we're going to want to do is to set mini-goals for you—landmarks that you can achieve along the way so you can see progress. Rather than focusing on the long-term goals, which probably feel daunting, let's shoot for a 10% weight loss. That would be about 25 pounds for you. And by focusing on a few targeted diet and exercise patterns to work on, we can come up with specific weekly goals. Have you ever used that strategy before?"

G: "Not really. I'm kind of an all-or-nothing guy."

Clinician: "Okay. Let's set some mini-goals for this week. That's what I want you to think about. Ready?"

G: "Yep. Let's go."

The People Pleaser

Description

People Pleasers are good-natured people who have a strong sense of responsibility and commitment to their family, work and volunteer causes. What's lacking, however, is their ability to take care of themselves and their own health at the same time. Because People Pleasers have trouble saying "no" to others, they end up putting everyone else's needs before their own. This leaves them last on their own "to do" list.

The Problem

Many of the People Pleasers we see are altruistic in nature, giving to their religious institutions, community, and volunteer causes, which leaves little time left over for themselves. According to Smith, women in particular are often conflicted about caring for themselves because they are altruistic (37). Many women are the caretakers of the family, caring for their children, spouse, parents, and even their coworkers before they spend time on their own needs. Lu and Wykle found that caregivers with high levels of stress had poorer self-rated health (38). Other People Pleasers are trying to seek approval. Overweight and obese people may suffer from the "doormat" syndrome, in which they become People Pleasers in an effort to be liked and to somehow make up for their excess weight (39). Different than the altruistic motive seen in the first example, low self-esteem can cause these People Pleasers to be taken advantage of and have difficulty asserting themselves. Both types of People Pleasers share a common problem that they don't spend enough time on their own health needs.

Strategies for People Pleasers

The following strategies may help People Pleasers succeed at weight loss and maintenance:

- Commit to self-care
- Plan your yeses
- Say "no" like a pro
- Assign tasks to others

Commit to Self-care

Some People Pleasers think that committing time to self-care is akin to being selfish. People Pleasers need to understand that when they take care of their own needs, they're acknowledging that they have needs, limits, and boundaries, such as needing time to be alone, to rest, to exercise, to plan healthful meals, etc (40). Taking care of oneself is not selfish, but an outgrowth of self-love and wanting to be as healthy as possible.

The following counseling suggestions may help People Pleasers commit to self-care:

- Encourage patients to verbalize how their People Pleaser tendencies take away time from their own self-care.
- Help patients think about participating in self-care as a form of self-preservation and discuss how investing in self-care means they'll be around longer to take care of the ones they love.
- Explain how many people take better care of their cars than they do of their bodies. See Self-Care Maintenance Tips in Box 6.8.
- Have patients verbalize their commitment to their own self-care needs.

Plan Your Yeses

Being busy can distract People Pleasers from remembering the things in life that truly excite them (41). Saying "yes" to everyone else can also distract People Pleasers from thinking about their own life passions and how they spend their time. When people are considering making healthful lifestyle changes, this is a perfect time for them to reevaluate their own life priorities.

The following counseling suggestions may help People Pleasers plan their yeses:

- Encourage patients to complete a Life Passions Inventory as a way to highlight personal life passions that may have eluded them (41). This involves completing the four columns (Relationships, Work, Spirituality, Self Care) in a table like the one in Table 6.4. In each of the columns, the person taking inventory writes down things that he or she is passionate about doing now or in the future.
- Encourage patients to discuss four aspects of their life (relationship, work, spirituality, and self-care) that take time and commitment and are important to them.
- Have patients use this inventory to rethink how they currently spend their time.
- Help patients to problem-solve ways to fit in more self-care activities.

Box 6.8 ✦ Self-Care Maintenance Tips

Just like a car, our bodies and minds need to be fueled properly, tuned up regularly, and not driven while on empty.

Table 6.4 ✦ Sample Life Passions Inventory for People Pleasers

Relationships	Work	Spirituality	Self-Care
Get married	Ask for a promotion	Volunteer at my church	Learn to play tennis
Get a pet	Attend professional development seminars	Attend services on the weekend	Take evening dance classes
Connect with relatives	Spend fewer hours at work	Attend religious retreat	Join a walking group
Take a vacation with friends	Get a new assistant	Read inspiring books	Take a healthy cooking class

Say "No" Like a Pro

Participating in self-care requires assertiveness to say "no" to others when needed; for many People Pleasers, this will be a new skill. People Pleasers need to understand that being assertive is a healthful trait because this means that they respect their own feelings and values as much as they respect the feelings and values of others (42). Learning to say "no" is a skill that can be practiced and learned.

The following counseling suggestions may help People Pleasers say "no" like a pro:

- Give patients permission to be assertive in their day-to-day decision-making (and say "no" when needed) as an important part of their healthy lifestyle program.

- Encourage patients to think about and voice typical situations when they have trouble saying "no."

- Have patients practice saying "no" by role-playing (with family members, work colleagues, or members of their spiritual community) situations they think will be difficult for them (41).

- Give patients sample responses to use when asked for a favor, such as "I need to check my calendar first" or "Let me think about it," as ways to buy themselves more thinking time (41).

Assign Tasks to Others

People Pleasers have a tendency to take on more than they can handle. For example, they may be the parents who are still making their teenagers' school lunches or cleaning up after their children when the children are old enough to take on more responsibility. Or, maybe they're doing more at work when others could pitch in. Being able to ask for help and delegate tasks to others will help to lighten their load—and make more time for themselves. Again, this will take some assertiveness to let others know their needs.

The following counseling suggestions may help People Pleasers assign tasks to others:

- Help patients understand that their family and friends are not mind-readers and they may need to confide in those close to them about how they take on too much and have a dilemma about saying "no."

- Teach patients how to help people in their lives understand that they need support to fulfill their own needs.

- Encourage patients to figure out how they can lighten their load at home and at work to make more time for themselves.

- Advise patients to be specific when they ask for help and delegate tasks, such as "Can you pick the kids up from soccer practice so I can get to my exercise class?" or "I'd like you to make your own lunches from now on so that I can use that evening time to make my lunch and plan our next day's dinner meal."

Questions Clinicians Ask During Counseling Sessions

The following questions may help the clinician and the patient decide which of the four strategies or combination of strategies will best target the patient's needs. With practice, these strategies will lead the patient to more healthful habits and improved coping skills.

- "Why do you think you are a People Pleaser?"
- "How does People Pleasing make you feel?"
- "How do you feel about taking time for yourself and your self-care?"
- "Why do you think you have trouble saying 'no'?"
- "Do you have any experiences saying 'no' and how that felt?"
- "Do you see any barriers that will make it hard for you to start saying 'no' when needed?"
- "What part of your life will likely be disrupted the most if you start saying 'no'?"
- "What types of self-care activities would you like to have more time to be engaged in?"
- "What types of tasks do you think you could delegate to others?"
- "Which of the four strategies sound most useful to start practicing?"
- "Which strategies stand out as being something you have wanted to adopt?"

Case Study

J is a 40-year-old woman, 5'1", who weighs 142 pounds with a BMI of 26.9. J is a middle school music teacher with two children, ages 15 and 12. In addition to her day job, she also teaches church choir on Sundays and carpools the children to their sports events and religious school classes. She has previously been successful following several commercial weight-loss programs, but regains the weight when she leaves the programs. She is now looking for a program that will help her change her lifestyle.

> **Clinician (after reviewing J's eating and exercise patterns):** "J, I would now like to turn to your coping pattern profile. The most dominant pattern I see is the People Pleaser. There are many positive attributes to people pleasing. It is a very altruistic quality—caring for people and giving of yourself. But we consider it a weight-gaining pattern when you always put others ahead of yourself and at the detriment of your own needs. If you're always at the bottom of the totem pole, your needs will not be taken care of. Does this sound like you?"

> **J:** "Yes, I have always been like that. I don't know if I am just a pushover or what, but it's really hard for me to say 'no'."

> **Clinician:** "Well, if you consider taking care of yourself a problem, then we need to address it. There are four strategies that we use to turn this around. Change starts with making a commitment to yourself. If you are not healthy, then you will not be able to help others. There is also an exercise that I would like you to do this week—it's called the Life Passions Inventory. I want you to think about all of the things you want to accomplish; activities that make you happy and fulfilled. The four areas of this inventory are relationships, work, spirituality, and self-care. Think about each of these areas in your life. Which ones need more time and nurturing? It will be a starting place for you to re-plan how you want to spend your time. Eventually, you will need to start saying 'no' to some things and 'yes' to others."

J: "Very interesting. This sounds like a very useful exercise. I've never done anything like this before."

Clinician: "I think you will enjoy it. It is very rewarding."

The Fast Pacer

Description

Fast Pacers are experts at multitasking and juggling. They're moving through life so fast that they really don't have time to think about or plan how to live more healthfully and lose weight. Fast Pacers feel scattered and frazzled and have trouble relaxing; they know they need to slow down and put balance back into their lives but they're not sure how to do so.

The Problem

The pace of life in America is increasing (11). Despite having so many time-saving devices like computers, cell phones, and home DVRs, we're feeling more rushed and strapped for time (43). Many individuals are working more and sleeping less, and this faster pace of life leads to more stress along with unhealthful eating and exercise habits (11). Thayer calls this condition *tense tiredness*, when your resources are depleted from hectic scheduling and at the same time you're feeling frazzled; this leads people to seek energy boosts through food with little time left over to stop work and exercise (11). Poor sleep habits have also been associated with weight gain and obesity (44). According to the National Sleep Foundation, short sleep duration is associated with weight gain, obesity, increased appetite, and increased risks of diabetes and heart problems (45).

Strategies for the Fast Pacer

The following strategies may help Fast Pacers succeed at weight loss and maintenance:

- Take a new look at your life
- Stay aware in the present
- Seek support
- Recharge and relax

Take a New Look at Your Life

To change behavior, one must begin with an awareness of the behaviors and life stressors that have shifted one's life out of balance. One way for patients to evaluate whether their lives are out of balance is to list and then analyze their life roles and identities (46). Joel and Michelle Levey suggest that individuals create a Life Roles Inventory (see Table 6.5) as a way to think about and record how they define themselves in four dimensions of their lives: relationships, work, spirituality, and self-care (46). By listing roles that describe who they are or want to be in each of the four dimensions, patients notice their life imbalances and gain awareness about ways to rebalance.

Table 6.5 ✦ Example of a Life Roles Inventory

Relationships	Work	Spirituality	Self-Care
Son	Teacher	Volunteer	Tennis player
Husband	Mentor	Fundraiser	Hiker
Brother	Coach	Church member	Healthy person
Friend	Tutor	Choir singer	Outdoor cook
Lover	Parent counselor	Spiritual person	Dog lover

The following counseling suggestions may help Fast Pacers take a new look at their lives:

- Instruct patients to complete a Life Roles Inventory like the one in Table 6.5, using the following questions to help guide them:
  - ▶ How invested are you in each of the four areas of your life?
  - ▶ Are you overextended in some areas?
  - ▶ Are some areas underdeveloped?
  - ▶ What areas are your greatest sources of stress?
  - ▶ What areas help you balance your stress by giving you joy and pleasure?
  - ▶ What areas do you want to develop more and what do you want to cut back on?

- Encourage patients to verbalize the things they want to do to put their life back in better balance, such as eat more, exercise more, sleep more, spend more time with their family and dog, attend church more often, etc.

- Have patients commit to taking the necessary steps to rebalance their life.

Stay Aware in the Present

Being more mindful allows people to live a more purposeful and balanced life. Mindfulness, defined as a state of being attentive to and aware of what is taking place in the present, has long been associated with psychological well-being (47). One study found that increased mindfulness resulted in an improvement in mood and a reduction in stress (47). Another study found that mindfulness meditation can be a powerful cognitive-behavior coping strategy for changing the way individuals respond to life events (48). An integrative medicine study of 154 outpatients with one or more known cardiovascular risk factors showed that multidimensional techniques including mindfulness meditation, relaxation training, stress management, and health education helped improve weight loss, increase exercise, and reduce risks of coronary heart disease among participants (49).

The following counseling suggestions may help Fast Pacers stay aware in the present:

- Encourage patients to think about being more mindful as a way to appreciate and enjoy every role they care about. When they're living in the moment, they're more focused and engaged with the people who surround them. This heightened sense of awareness or mindfulness helps them to connect better with others and as a result they even feel more at ease with themselves.

- Encourage patients to use mindful breathing when they find themselves focusing elsewhere to slow down and bring their attention back to the here and now.

- Have patients practice using mindful breathing as a relaxation skill. See Relaxation Breathing Tips in Box 6.9 (50).

- Help patients value meals and working out as "sacred" times, which honor their body and health, rather than "just something to fit into my day."

- Encourage patients to pay attention to how much time they spend worrying about the past (eg, past diets that didn't work or past overeating episodes) or thinking about the future (eg, "What if I'm unable to lose weight?" or "What if I gain all my weight back?") instead of living in the moment or focusing on the present (eg, "What small thing can I do today to help myself stay on track?").

Seek Support

Many Fast Pacers are used to getting things done themselves and not relying on others for support. Going it alone can easily make people feel overwhelmed. One study found that men and women with low levels of social support at work and who were exposed to job strain seemed to be at higher risk for increases in blood pressure compared with those who had social support (51). Lack of social support to eat healthfully and exercise is a well-known barrier to losing weight and keeping it off (52).

The following counseling suggestions may help Fast Pacers seek support:

- Encourage patients to talk to supportive people they trust about ways they can slow down and prioritize more healthful behaviors into their hectic schedules. Suggest they ask loved ones at home for help, find a walking buddy at work, or delegate work to coworkers or hire a work assistant.

- Encourage patients to spend social time with people they enjoy and less time with those who drain their energy.

- Have patients combine activities so they get more out of their limited time (eg, schedule walks with a friend, spouse, or child; meet friends at the fitness club; sign up for class with spouse or friend).

Recharge and Relax

Getting enough restful sleep will help recharge the Fast Pacer's batteries, which normally run on overdrive. This will help Fast Pacers make better eating and exercise choices during the day. Engaging in mind/body type activities like yoga, tai chi, progressive relaxation exercises, meditation, or massage has

---

Box 6.9 ✦ Relaxation Breathing Tips

Relaxation exercises can quiet the mind and relax the body. Here are some tips to guide you:

- Find a quiet room, wear loose clothing and sit or lie on the floor.
- Close your eyes and get comfortable. As you focus on your breathing, relax your muscles starting with your head and face and moving down your neck, shoulders, arms, trunk, abdominals, legs, feet, and toes. Stay relaxed as you repeat a positive or neutral word such as peace " or "calm" while slowly breathing in and out. Continue slow, natural breathing for 10 to 20 minutes. If thoughts come to your mind, silently repeat your chosen word and focus on your breathing.
- Try a shorter version or mini-relaxation session during times of high stress, such as in the middle of a hectic workday.
- If you practice these exercises regularly (some people do them daily, others a few times per week), you should experience relaxing and calming effects.
- To purchase relaxation CDs, tapes, and exercises to help with managing stress, contact the Benson-Henry Institute for Mind Body Medicine (http://www.mbmi.org/shop/listproducts.asp?fam=4) or do an Internet search to find other relaxation resources.

Source: Data are from reference 50.

also been shown to help individuals relax and unwind. For many Fast Pacers, taking time to exercise regularly can be the best way to recharge their batteries and lift their mood.

The following counseling suggestions may help Fast Pacers relax and unwind:

- Talk with patients about their sleep habits and the importance of getting enough restful hours of sleep each night. According to the National Sleep Foundation, sleep needs vary across populations and individuals. Sleep quality seems to be more important than sleep quantity. If individuals find they are sleepy during the day, they probably are not getting enough restful hours of sleep (45). See Box 6.10 for good sleep tips (53).

- Discuss with patients their interests in engaging in mind/body exercises.

- Have patients discuss their plans for fitting more regular exercise into their lifestyle.

Questions Clinicians Ask During Counseling Sessions

The following questions may help the clinician and the patient decide which of the four strategies or combination of strategies will best target the patient's needs. With practice, these strategies will lead the patient to more healthful habits and improved coping skills.

- "Why do you think your pace of life is so fast?"
- "How does this fast-paced life make you feel?"
- "Have you tried to slow down?"
- "Has anything helped you to slow down or feel better in the past?"
- "Do you have ideas about how you would like to reprioritize your life?"
- "What are the barriers you see to doing so?"
- "Do you know what mindfulness is?"
- "Would being more mindful help you?"
- "Do you have supportive people in your life to turn to for help?"
- "Have you ever tried engaging in a mind/body type of activity, such as yoga, tai chi, or meditation?"
- "How do you feel when you can fit in your exercise time?"
- "Would you say you get enough hours of restful sleep each night?"
- "Of the four strategies, which ones are you most confident you can adopt?"
- "Have you been successful at using any of these strategies in the past?"

Box 6.10 ✦ Good Sleep Tips

- Avoid caffeine (coffee, tea, soft drinks, and chocolate) and nicotine close to bedtime; some caffeine-sensitive people may need to stop caffeine much earlier in the day.
- Avoid alcohol because it can disrupt sleep.
- Exercise regularly, but preferably not within the 3 hours before bedtime.
- Establish a regular, relaxing bedtime routine such as taking a warm bath.
- Create a sleep-conducive environment that is quiet, dark, and comfortable.

Source: Tips are from the National Sleep Foundation (53).

Case Study

S is a 35-year-old woman, 5′ 5″, who weighs 186 pounds with a BMI of 31. S has been working with a weight-loss counselor for 3 months and has not made much progress losing weight. Although she understands what to do, she has been overloaded with her work (she is a residential real estate agent), and is married with two children ages 10 and 8. S seems frustrated that she has not been more successful despite feeling excited and motivated after each counseling visit.

> **Clinician:** "S, I know that you are frustrated about your weight. I am concerned that you will not be successful unless you carve out more time to take care of yourself. You are a Fast Pacer—that means that your days are overloaded with responsibilities and tasks."
>
> **S:** "I agree. I literally run ragged all day. I really don't know what to do."
>
> **Clinician:** "There's an exercise that I have many of my patients do to help them sort out their so-called life imbalances. In other words, if you had a better idea of what you want to do and what you can let go of, it will give you a road map for change. It's called a 'Life Roles Inventory.' What I want you to do is make a list with four column headings: Relationships, Work, Spirituality, and Self-Care. Under each heading, list your life roles, that is, how you see yourself. For example, being a healthy person would go under Self-Care. After you do this exercise, look at the chart and think about how you prioritize where you spend your time. Balancing your roles and priorities will probably require asking for more help for some things and giving up some other things."
>
> **S:** "I've never done something like this before."
>
> **Clinician:** "After 3 months of working with you, I think this is the most important thing to do. I would also suggest that you share your inventory with your husband. Problem-solve with him about where you need help. Maybe the kids can take on more responsibility for things around the house."
>
> **S:** "Good idea."
>
> **Clinician:** "That's the goal for this week. We'll talk about some of your decisions on your next visit."

The Doubtful Dieter

Description

Doubtful Dieters are pessimistic thinkers who feel hopeless about their ability to lose weight and keep it off—they typically say they've tried everything and nothing ever works. Doubtful Dieters have developed a self-defeating attitude that no one can help them and at the same time they feel powerless to change their negative thinking and behaviors. When life difficulties arise, they look at them as hurdles and barriers instead of as challenges and opportunities.

The Problem

Whereas optimism has been shown to protect one's health, pessimism has been linked to poor physical health (54). Studies show that pessimists give up more easily and get depressed more often (55). Scheier et al found that pessimists coped with stress by using denial and distancing, by focusing on the stressful feelings and by disengaging from the goal with which the stressor was interfering (56). Middle-aged adults who felt pessimistic about the effort required to prevent further weight gain were deterred from helping themselves (57). Chronic negative emotions that deplete energy and impair coping can be self-sustaining (8). Maruta et al found a significant association between pessimistic thinking and poorer physical and mental functioning after a 30-year follow-up of 447 general medical outpatients (58). Pessimism has been found to affect heart health as well. Along with hopelessness, rumination, anxiety, and anger, pessimism was one of five negative states linked with cardiovascular disease (59). For the clinician, it is important to distinguish between pessimism as a ubiquitous personality trait from pessimism that is isolated to the failure of weight management.

Strategies for Doubtful Dieters

The following strategies may help Doubtful Dieters succeed at weight loss and maintenance:

- Alter your fate
- Confront your beliefs
- Distract and dispute
- Help yourself

Alter Your Fate

Pessimism is a powerful habit that, if left unchecked, can seal the fate of its sufferers by keeping them lost in self-doubt and helplessness. To shape this habit into a more healthful one, one must begin by realizing the power we all have to exert personal control over our own lives. Doubtful Dieters may be surprised to learn that optimists have better health than pessimists, catch fewer infections, and even live longer (55). Vitality, a positive state that is associated with a sense of enthusiasm and energy, is a composite of positive emotions (60). At the core of changing the Doubtful Dieter's coping pattern is belief in the power of personal control and ability to alter one's fate by changing thinking patterns and reactions to life's difficulties.

The following counseling suggestions may help Doubtful Dieters alter their fate:

- Discuss with patients how their feelings of helplessness and self-doubt can become a self-fulfilling prophecy because negative thinking encourages negative outcomes.

- Help patients make the connection between how they think and respond to life stresses and their physical health.

- Explain to patients that people who can respond to life difficulties with less pessimism (ie, optimistically) tend to be healthier, catch fewer infections, and live longer.

- Ask patients whether they are committed to doing the work needed to follow through with these strategies so they can start taking control, altering their fate, and improving their outcomes.

Confront Your Beliefs

When people encounter difficulties, they first react by thinking about the difficulties and as time passes their thoughts become their beliefs (55). Seligman discusses how these beliefs can either cause people to take positive action or give up. For some people, negative beliefs can become so habitual that they don't really notice them until they're asked to focus on and track them.

The following counseling suggestions may help Doubtful Dieters confront their beliefs:

- Have patients pay attention to the aspects of negative thinking that keep Doubtful Dieters feeling hopeless and helpless:
  - ▶ They personalize adversity by blaming themselves.
  - ▶ They make the problem bigger than it is.
  - ▶ They make the problem sound permanent and unfixable.

- Suggest that patients keep an ABC record (A is for the adversity, B is for the beliefs, and C is for the consequences) as a way to track their negative beliefs (55). (See example in Box 6.11.) Encourage them to keep this record for a few days or for as long as it takes to identify five ABCs from their own life that relate their diet behaviors to their eating, exercise, or mood.

- Have patients read over their ABCs and make the link between their pessimistic beliefs and not taking positive actions. If this is difficult for them to do on their own, encourage them to bring in their ABC record to review at the next counseling visit.

Distract and Dispute

Distraction and disputation are two methods that can help people deal with pessimistic beliefs once they're aware of them (55). Distraction involves trying to do something else to divert your attention away from the pessimistic beliefs whereas disputation involves arguing with yourself as to why your pessimistic belief must be false. In helping people become more optimistic, Seligman teaches that disputing beliefs is more effective in the long run than using distractions because people can use disputation to learn more healthful ways to react to adverse situations (55). Once people realize that their beliefs are not facts, they become more open to learning the important skill of how to dispute their own beliefs.

The following counseling suggestions may help Doubtful Dieters distract and dispute:

- Teach patients the STOP (*S*low down, *T*ake a breath, *O*bserve objectively without attitude or emotion, *P*lan a different response) method of distracting their attention from their pessimistic beliefs when they occur. Patients can pair this with snapping a rubber band on their wrists or writing down their negative beliefs the moment they occur (55).

Box 6.11 ✦ Sample ABC Records for Doubtful Dieters

Example 1

Adversity	I went to a party and noticed all the slim women talking and having fun.
Belief	Why did I decide to come here? Who would ever want to talk to me the way I look? I will never be able to socialize with normal people.
Consequences	I left after 5 minutes because I felt so out of place.

Example 2

Adversity	While at work, I couldn't resist and ate two doughnuts.
Belief	I am so weak. My coworkers know I'm on a diet and must think I'm a real pig.
Consequences	After work, I headed straight for the ice cream and ate three bowls since I already ruined my diet.

- Encourage patients to give themselves permission to schedule a later time to think about the adverse situation and what transpired; this will help to diminish the seriousness of the actual situation (55).

- Have patients practice disputing their beliefs by evaluating the evidence and realizing that their beliefs are factually incorrect or by thinking of alternative causes that are changeable and less personal (56).

- Discuss with patients that their coping responses will become more positive and effective once they're able to dispute their negative beliefs.

Help Yourself

Self-doubt can be paralyzing and lead many Doubtful Dieters to suffer from feelings of helplessness. As Doubtful Dieters learn to challenge their negative beliefs and cope more effectively, they will start taking positive steps and helping themselves. Seligman suggests expanding an ABC record to become an ABCDE record by adding a D (disputation) and E (energization) (55).

The following counseling suggestions may help Doubtful Dieters help themselves:

- Encourage patients to keep an ABCDE record as a way to practice disputing their beliefs and developing more positive coping responses. See Box 6.12 for an example.

- Ask patients bring their ABCDE records to discuss at their next visit.

- If patients indicate that they need more help with their pessimistic thinking, discuss available resources, such as the book *Learned Optimism* by Seligman (55) or mental health professionals with experience in this area.

Box 6.12 ✦ Sample ABCDE Record for Doubtful Dieters

Example 1

Adversity	I went to a party and noticed all the slim women talking and having fun.
Belief	Why did I decide to come here? Who would ever want to talk to me the way I look? I will never be able to socialize with normal people.
Consequences	I left after 5 minutes because I felt so out of place.
Disputation	I was at a work party last week where I socialized and had fun for hours so it's not true that I can't socialize with people. People talked to me then and I looked the same as I look now.
Energization	I guess the real issue was that I didn't feel comfortable because I didn't recognize anyone when I first got there. At the other party, I waited a few minutes and then all of my friends started to arrive and I was able to relax and have fun.

Example 2

Adversity	While at work, I couldn't resist and ate two doughnuts.
Belief	I am so weak. My coworkers know I'm on a diet and must think I'm a real pig.
Consequences	After work, I headed straight for the ice cream and ate three bowls since I already ruined my diet.
Disputation	Okay, so I skipped my 350-calorie breakfast this morning and I was starving and had 600 calories from doughnuts instead. That's only one meal and doesn't mean I blew my diet.
Energization	At noon, I got right back on track with my healthy lunch I brought from home. It's easier to make good food choices when I'm not starving. I also reminded myself that if I eat my breakfast, I'll be less vulnerable to making poor food choices.

Questions Clinicians Ask During Counseling Sessions

The following questions may help the clinician and the patient decide which of the four strategies or combination of strategies will best target the patient's needs. With practice, these strategies will lead the patient to more healthful habits and improved coping skills.

- "Why do you think you are so pessimistic when it comes to your weight?"
- "Do you consider yourself a pessimistic person or just when it comes to your weight?"
- "What types of situations make you doubt yourself?"
- "Do you feel that your negative thinking impacts negative outcomes?"
- "Have you ever tracked your beliefs and tried to dispute them?"
- "Has anything ever helped change your negative beliefs?"
- "Are you opposed to keeping a journal to better understand your negative beliefs?"
- "Which strategies are you most confident you can start adopting immediately?"
- "Which of the four portioning strategies do you find the easiest? Hardest?"

Case Study

A is a 29-year-old single woman, 5'7", who weighs 218 pounds with a BMI of 34.1. A is a social worker and lives alone. She has been battling her weight since high school and has tried several different diets. She often loses 15 to 30 pounds but then regains weight, ending up heavier than she was before the diet. While she doesn't consider herself a pessimist when it comes to life in general (although she isn't particularly hopeful that she will ever get married), she scored high on the Doubtful Dieter coping pattern.

Clinician: "A, I want to talk about one pattern that was particularly high on your coping pattern profile—the Doubtful Dieter. Tell me about that."

A: "Doubtful about ever being able to lose weight! Well yeah. Why shouldn't I feel that way? I can't lose weight. It's so depressing."

Clinician: "I can understand why you developed a pessimistic attitude about losing weight. You've been trying hard and you haven't been as successful as you would like. Is self-doubt something you generally struggle with?"

A: "You mean in everything I do? Not really. It's just my weight."

Clinician: "Well, weight loss is the long-term goal and I'm going to guide you through a diet and physical activity program you can follow. But I also want to address your pessimism because it can get in the way of success. Can you tell me the situations where you feel it most?"

A: "I guess when I blow my diet. It's usually toward the end of the day after my last client. I grab a candy bar or bag of chips to deal with stress, then feel that I'm a complete failure and I'll never get my weight under control. At night then, I feel what's the use and I eat a lot of bad stuff."

Clinician: "Okay. Here's the exercise I want you to do to directly confront those situations. It's called keeping an ABCDE record. Pretty easy to remember. Let me take you through it. Let's use what you just told me as an example. A is for adversity. In your case, the adversity is stress at the end of the day."

A: "Right."

Clinician: "B is for belief. You turn to a candy bar or a bag of chips to deal with the stress and then you tell yourself that you're a failure and you'll never lose weight."

A: "Correct. I just get so mad at myself."

Clinician: "C is for consequences. Because your negative beliefs magnified your own self-doubt, this makes you want to throw in the towel and then when you get home you eat more unhealthy foods because you feel you've already blown your diet."

A: "Yes. That's the typical sequence of events. That's me!"

Clinician: "Okay. Here is where the healing begins. D is for disputation. I want you to deliberately dispute the negative beliefs that feed negative behaviors. Is it true that you are a failure and will never lose weight because you had one candy bar?"

A: "Well, no."

Clinician: "Why?"

A: "Because the candy bar is only one bad choice. I can make better choices the rest of day. And I don't have to have a candy bar every day."

Clinician: "Good. And the last letter is E which stands for energization. How can you plan to energize yourself to feel better and start taking some positive steps?"

A: "Well, I think the real problem is that I never have any healthy food options with me when I feel stressed. If I keep some fruit on hand or a meal replacement bar, then I would be less tempted to make bad choices."

Clinician: "Exactly. By planning, thinking ahead, and using this ABCDE exercise, I think you can turn self-doubt into more positive behaviors."

The Overreaching Achiever

Description

Overreaching Achievers have achieved a high degree of success in their work and at home, and they expect the same level of success with their weight. However, for many Overreaching Achievers, their weight is the only part of their life that makes them feel unsettled. Regardless of the progress they make losing weight, it's never enough. High expectations leave them feeling frustrated and discouraged.

The Problem

A review of studies has shown that unrealistic weight goals are among the psychological factors that have an impact on weight maintenance and relapse behaviors in obesity (61). Foster et al (62) and Wadden et al (63) have shown that patients' expectations for weight loss (what they call "dream weight") greatly exceed what can be reasonably achieved through lifestyle treatment alone. In Foster et al's 48-week study of 60 obese women, mean weight loss was 16 kg (16% of initial body weight), but nearly half of patients did not achieve even what they considered a disappointed weight, one that "they could not view as successful in any way" (62). Cooper et al agree that when trying to lose weight, unrealistic weight goals create a major obstacle to successful weight maintenance because patients see their lower weight as not worth maintaining (19). Setting unrealistically high performance standards and being unable to achieve these personal goals can trigger negative psychological states and performance dissatisfaction (64).

Strategies for Overreaching Achievers

The following strategies may help Overreaching Achievers succeed at weight loss and maintenance:

- Describe weight goals
- Find new measures of success
- Trim goals
- Accept limits

Describe Weight Goals

Clinicians need to help patients set goals that are realistic and attainable. It's not unusual, however, for patients to have lofty goals such as the 55-year-old salesman who wants to weigh what he did when graduating college or the 42-year-old mother of four who wants to weigh what she did when she got married. Polivy has found that it's important for people to learn to distinguish between realistic and impossible self-change goals in order to avoid overconfidence and false hope that can lead to failure and distress (65). The Overreaching Achiever strategies are best discussed when, for no clear reason, the patient's rate of weight loss has lessened or even hit a plateau after a reasonable period (eg, 4–6 months) of weight loss (19).

The following counseling suggestions may help Overreaching Achievers describe weight goals:

- Encourage patients to discuss four goal weights as a way to encourage dialogue about their weight-loss expectations (62):
  - ▶ Their ideal or "dream" weight—ie, a weight they would choose if they could weigh whatever they wanted.
  - ▶ Their "happy" weight—ie, a weight that is not as ideal as the first one, but a weight they would be happy to achieve.
  - ▶ Their "acceptable" weight—ie, a weight that they would not be particularly happy with, but one that they could accept because it is less than their current weight.
  - ▶ Their "disappointed" weight—ie, a weight that is less than their current weight but one they would not view as successful in any way.

- Discuss with patients how they selected these weights (such as through a BMI chart, a physician recommendation, or a previous weight-loss attempt) along with the consequences of reaching that weight (eg, effects on clothing size and choice, health, work, social life, self-confidence) or not reaching that weight (eg, would they be so discouraged they would abandon their program?) (19).

- Encourage patients to discuss how hard they think it will be to achieve their goals.

- Reinforce to patients that this exercise gives the clinician a better idea of the patients' goals.

Find New Measures of Success

Clinicians should encourage patients to appreciate that some weight-management goals can be achieved without losing a specific number of pounds or hitting a target weight. For example, patients can aim to feel more confident, more energetic; they can measure success as being able to get down on the ground and play with their kids or being able to climb the stairs without shortness of breath; they can focus on feeling more in shape, younger, and attractive; or they can strive to be fit enough to take a dance class with their spouse. Cooper et al call these "primary" goals because they can be easier to achieve and provide patients with more immediate benefits than goals defined in terms of pounds lost (19).

The following counseling suggestions may help Overreaching Achievers find new measures of success:

- Have patients discuss other ways to define success (in addition to weight lost), such as feeling more confident, having more energy, clothes fitting looser, sleeping better, feeling more in control.

- Remind patients that paying attention to these goals (especially if weight loss doesn't seem to be occurring quickly enough) will help boost their motivation.

Trim Goals

Losing 10% of one's body weight has been shown to improve appearance, self-esteem, sense of well-being, blood pressure, blood lipids, and blood glucose, and decrease waist size (66). A 10% weight-loss goal is not only beneficial but also realistic and achievable for most people. For example, the subgoal for a patient who weighs 180 pounds would be weight loss of 18 pounds and a target weight of 162. For some Overreaching Achievers, setting 10% subgoals or mini-goals helps them focus and maintain motivation.

The following counseling suggestions may help Overreaching Achievers trim goals:

- Share with patients the list of proven benefits of moderate weight loss.

- Encourage patients to consider setting a 10% weight-loss mini-goal. Advise them that such a goal is practical, realistic, and achievable and will be less stressful to approach than a goal based on expectations that are too high. Explain that once this mini-goal is achieved, they can set another 10% goal.

- Encourage patients to focus on the process of reaching their goals, aiming for progress not perfection.

Accept Limits

Once patients have made healthful lifestyle changes, there comes a time when they need to accept the weight they have reached and the shape produced by these changes (67). Wilson explains that acceptance is an active process that can be nurtured; it does not simply mean one resigns oneself to an unhappy fate (67). Clinicians need to help patients accept that losing weight provides benefits but these benefits are not limitless.

The following counseling suggestions may help Overreaching Achievers accept limits:

- Discuss with patients what cannot be changed through a weight-loss program, such as one's genetics or bone structure.

- Ask patients whether, based on the work they've done and the goals they've met, they want to consider a higher goal for their desired weight.

- Encourage patients to think and talk about how they'd feel about themselves if indeed their desired weight goal was set higher. For example, would they feel motivated or discouraged if the desired weight goal was increased? According to Cooper et al, this exercise helps identify any obstacles that could prevent patients from accepting a more moderate weight goal (19).

- Help patients accept higher weight goals by pointing out the successes they've achieved so far and encouraging them to understand that some things are simply not changeable and are therefore out of their control.

- Encourage patients to accept a more moderate weight goal (even if they believe that another, more ambitious goal would be preferable) as a way to form a new reality (19).

Questions Clinicians Ask During Counseling Sessions

The following are potential questions to help the clinician and the patient decide which of the four strategies or combination of strategies will best target the patient's needs. With practice, these strategies will lead the patient to more healthful habits and improved coping skills.

- "Why do you think you've been unable to feel successful or happy when it comes to your weight?"
- "When you feel like you aren't reaching your goals, do you attribute this to specific barriers? If you do, what are these barriers?"
- "What can't you do at this weight compared to a lower body weight?"
- "Did it help you to describe your three weight goals?"
- "Does it help you to pay attention to other measures of success?"
- "How do you feel about setting a percentage weight goal?"
- "How do you feel about accepting your limitations?"
- "Which strategies can you see yourself using successfully?"
- "All four strategies can be helpful, but which do you want to start trying now?"

Case Study

J is a 50-year-old woman, 5'3", who weighs 163 pounds with a BMI of 28.9. J has already lost 22 pounds (or 12%) of her initial body weight of 185 pounds and kept the weight off for 4 months, but she is not happy. Before she entered the program, she set a goal weight of 130 pounds, her weight before having children. J scored high on the Overreaching Achiever pattern when she entered the program, and she has continually mentioned her desire to lose more weight.

>**Clinician:** "J, you have done really well in the program, losing 12% of your initial body weight. To give you some perspective, most people in a lifestyle management program lose about 10% of their weight. Congratulations!"

>**J:** "That's fine, but it's not enough. I'm not done losing weight yet."

>**Clinician:** "I know you said that your personal goal is 130 pounds, that's 33 more pounds to lose. If you lost that much weight, it would be equivalent to a 30% weight loss. That is the amount of weight that people usually achieve with bariatric surgery. I'm not a fortune-teller and I am not going to get in the way of your efforts to lose more weight, but a weight of 130 may not be realistic. The reason that I am bringing this up now is because I want you to celebrate the success that you have already achieved rather than dwell on the disappointment.

>**J:** "It is hard for me to accept my current weight. I still feel so big."

>**Clinician:** "J, I want you to think about all the positive changes you have experienced other than the scale weight. For example, do your clothes fit differently?"

>**J:** "Absolutely! I can get into outfits that have been sitting in my closet for years."

>**Clinician:** "What else?"

>**J:** "My husband gives me praise all the time. And so do my friends."

Clinician: "And what about your health?"

J: "I'm off of my water pill and the pill I took for heartburn."

Clinician: "Exactly. The benefits that you have already achieved are fabulous. Take credit for them and enjoy your health. For this week, I want you to complete the list of all of the positive changes that have occurred over the past months in addition to your weight loss and bring it with you at your next visit. Okay?"

J: "Okay. I can do that."

Summing Up the Coping Domain

In this chapter, you have learned how to help your patients attain more healthful coping styles and skills. Whether your patients turn to food to soothe their emotions, have a poor body image that impairs their self-esteem, procrastinate, put everyone else's needs before their own, are juggling too many roles, doubt anyone can help them, or have unrealistic goals, you are now equipped to counsel them to develop a plan that meets their needs. For counseling in the coping domain to be effective, clinicians need to help patients better understand their coping "personality," their unique combination of different coping patterns. With the right counseling strategies, clinicians can help patients prioritize which pattern to work on first, progress through their program, and target different patterns as needs arise. When appropriate, clinicians can also help patients find additional professional help with coping skills.

In the next chapter, you will learn how to follow-up with patients using the Lifestyle Patterns Approach. This chapter discusses how to track patients' progress, conduct follow-up visits, deal with behavior and weight-gain relapses and weight plateaus, and address ongoing monitoring considerations and family patterns.

References

1. Foreyt JP, Poston WS 2nd. What is the role of cognitive-behavior therapy in patient management? *Obes Res.* 1998;6(Suppl 1):18S-22S.

2. Elfhag K, Rössner S. Who succeeds in maintaining weight loss? A conceptual review of factors associated with weight loss maintenance and weight regain. *Obes Rev.* 2005;6:67-85.

3. Drapkin RG, Wing RR, Shiffman S. Responses to hypothetical high risk situations: do they predict weight loss in a behavioral treatment program or the context of dietary lapses? *Health Psychol.* 1995;14:427-434.

4. WK Bickel, RE Vuchinich, eds. Reframing Health Behavior Change with Behavioral Economics. Mahwah, NJ: Lawrence Erlbaum Publishers; 2000.

5. Tosevski DL, Milovancevic MP. Stressful life events and physical health. *Curr Opin Psychiatry.* 2006;19:184-189.

6. Folkman S, Moskowitz JT. Coping: pitfalls and promise. *Annu Rev Psychol.* 2004;55:745-774.

7. Beutler LE, Moos RH, Lane G. Coping, treatment planning, and treatment outcome: discussion. *J Clin Psychol.* 2003;59:1151-1167.

8. Rozanski A, Kubzansky LD. Psychologic functioning and physical health: a paradigm of flexibility. *Psychosom Med.* 2005;67(Suppl 1):S47-S53.

9. Cheng C. Assessing coping flexibility in real-life and laboratory settings: a multimethod approach. *J Pers Soc Psychol.* 2001;80:814-833.

10. Shaw K, O'Rourke P, Del Mar C, Kenardy J. Psychological interventions for overweight and obesity. *Cochrane Database Syst Rev.* 2005;(2):CD003818.

11. Thayer RE. *Calm Energy: How People Regulate Mood with Food and Exercise.* New York, NY. Oxford University Press; 2001.

12. Oliver G, Wardle J, Gibson EL. Stress and food choice: a laboratory study. *Psychosom Med.* 2000;62:853-856.

13. Epel E, Lapidus R, McEwen B, Brownell K. Stress may add bite to appetite in women: a laboratory study of stress-induced cortisol and eating behavior. *Psychoneuroendocrinology.* 2001;26:37-49.

14. Blair AJ, Lewis VJ, Booth DA. Does emotional eating interfere with success in attempts at weight control? *Appetite.* 1990;15:151-157.

15. Kayman S. Maintenance and relapse after weight loss in women: behavioral aspects. *Am J Clin Nutr.* 1990;52:800-807.

16. *Diagnostic and Statistical Manual of Mental Disorders DSM-IV-TR.* 4th ed. Arlington, VA: American Psychiatric Association; 2000.

17. Yanovski SZ. Binge eating in obese persons. In: Fairburn CG, Brownell KD. *Eating Disorders and Obesity. A Comprehensive Handbook.* 2nd ed. New York, NY: Guilford Press; 2002:403-407.

18. Wadden TA, Crerand CE, Brock J. Behavioral treatment of obesity. *Psychiatr Clin N Am.* 2005;28:151-170.

19. Cooper Z, Fairburn GG, Hawker DM. *Cognitive Behavioral Treatment of Obesity: A Clinician's Guide.* New York, NY: Guilford Press; 2003.

20. Thayer RE, Newman JR, McClain TM. Self-regulation of mood: strategies for changing a bad mood, raising energy, and reducing tension. *J Pers Soc Psychol.* 1994;67:910-925.

21. Pawlow LA, Jones GE. The impact of abbreviated progressive muscle relaxation on salivary cortisol. *Biol Psychol.* 2002;60:1-16.

22. Gupta N, Khera S, Vempati RP, Sharma R, Bijlani RL. Effect of yoga-based lifestyle intervention on state and trait anxiety. *Indian J Physiol Pharmacol.* 2006;50:41-47.

23. Rosen JC. Obesity and body image. In: Fairburn CG, Brownell KD. *Eating Disorders and Obesity. A Comprehensive Handbook.* 2nd ed. New York, NY: Guilford Press; 2002:399-402.

24. Friedman KE, Reichmann SK, Costanzo PR, Musante GJ. Body image partially mediates the relationship between obesity and psychological distress. *Obes Res.* 2002;10:33-41.

25. Kiernan M, King AC, Kraemer HC, Stefanick ML, Killen JD. Characteristics of successful and unsuccessful dieters: an application of signal detection methodology. *Ann Behav Med.* 1998;20:1-6.

26. Bacon L, Stern JS, Van Loan, MD, Keim NL. Size acceptance and intuitive eating improve health for obese female chronic dieters. *J Am Diet Assoc.* 2005;105:929-936.

27. Stewart TM, Williamson DA, White MA. Rigid vs. flexible dieting: association with eating disorder symptoms in nonobese women. *Appetite.* 2002;38:39-44.

28. Rosen-Grandon JR. Resolving to change ourselves. Dr. Jane's Notebook. 1995. http://www.dr-jane.com/chapters/Jane118.htm. Accessed September 28, 2007.

29. Parham ES. Promoting body size acceptance in weight management counseling. *J Am Diet Assoc.* 1999;99:920-925.

30. Cash TF. *The Body Image Workbook: Second Edition.* Oakland, CA: New Harbinger Publications; 2008.

31. Delinsky SS, Wilson GT. Mirror exposure for the treatment of body image disturbance. *Int J Eat Disord.* 2006;39:108-116.

32. Sarwer DB, Thompson JK. Obesity and body image disturbance. In: Wadden TA, Stunkard AJ, eds. *Handbook of Obesity Treatment.* New York, NY: Guilford Press; 2002:458-464.

33. Steel P. The nature of procrastination: a meta-analytic and theoretical review of quintessential self-regulatory failure. *Psychol Bull.* 2007;133:65-94.

34. Marano HE. Getting out from under. *Psychol Today.* Mar/Apr 2006. http://psychologytoday.com/rss/index.php?term=pto-20060324-000001&print=1. Accessed September 28, 2007.

35. Olsen S. A formula for procrastination. CNET Networks. January 12, 2007. http://www.news.com/2102-1008_3-6149636.html?tag=st.util.print. Accessed September 28, 2007.

36. Rippe J.M. ed. *Lifestyle Medicine.* Malden, MA: Blackwell Science; 1999.

37. Smith A. An analysis of altruism: a concept of caring. *J Adv Nurs.* 1995;22:785-790.

38. Lu YF, Wykle M. Relationships between caregiver stress and self-care behaviors in response to symptoms. *Clin Nurs Res.* 2007;16:29-43.

39. Johnson C. Obesity, weight management, and self-esteem. In: Wadden TA, Stunkard AJ, eds. *Handbook of Obesity Treatment.* New York, NY: Guilford Press; 2002:480-493.

40. Rosen-Grandon JR. Is taking care of you selfish? Dr. Jane's Notebook. 1995. http://www.dr-jane.com/chapters/Jane109.htm Accessed September 28, 2007.

41. Breitman P, Hatch C. *How to Say No without Feeling Guilty: And Yes to More Time, More Joy and What Matters Most to You.* New York, NY: Broadway Books; 2000.

42. Coping.org: Tools for Coping with Life's Stressors. Improving Assertive Behavior. 2007. http://www.coping.org/relations/assert.htm#What Accessed 9/28/07.

43. Glick J. *Faster: The acceleration of just about everything.* New York: Pantheon Books 1999.

44. Patel SR, Malhotra A, White DP, Gottlieb DJ, Hu FB. Association between reduced sleep and weight gain in women. *Am J Epidemiol.* 2006;164:947-954.

45. The National Sleep Foundation. 2007. How Much Sleep Do We Really Need? http://www.sleepfoundation.org/site/c.huIXKjM0IxF/b.2417325/k.3EAC/How_Much_Sleep_Do_We_Really_Need.htm. Accessed September 28, 2007.

46. Levey J, Levey M. *Living in Balance: A Dynamic Approach for Creating Harmony and Wholeness in a Chaotic World.* Berkeley, CA: Conari Press, 1998.

47. Brown KW, Ryan RM. The benefits of being present: mindfulness and its role in psychological well-being. *J Pers Soc Psychol.* 2003;84:822-848.

48. Astin JA. Stress reduction through mindfulness meditation. Effects on psychological symptomatology, sense of control and spiritual experiences. *Psychother Psychosom.* 1997;66:97-106.

49. Edelmann D, Oddone EZ, Liebowitaz RS, Yancy WS, Olsen MK, Jeffreys AS, Moon SD, Harris AC, Smith LL, Quillian-Wolever RE, Gaudet TW. A multidimensional integrative medicine intervention to improve cardiovascular risk. *J Gen Intern Med.* 2006;21:728-734.

50. Benson-Henry Institute for Mind Body Medicine. Elicit the Relaxation Response. http://www.mbmi.org/basics/whatis_rresponse_elicitation.asp. Accessed December 14, 2007.

51. Guimont C, Brisson C, Dagenais GR, Milot A, Vezina M, Masse B, Moisan J, Laflamme N, Blanchette C. Effects of job strain on blood pressure: a prospective study of male and female white-collar workers. *Am J Public Health.* 2006;96:1436-1443.

52. Andajani-Sutjahjo S, Ball K, Warren N, Inglis V, Crawford D. Perceived personal, social and environmental barriers to weight maintenance among young women: a community survey. *Int J Behav Nutr Phys Act.* 2004;1:1-15.

53. National Sleep Foundation. Healthy Sleep Tips. http://www.sleepfoundation.org/site/c.huIXKjM0IxF/b.2417321/k.BAF0/Healthy_Sleep_Tips.htm. Accessed September 28, 2007.

54. Kubzansky LD, Sparrow D, Vokonas P, Kawachi I. Is the glass half empty or half full? A prospective study of optimism and coronary heart disease in the Normative Aging study. *Psychosom Med.* 2001;63:910-916.

55. Seligman ME. *Learned Optimism: How to Change Your Mind and Your Life.* New York, NY: Vintage Books; 2006.

56. Scheier MF, Weintraub JK, Carver CS. Coping with stress: divergent strategies of optimists and pessimists. *J Pers Soc Psychol.* 1986;51:1257-1264.

57. Ziebland S, Robertson J, Jay J, Neil A. Body image and weight change in middle age: a quantitative study. *Int J Obes Relat Metab Disord.* 2002;26:1083-1091.

58. Maruta T, Colligan RC, Malinchoc M, Offord KP. Optimism-pessimism assessed in the 1960s and self-reported health status 30 years later. *Mayo Clin Proc.* 2002;77:748-753.

59. Kubzansky LD, Davidson KW, Rozanski A. The clinical impact of negative psychological states: expanding the spectrum of risk for coronary artery disease. *Psychosom Med.* 2005;67(Suppl 1):S10-S14.

60. Rozanski A, Kubzansky LD. Psychologic functioning and physical health: a paradigm of flexibility. *Psychosomc Med.* 2005;67(Suppl 1):S47-S53.

61. Byrne SM. Psychological aspects of weight maintenance and relapse in obesity. *J Psychosom Res.* 2002;53:1029-1036.

62. Foster GD, Wadden TA, Vogt RA, Brewer G. What is a reasonable weight loss? Patients' expectations and evaluations of obesity treatment outcomes. *J Couns Clin Psychol.* 1997;65:79-85.

63. Wadden TA, Womble LG, Sarwer DB, Berkowitz BI, Clark VL, Foster GB. Great expectations: "I'm losing 25% of my weight no matter what you say." *J Couns Clin Psychol.* 2003;71:1084-1089.

64. Ward CH, Eisler RM. Type A behavior, achievement striving, and a dysfunctional self-evaluation system. *J Pers Soc Psychol.* 1987;53:318-326.

65. Polivy J. The false hope syndrome: unrealistic expectations of self-change. *Int J Obes Relat Metab Disord.* 2001;25(Suppl 1):S80-S84.

66. National Heart, Lung, and Blood Institute. Clinical guidelines on the identification, evaluation, and treatment of overweight and obesity in adults. The evidence report. *Obes Res.* 1998;6(Suppl 2):51S-210S.

67. Wilson GT. Acceptance and change in the treatment of eating disorders and obesity. *Behav Ther.* 1996;27:417-439.

Chapter 7

✦ ✦ ✦

Follow-up and Monitoring

Overview

This chapter outlines how to document, organize, and monitor patients' progress during each follow-up appointment to determine whether patients are achieving desired behavior, weight, and health outcomes. The chapter introduces the Progress Tracking Chart and explains how to use the Lifestyle Patterns Approach in follow-up visits. It also describes the value of readministering the Lifestyle Patterns Quiz to evaluate patient progress throughout the treatment process.

Progress Tracking Chart

The Progress Tracking Chart is available on the CD-ROM. Clinicians are encouraged to review the form as we discuss its use. Let's first look at how to organize and document your patients' progress. To keep an organized assessment of each patient's progress, a Progress Tracking Chart can be used at the beginning of each appointment. (Note: On the Lifestyle Patterns Progress Note introduced in Chapter 3, there is a prompt/check box to remind the clinician to complete the Progress Tracking Chart.) To complete the chart, fill in the date and weight of the patient and then ask the patient to assign a letter grade (A, B, C, D, or F) to the progress of his or her "homework" strategies. In our experience, this exercise is very useful because it encourages patient reflection and meaningful dialogue about goals and progress.

For each Lifestyle Pattern the patient is trying to improve, the provider should ask, "Based on the changes you have made since our last visit, what letter grade (A, B, C, D, or F) would you give yourself?" If the patient is successfully practicing new healthful behaviors most of the time and assigns high letter grades, it is likely that there will be an associated weight loss. On the other hand, if a patient has encountered barriers to changing behaviors, is finding the strategies difficult, and is reporting low letter grades, no weight loss or weight gain would be expected. After assessing progress and discussing the assigned patterns and corresponding strategies, it is possible to refocus and set a new agenda of dominant patterns and targeted strategies.

Follow-up Visits, Accountability, and Self-Monitoring

The recommended frequency of follow-up visits depends on various factors, including financial resources, insurance coverage, and clinician and patient availability. The US Preventive Service Task Force recommends high-intensity counseling, which is defined as meeting with patients more than once per month for the first 3 months of treatment (1).

The following dialogue illustrates how the Progress Tracking Chart can be used in a follow-up visit.

Clinician: "Nice to see you; it has been about 3 weeks since out last visit together. You have lost 3½ pounds and that leads me to believe you are doing well with the strategies we discussed last time. I would like to review your progress—what are you doing that you are proud of and what are you having difficulty with? Here is a Progress Tracking Chart [see Figure 7.1] that we will fill out together. It will help us focus our visit today and your "homework" for next time."

Patient: "Well, I lost 3½ pounds, which is great because I can honestly say that I am surprised at how easy most of these strategies were. I definitely don't feel like I am on a diet."

Clinician: "That's good to hear because the changes we discussed should be manageable—not impossible or overwhelming. Let's go over the two dominant patterns we discussed last visit: Fruitless Feaster and Rain Check Athlete. Can you assign a letter grade—A, B, C, D, or F—to your progress with each of them, just like when you were in school?"

Patient: "In other words, if I did well and am proud of what I accomplished I would get an A or a B and if I wasn't doing too well I would get a D or F?"

Clinician: "Yes, exactly. When you rate your progress, we will be able to know what we should congratulate you on and what still needs our attention and will be back on your 'homework' assignments after our visit today."

Patient: "I would give myself a C for the Fruitless Feaster—I could have done better. I give myself a B+ for the Rain Check Athlete. I have been fitting in 20 minutes of walking on most days, but I remember that you wanted me to get at least 30 minutes daily so I'm not there yet. Overall, I would give myself a B. I guess I have done pretty good these past 3 weeks so it makes sense that I lost 3½ pounds."

Clinician: "Congratulations on your progress! What can I help you with today to change the Fruitless Feaster C into an A or a B?"

Patient: "I did a good job of buying and eating fruit, but I guess I really don't know what to do with vegetables. After having broccoli too many times, I got sick of it."

Clinician: "Okay, today we will definitely review how to increase the variety of your vegetables and quick ways to prepare them. I will make a list for you of vegetables to buy and seasonings, marinades, herbs, and spices to add bursts of flavor. In addition to helping you with that, I think we need to talk about how you are going to make time to fit in at least 30 minutes of walking daily. Have you thought about this?"

Patient: "I have talked to my wife about this and I think it's time to hire an assistant at work, which is something I probably should have done years ago. This will give me more time to devote to exercise. I may even join our local gym. I was also wondering if we could go over goals for the Hearty Portioner because I was at a family dinner and noticed how much more I ate than many people and how much faster I eat, too."

Clinician: "Okay, then for the rest of our visit today, let's discuss eating more vegetables and how to manage portions."

Date	4/16/08	5/8/08							
Weight	212.3	208.8							
Eating Patterns									
Meal Skipper									
Nighttime Nibbler									
Convenient Diner									
Fruitless Feaster	I	C							
Steady Snacker									
Hearty Portioner									
Swing Eater									
Exercise Patterns									
Couch Champion									
Uneasy Participant									
Fresh Starter									
All-or-Nothing Doer									
Set-Routine Repeater									
Tender Bender									
Rain Check Athlete	I	B+							
Coping Patterns									
Emotional Stuffer									
Self-Scrutinizer									
Procrastinator									
People Pleaser									
Fast Pacer									
Doubtful Dieter									
Overreaching Achiever									
Overall Progress Self-Evaluation		B							

Figure 7.1 Progress Tracking Chart example from case study.

Accountability *throughout* a weight control program (not just at follow-up visits) can contribute to successful weight loss and maintenance. Web-based weight control programs (see Box 7.1) can be effective tools for patients who desire additional accountability to the face-to-face visits (2). In addition, the Progress Tracking Chart can be used by patients to self-evaluate and be accountable for their success each week. Patients who are doing other types of self-monitoring may not want to use this tracking form for self-assessment, but it is an option for those patients who would find it helpful to evaluate their progress by assigning a letter grade weekly and not just in the office with the clinician.

Self-monitoring, whether it uses the Progress Tracking Chart or another type of self-monitoring form, is an important part of successful weight-control programs. Patients who regularly monitor their behaviors lose more weight than those who do not monitor behaviors. In a study by Carels et al, 40 obese (body mass index $\geq$ 30) sedentary patients completed a 6-month behavioral weight loss program. The study participants who regularly self-monitored lost nearly twice as much weight as those who did not monitor behaviors (10.5 kg vs 5.5 kg in 6 months) (3).

Behavior Lapses and Weight Gain Relapses

Wing and Phelan define successful long-term weight loss as losing 10% body weight and keeping it off for at least 1 year. They estimate that about 20% of overweight individuals are successful at long-term weight loss (4). Health care providers should not expect patients to always lose weight between appointments. Even the most talented clinician with the most motivated and dedicated patient will have setbacks.

A *lapse* is a normal setback and is just a slight error or slip in behavior. It is an isolated event such as indulging in a high-calorie food, not exercising as much as scheduled, or overeating while watching television. A lapse is an opportunity to learn, refocus, and further strategize a particular pattern. If a patient sees the lapse as a temporary issue and resolves it by problem-solving with his or her health care provider, it will not turn into a *relapse*. A *relapse* is a number of lapses strung together that causes a return to the former way of eating, exercising, or coping. If a relapse continues over an extended period of time, it is called a *collapse* and there is little hope of reversing the negative trend.

Preventing small lapses and weight regains from becoming larger relapses seems critical to successful weight loss and long-term weight maintenance. Wing and Phelan evaluated members of the National Weight Control Registry (NWCR), a self-selected group of more than 4,000 adults who have lost at least 30 pounds and kept it off for at least 1 year. They found that only 11% of people in the NWCR were able to recover from weight gain of even just 5 pounds or less (4). The key message to clinicians and patients: it is normal to lapse but quick problem-solving to counter lapses is critical because most people will not recover from even small weight regains.

To decrease the likelihood of relapses and weight regain, clinicians should meet with patients regularly and teach them a technique called *self-regulation*. Self-regulation involves two things: *daily* self-

---

Box 7.1 ✦ Web-Based Lifestyle Patterns Program

The Lifestyle Patterns program is available online through Diet.com (http://www.diet.com) as a fee-based program, with expert support and Lifestyle Pattern–specific meal plans and strategies. Diet.com also has free social support, group weight loss challenges, tracking tools, healthy recipes, fitness videos, and daily blogs. See the Resources section in Appendix F for more information on this and other Web-based forms of support.

weighing and an action plan to follow if the scale shows a 3- to 5-pound weight gain. Wing and colleagues recruited 314 successful dieters (people who lost at least 10% of their body weight during the 2 years prior to enrolling in this study) and split them into one of three groups: control, face-to-face intervention, and Internet intervention (5). In the two intervention groups, the participants received a scale, guidelines on how to weigh themselves daily, encouragement to make behavior changes if their weight increased (called self-regulation), and a tool kit with items such as food and exercise diaries and a pedometer to use if they gained more than 5 pounds. The study participants' weight was tracked for 18 months. In the control group (not weighing themselves daily), 72% regained more than 5 pounds over the period of 18 months. However, only 26% of the participants regained 5 pounds or more when they weighed themselves daily with an action plan for weight gain (self-regulation) and had monthly face-to-face visits with their health care provider.

Although Wing et al's study shows daily weighing to be beneficial, we know that some patients prefer weekly weighing. Clinicians should outline an action plan for each patient based on his or her lifestyle patterns. For example, if a patient is primarily a Steady Snacker, the action plan for a weight gain of 3 to 5 pounds would be to review and restart the four targeted strategies for the Steady Snacker: keep a snacking log, preplan snacks, stock up on healthy snack choices, and tame what triggers to much snacking.

In addition to regular appointments and self-regulation techniques, clinicians should be mindful and monitor patients' moods. Wing and Phelan found that patients with more depression and negative affect ("feeling blue") were at higher risk for continued relapse and weight regain (4). Elfhag and Rossner reviewed almost 60 studies to determine factors associated with weight regain (6). Based on their findings, clinicians should also be mindful of monitoring the following factors with their patients:

• Perceived barriers for weight-loss behaviors

• Sedentary lifestyle

• Lack of social support

• Lack of self-confidence

• Dichotomous (black-and-white) thinking

• History of weight cycling

• Disinhibited eating (overeating foods typically limited or restricted)

• Binge eating (eating a large amount of food in a short period of time and feeling a lack of control)

• Excessive complaints of hunger

• Eating in response to negative emotions and stress

• Passive reactions to problems

This is also a good time to use the behavior theories and methods reviewed in Chapter 1. Depending on the patient's particular barriers or obstacles toward making further lifestyle changes, several techniques are useful in helping the patient address ambivalence and making a specific plan of action. These techniques include motivational interviewing (express empathy, develop discrepancy, support self-efficacy, roll with resistance), using the theory of planned behavior (assessing patient's attitude about the behavior to be changed, normative beliefs, perceived and actual behavioral control and intention), and cognitive-behavior therapy (self-monitoring, stimulus control, cognitive restructuring). In addition, assure patients that although weight loss and maintenance are difficult and require continual diligence, they will get easier over time. Wing and Phelan found that people who maintained weight loss for 2 years reduced their risk of subsequent regain by nearly 50% (4).

Weight Plateaus

A weight-loss plateau occurs when a person is in energy balance (calories eaten are equal to the calories burned) and therefore no weight loss occurs. A weight-loss plateau can be frustrating to patients, but it is a normal part of the weight-loss process. As people lose weight, they lose muscle mass (in addition to fat and water), which results in a lower metabolic rate. Additionally, at their new lower body weight, they burn fewer calories doing the same physical activity. Research suggests that people burn approximately 50 kcal less per day with a 10% reduction in body weight (7).

It is important to help patients understand that plateaus are both a normal and expected part of the weight-loss process. At a plateau, patients can decide to take one of two actions: (*a*) continue with current changes and work toward successful *maintenance* of the weight loss, or (*b*) reevaluate and refocus efforts toward eating, exercise, and coping patterns to shift energy balance to produce additional weight *loss*. If a patient desires further weight loss, more effort and strategies can be put toward existing identified patterns or the Lifestyle Patterns Quiz may be re-administered to measure progress and potentially identify any new emerging patterns.

Re-administering the Lifestyle Patterns Quiz

To provide measurement of progress, we recommend that the entire 50-question Lifestyle Patterns Quiz be re-administered after patients lose 5% to 10% of their body weight, and periodically thereafter. Alternatively, clinicians who are helping patients to focus on only one or two lifestyle dimensions may choose to administer individual sections (eating, exercise or coping) of the full quiz. Many patients experience a weight-loss plateau after losing 10% of their body weight. Retaking the test allows the patient and clinician the opportunity to reflect on accomplishments and also begin to set a new agenda for continued treatment. The following is an example of a clinician-patient dialogue regarding the re-administration of the quiz.

> **Clinician:** "We have worked together about 5 and a half months and congratulations are in order because you have lost 10% of your body weight. I would like to give you the 50-question Lifestyle Patterns Quiz again, the one you took the first time we met, so we can reflect on what you have accomplished and identify which areas may still need our attention and strategizing."

> **Patient:** "I feel like a different person than when I took that quiz the first time. I am anxious to see if my new test results reflect all of the changes I have made. Actually, I am surprised that I haven't lost more weight with all of the changes I have made."

> **Clinician:** "Here are the results. [See printed quiz results in Figures 7.2–7.4.] Let's review the changes. The first time you took the quiz, the dominant patterns for eating were Fruitless Feaster and Hearty Portioner. Those both have gone down below 33%. That's what we would have expected because you have worked so hard to correct these problematic behaviors. But look at this, Convenient Diner has increased."

> **Patient:** "Oh, that makes sense because I have been traveling much more with my new job. This is a good reminder that I could use help on healthy dining out tips."

> **Clinician:** "For exercise the dominant patterns were Uneasy Participant and Rain Check Athlete when you previously took the quiz, but they are both under 33% now. The Set-Routine Repeater, however, jumped up and is something you and I can talk about—getting more variety in your exercise routine is important to long-term success."

Patient: "Yes, I am doing very well with exercise but I am starting to get a little bored. I would like to discuss other options."

Clinician: "Finally, when you first took the quiz, your dominant coping patterns were Persistent Procrastinator, People Pleaser, and Overreaching Achiever. The Persistent Procrastinator and People Pleaser have decreased, but the Overreaching Achiever is still quite high. Even before you re-took the quiz, you mentioned you were surprised you haven't lost more weight and you seem disappointed in your results, even though they are exactly on track with where they should be at 6 months. We definitely will address whether your expectations are too ambitious today."

Patient: "Okay, I need reminding that I am on track and where I should be. It feels good to hear that. It was helpful for me to see how the quiz results changed with all of my hard work over the past few months. I am anxious to talk about and get the handouts for the next three major habits, Convenient Diner, Set-Routine Repeater, and Overreaching Achiever. I hope I can do as well with these three, but I'm not sure. I guess time will tell."

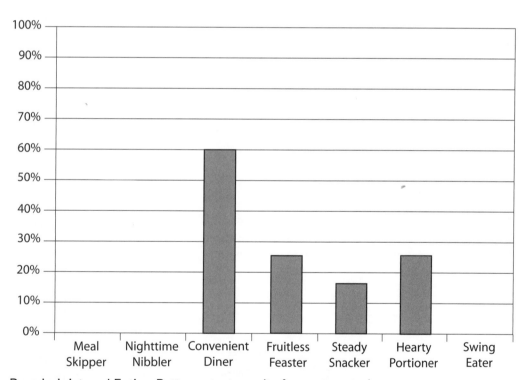

Figure 7.2 Re-administered Eating Patterns test results from case study.

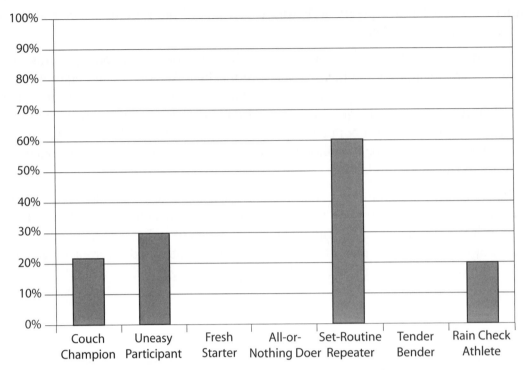

Figure 7.3   Re-administered Exercise Patterns test results from case study.

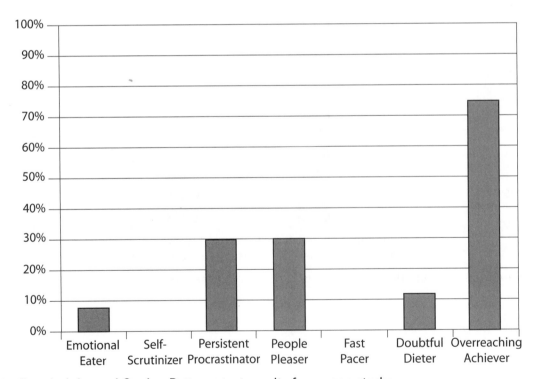

Figure 7.4   Re-administered Coping Patterns test results from case study.

Ongoing Monitoring Considerations

With all of the Lifestyle Patterns, ongoing monitoring of clients requires attention to the following topics: weight and health outcomes, high-risk situations, spillover benefits, and weight maintenance.

Weight and Health Outcomes

Although we tell our patients that losing 1 to 2 pounds per week is a healthful rate of weight loss, patients need to know that losing zero pounds one week but then losing 3 pounds the next means they're still within those guidelines. Help patients understand that you can't predict body weight changes the way you would be able to predict changes in a room's temperature by resetting a thermostat. Changes in body weight are physiologically determined, and the body is always adapting and adjusting along the way. Sometimes a simple explanation regarding how each person's body reacts uniquely is all that is needed to mollify patient's frustration and concerns. Patience is a virtue that we need to encourage among our patients as they are working on their healthful lifestyle strategies.

What weight goal should clinicians help their patients work toward achieving? As discussed in the Overreaching Achiever strategies in Chapter 6, losing 10% of one's body weight is the "gold standard" when it comes to setting a goal that is realistic, attainable, and doable. We encourage clinicians to help their patients meet their 10% goals. After that, if further weight loss would be beneficial and patients are willing to make more modifications in their daily diet and physical activity, then another 5% goal can be set. Clinicians need to tell patients that this 10% weight loss can decrease blood pressure, blood glucose, and lipid levels; improve mobility; and even decrease the need for some medications. Encouraging patients to pay attention to these health-related outcomes reinforces the value and benefit of weight loss and weight maintenance as important therapeutic strategies.

High-Risk Situations

As part of the monitoring process, health care providers must help patients plan ahead for high-risk situations. Whether they're having out-of-town guests, attending a holiday celebration, recovering from an injury, or dealing with a major life change like divorce or a serious illness, patients will look to clinicians for guidance regarding how their weight-loss plan and strategies may be affected. Clinicians need to be sensitive to the shifting needs of their patients as their lives and situations change. Using shared decision-making, clinicians can help their clients develop a list of core behaviors that, despite their current life stressors, they can still do faithfully to keep themselves feeling in control. One patient's core behaviors may be eating breakfast each day and wearing a pedometer, whereas another person's may be keeping a food log (even if they only have time to scribble something on a piece of paper at the end of the day) and carrying a water bottle with them as a reminder to stay hydrated. Patients need to know that it's okay that they will not always be up for following all of their strategies, but they should be ready to ramp-up their program once their life stressors decrease. At such times, clinicians can emphasize to patients the importance of building their support team at work, at home, and even online. An online diet support community can offer patients a place where they can talk to other people trying to lose weight or maintain weight loss, feel like they're not alone, and keep their motivation high despite their changing circumstances. See Appendix F for online diet support community resources.

Spillover Benefits

Although we typically discuss the 21 Lifestyle Patterns as being distinct entities, clinicians will likely see some overlap and some welcome spillover benefits among patterns as they evaluate and monitor their patients. For example, the People Pleaser may learn to be more assertive, which may help her emotional eating tendencies that occur when people try to take advantage of her at work. Or the Meal Skipper may use meal replacement bars as a quick meal on the run, which may also help his Hearty Portioner tendencies. The Uneasy Participant who is more comfortable working out at home may find that this is also a time-saving strategy that is good for her Rain Check Athlete personality type. Additionally, we know that healthful behaviors tend to cluster together as the patient improves self-care. The patient who is choosing a more healthful diet is also more likely to be more physically active and have an increased sense of self-control. We encourage clinicians to pay attention to these spillover benefits and point them out to patients as a way to support and encourage their continued progress.

Weight Maintenance

During weight maintenance, patients change their focus to the strategies and skills needed to balance calorie intake with the amount of calories burned. The motivation and reward of weight loss must be replaced with the long-term benefits of maintaining the lower body weight. Ideally, weight maintenance occurs after the patient has reached his or her desired weight-loss goal. Unfortunately, as discussed in the Overreaching Achiever strategies in Chapter 6, patients often set their weight goals so low that they may never meet them. In a weight-management program, body weight will more often plateau or stabilize before the patient has reached his or her desired goal weight. This typically occurs after approximately 6 months of treatment. For these patients, weight maintenance may be a preferred strategy for a period of time, at least until they can apply new strategies or modalities to enhance further weight loss. In sum, weight maintenance begins at the point when the patient is unable to lose further weight—it is rarely a predetermined decision.

Family Health and Weight Patterns

Up to this point, we have discussed the Lifestyle Patterns Approach in the context of helping adults with weight management. However, as adults develop more healthful eating, exercise, and coping habits, their families can also benefit from those changes. Therefore, it is important to encourage patients following the Lifestyle Patterns Approach to practice the more healthful habits with the whole family. For example, if a Steady Snacker mom restocks the house with more healthful snacks, the whole family has the opportunity to participate in this change and enjoy eating those snacks. If a Fruitless Feaster dad is working on eating more flavorful vegetables with meals, the whole family can join him in his attempt to eat more produce. If a Nighttime Nibbler parent is trying to not snack while watching television, everyone in the family should be asked to try this strategy. Ideally, the Lifestyle Patterns Approach does not isolate one member of a family; rather, it can be an approach that allows the whole family to make healthful changes together.

Having overweight parents increases a child's risk of becoming an obese adult. Agras et al studied 150 children from birth to age 9.5 years and found that children with an overweight parent had a 48% chance that they would be overweight or obese, whereas children with normal-weight parents had a 13% chance of becoming overweight or obese (8). Additionally, if children had overweight parents *and* the parents did not have concern regarding the child's weight, those children had a 63% chance of becoming overweight or obese.

Although the tendency of overweight children to become overweight adults can be partially explained by genetics, there is also a powerful behavioral and environmental component. Parents are role models for their children's behavior. Parents influence children's access to food and opportunities for physical activity. Davison et al looked at data from 9- to 11-year-old girls in 192 families and concluded that girls from "obesigenic families" (parents with high caloric intake and low physical activity) had diets higher in fat and watched more television than girls from nonobesigenic families (9).

Health care providers should teach patients that small changes for the whole family can be a successful way to prevent weight gain in both parents and children (10). The American Dietetic Association reviewed 28 studies on weight reduction in children between ages of 5 and 12 years. The results consistently showed significant weight reduction when parents were involved in the eating and exercise behavior changes (11). Although there are many resources and recommendations for improving the health of American families, research highlights and emphasizes six primary areas: (*a*) limit screen time, (*b*) increase active time, aiming for at least 60 minutes most days, (*c*) keep healthful food available and accessible, (*d*) repeat exposure to healthful foods, (*e*) model healthful eating habits, and (*f*) sit down together for family meals. A comprehensive resource for families is the program called *We Can!* (Ways to Enhance Children's Activity and Nutrition) from the National Institutes of Health (12). This Web site contains realistic ideas, tips, and resources to help families eat healthfully and get active.

Energy Out—Healthy Family Style

In a survey of more than 2,000 children, the Kaiser Family Foundation found that children spend approximately 6 hours a day in front of a screen: 4 hours in front of the television, 1 hour in front of the computer, and 1 hour playing video games (13). The 6 hours of reported screen time is three times the 2-hour maximum that the American Academy of Pediatrics (AAP) recommends for children (14).

Leading health organizations, such as the Centers for Disease Control and Prevention, US Department of Agriculture, National Institutes of Health, National Cancer Institute, and AAP, recommend 60 minutes of physical activity for children every day. It is important to educate parents about strategies to be more active as a family. Give patients ideas for family activities, such as riding bikes to the library; training for a charity walk; celebrating birthdays and holidays with activities such as a bean bag toss, volleyball game, or Frisbee match; washing the car; or going on a weekend family hike.

Energy In—Healthy Family Style

Healthful family eating habits begin with keeping healthful food available in the house *and* having the healthful food accessible to kids. For example, it is not enough to have whole oranges in the house; they should be peeled and put at kids' eye level in the refrigerator, within their reach. Blanchette and Brug reviewed 15 studies and found availability and accessibility of healthful foods were more consistently and positively correlated to actually eating a more healthful diet than any other factors, such as peer influence, specific knowledge of recommended servings and television advertisements (15).

In addition to having healthful foods available and accessible, parents need to have patience and also eat these foods themselves. Many parents stop offering healthful foods to kids if their children seem to dislike those foods, but preference for healthful foods can be taught. With repeated exposure to a healthful food, children will increasingly like and eat more of it. Wardle et al found that after giving kids a vegetable 14 times, the children began to like it and eat more of it (16). Health care providers need to encourage parents to positively and gently continue to offer their kids small bites of healthful foods even

---

Box 7.2 ✦ Tips for Having a Healthy Family

- Set a 2-hour limit on total daily screen time—television, video games, and computer.
- Get active as a family. Children need at least 60 minutes of activity most days.
- Keep healthful foods in the home *and* easy for kids to grab.
- Offer healthful foods to kids many, many times—it can take 14 exposures to a food before they start liking and eating it.
- Parents are the role model. If parents eat healthful foods and are active, kids will follow their lead.
- Make time for family meals most if not all days of the week.

---

if at first they seem to dislike them. Parents also need to eat the healthful foods that they are offering to their children. Wardle and colleagues also found that there was a positive association between parental fruit and vegetable intake and children's intake (16).

An innovative way to encourage families to eat healthful foods is to try flavor-flavor learning. This involves pairing an undesirable food with a food that has a flavor family members like. For example, if an adult or child likes peanut butter but does not like broccoli or cauliflower, suggest putting peanut butter sauce on broccoli and cauliflower (17).

Finally, health care providers need to encourage parents to plan meals and find time to sit down together for family meals. Boutelle et al found that meal planning in advance is associated with higher fruit and vegetable consumption (18). Of the nearly 300 families in this study, 46% of parents did *not* plan meals. Although parents thought family meals were important, one in three felt they had no time to eat together.

In the study by Boutelle et al, the more nights per week a family ate dinner together, the greater the likelihood that they ate a healthful meal (defined as high in fruits and vegetables and low in fat) (18). Television should not be part of preplanned family meals. As the number of nights per week the television is on during dinner increases, consumption of fruits and vegetables decreases (19).

The bottom line for health care providers: parents need to be reminded that they are the primary role models for their children. Healthful changes in parents' patterns spark change in the whole family's patterns. See Box 7.2 for Tips for Having a Healthy Family.

Summing Up Follow-up and Monitoring

In this chapter, you have learned how to follow-up with patients using the Lifestyle Patterns Approach. The Progress Tracking Chart is a valuable tool to document, organize, and monitor patients' progress with eating, exercise, and coping behaviors and weight changes. Re-administering the Lifestyle Patterns Quiz is valuable when patients lose 10% of their body weight, hit a plateau, or any time evaluation of progress is needed. This chapter outlined techniques and resources to handle common challenges such as behavior lapses, weight gain relapses, plateaus, ongoing monitoring considerations, and family health and weight patterns.

Chapter 8 will review disease-specific guidelines for type 2 diabetes mellitus, hypertension, dyslipidemia, and metabolic syndrome as they relate to the Lifestyle Patterns Approach, and then review adjunctive use of very–low-calorie diets, pharmacotherapy, and bariatric surgery.

References

1. US Preventive Service Task Force. Screening for obesity in adults. *Ann Intern Med.* 2003;139:930-932. http://www.ahrq.gov/clinic/3rduspstf/obesity/obesrr.pdf. Accessed September 23, 2007.

2. Harvey-Berino J, Pintauro S, Buzzell P, Gold EC. Effect of internet support on the long-term maintenance of weight loss. *Obes Res.* 2004;12:320-329.

3. Carels RA, Darby LA, Rydin S, Douglass OM, Cacciapaglia HM, O'Brien WH. The relationship between self-monitoring, outcome expectancies, difficulties with eating and exercise, and physical activity and weight loss treatment outcomes. *Ann Behav Med.* 2005;30:182-190.

4. Wing RR, Phelan S. Long-term weight loss maintenance. *Am J Clin Nutr.* 2005;82(1 Suppl):222S-225S.

5. Wing RR, Tate DF, Gorin AA, Raynor HA, Fava JL. A self-regulation program for maintenance of weight loss. *N Engl J Med.* 2006;355:1563-1571.

6. Elfhag K, Rossner S. Who succeeds in maintaining weight loss? A conceptual review of factors associated with weight loss maintenance and weight regain. *Obes Rev.* 2005;6:67-85.

7. Heilbronn LK, Jonge L, Frisard MI, DeLany JP, Larson-Meyer E, Rood J, Nguyen T, Martin CK, Volaufova J, Most MM, Greenway FL, Smith SR, Deutsch WA, Williamson DA, Ravussin E; Pennington CALERIE Team. Effect of 6-month calorie restriction biomarkers on longevity, metabolic adaptation, and oxidative stress in overweight individuals: a randomized controlled trial. *JAMA.* 2006;295:1539-1548.

8. Agras WS, Hammer LD, McNicholas F, Kraemer HC. Risk factors for childhood overweight: a prospective study from birth to 9.5 years. *J Pediatr.* 2004;145:20-25.

9. Davison KK, Francis LA, Birch LL. Reexamining obesigenic families: parents' obesity-related behaviors predict girls' change in BMI. *Obes Res.* 2005;13:1980-1990.

10. Rodearmel SJ, Wyatt HR, Barry MJ, Dong F, Pan D, Israel RG, Cho SS, McBurney MI, Hill JO. A family-based approach to preventing excessive weight gain. *Obesity.* 2006;14:1392-1401.

11. Position of the American Dietetic Association: individual-, family-, school-, and community-based interventions for pediatric overweight. *J Am Diet Assoc.* 2006;106:925-945.

12. National Institutes of Health. "We Can" program Web site. http://www.nhlbi.nih.gov/health/public/heart/obesity/wecan/. Accessed September 23, 2007.

13. Kaiser Family Foundation. Executive Summary: Media in the Lives of 8-18 year olds. March 2005. http://www.kff.org/entmedia/7250.cfm. Accessed September 23, 2007.

14. Council on Sports Medicine and Fitness; Council on School Health. Active healthy living: prevention of childhood obesity through increased physical activity. *Pediatrics.* 2006;117:1834-1842.

15. Blanchette L, Brug J. Determinants of fruit and vegetables consumption among 6–12-year-old children and effective interventions to increase consumption. *J Hum Nutr Diet.* 2005;18:431-443.

16. Wardle J, Cooke L, Gibson EL, Sapochnik M, Sheiham A, Lawson M. Increasing children's acceptance of vegetables; a randomized trial of parent-led exposure. *Appetite.* 2003;40:155-162.

17. Havermans RC, Jansen A. Increasing children's liking of vegetables through flavour-flavour learning. *Appetite.* 2007;48:259-262.

18. Boutelle KN, Birnbaum AS, Lytle LA, Murray DM, Story M. Associations between perceived family meal environment and parent intake of fruit, vegetables, and fat. *J Nutr Educ Behav.* 2003;35:924-929.

19. Fitzpatrick E, Edmunds LS, Dennison BA. Positive effects of family dinner are undone by television viewing. *J Am Diet Assoc.* 2007;107:666-671.

Chapter 8

✦ ✦ ✦

Special Patient Populations

Overview

Because overweight and obesity are associated with an increased risk of numerous health problems that affect at least nine organ systems (1), attention to these conditions is essential when instituting a weight-loss treatment plan. Although individuals will vary, the number and severity of organ-specific comorbid conditions usually increases as weight increases (2). Treatment guidelines for the most commonly associated diseases, including type 2 diabetes mellitus, hypertension, dyslipidemia, and metabolic syndrome, identify weight management as one of the most important therapeutic components of care. Similarly, engaging in increased levels of physical activity and choosing a healthful diet form the foundation of lifestyle management (3,4). Beyond these general principles, each of the aforementioned comorbid conditions has specific dietary recommendations that have been shown to improve treatment outcomes. Accordingly, clinicians should consider disease-specific counseling when using the Lifestyle Patterns Approach in patients who present with comorbid conditions.

Although treatment of obesity must always include lifestyle management (the central focus of this book), adjunctive use of very–low-calorie diets (VLCDs), pharmacotherapy, or referral for bariatric surgery may be considered for select patients. Because these modalities alter the patient's diet and eating style, the Lifestyle Patterns Approach may need to be adapted to help patients make the necessary changes. This chapter will briefly review the disease-specific guidelines for type 2 diabetes mellitus, hypertension, dyslipidemia, and metabolic syndrome as they relate to the Lifestyle Patterns Approach, and then review adjunctive use of VLCDs, pharmacotherapy, and bariatric surgery.

Type 2 Diabetes Mellitus

Evidence-based nutrition recommendations and interventions for diabetes were updated in 2006 (5). A summary of the recommendations are listed in Box 8.1. Table 8.1 summarizes eating patterns that are pertinent to review in patients with type 2 diabetes. The issues noted in this table are particularly relevant if the patient takes insulin or insulin secretagogues.

Box 8.1 ✦ Key Nutrition Recommendations and Interventions for Type 2 Diabetes

- Moderate weight loss (7% body weight) is recommended for overweight and obese insulin-resistant individuals.
- Regular physical activity (150 min/week).
- A dietary pattern that includes carbohydrate from fruits, vegetables, whole grains, legumes, and low-fat milk is encouraged.
- Monitoring carbohydrate, whether by carbohydrate counting or exchanges remains a key strategy in achieving glycemic control.
- Limit saturated fat to < 7% of total calories and dietary cholesterol to < 200 mg/d.
- Two or more servings of fish per week are recommended to provide n-3 polyunsaturated fatty acids.
- The best mix of carbohydrate, protein, and fat seems to vary depending on individual circumstances.

Source: Data are from reference 5.

Table 8.1 ✦ Eating Patterns Counseling Considerations in Patients with Type 2 Diabetes

Eating Patterns	Special Consideration
Convenient Diner	• Foods eaten out are generally larger portions and higher in calories than foods served at home. Dietary carbohydrate is the major determinant of postprandial glucose levels; therefore, monitoring the amount and type of carbohydrate in meals is important.
Fruitless Feaster	• Fruits and vegetables are recommended as a good source of carbohydrate.
Hearty Portioner	• Carbohydrate content of large meals may be high. • Dietary carbohydrate is the major determinant of postprandial glucose levels; therefore, monitoring the amount and type of carbohydrate in meals is important.
Meal Skipper, Nighttime Nibbler, Steady Snacker	• The timing of meals and snacks and adherence to a structured meal pattern are important to achieve optimal glycemic control and to avoid hyperglycemia and hypoglycemia.
Swing Eater	• Many patients with diabetes think in terms of "good" and "bad" carbohydrates or "cheating" when they consume sweets. This black-and-white thinking often leads to over-restriction and rebound overeating. Hypoglycemic episodes may also be considered as acceptable occasions for excess consumption of sweets.

Physical activity is vital for the prevention as well as the management of type 2 diabetes (6-8). Physical activity reduces blood glucose and decreases insulin resistance. See Table 8.2 for the exercise patterns that require special attention in patients with type 2 diabetes, particularly if the patient takes insulin or insulin secretagogues.

Emotional issues play an important role in the lives of people with diabetes because the disease increases demands on day-to-day self-care (9). Living with diabetes may generate considerable psychological stress. Table 8.3 identifies coping patterns to review most carefully in patients with diabetes.

Table 8.2 ✦ Exercise Patterns Counseling Considerations in Patients with Type 2 Diabetes

Exercise Patterns	Reasons for Concern
All-or-Nothing Doer	Patients may experience hypoglycemia with inconsistent, vigorous workouts.
Couch Champion, Rain Check Athlete, Tender Bender, Uneasy Participant	Physical inactivity is implicated in the development of type 2 diabetes, and physical activity is associated with improved diabetes care.
Fresh Starter, Set-Routine Repeater	Patients may not be engaging in resistance training, an important component of exercise that can increase insulin sensitivity.

Table 8.3 ✦ Coping Patterns Counseling Considerations in Patients with Type 2 Diabetes

Coping Patterns	Reason for Concern
Doubtful Dieter, Fast Pacer	People with diabetes may feel frustrated, overwhelmed, burned out and even pessimistic about all they need to do to care for themselves.
Emotional Eater	Diabetes-related emotional distress may lead to unplanned eating.
Persistent Procrastinator	Diabetes is often a silent disease without symptomatic reminders.
Overreaching Achiever	Some patients with diabetes may get upset or frustrated when they get occasional high blood glucose readings, expecting to maintain normal glucose level at all times.

Hypertension and Cardiovascular Disease Risk Reduction

In 2006 the American Heart Association (AHA) published evidence-based recommendations for diet-related lifestyle modifications for people with hypertension (10). (See Box 8.2.) The AHA has also recently updated its diet and lifestyle recommendations for cardiovascular disease risk reduction (11). (See Box 8.3.) Table 8.4 (12-18) identifies eating, exercise, and coping patterns that should be reviewed most carefully in patients with cardiovascular disease or hypertension.

Box 8.2 ✦ Key Nutrition Recommendations for Hypertension

- For overweight or obese persons, lose weight, ideally attaining a BMI < 25; for nonoverweight persons, maintain desirable BMI < 25
- Lower salt (sodium chloride) intake as much as possible, ideally to ~ 65 mmol/d sodium (corresponding to 1.5 g/d of sodium or 3.8 g/d sodium chloride)
- Consume a diet rich in fruits and vegetables (6–10 servings/d), rich in low-fat dairy products (2–3 servings/d), and reduced in saturated fat and cholesterol
- Increase potassium intake to 120 mmol/d (4.7 g/d), which is also the level provided in DASH-type diets
- For those who drink alcohol, consume ≤ 2 alcoholic drinks/d (men) and ≤ 1 alcoholic drink/d (women)

Source: Data are from reference 10.

Box 8.3 ✦ American Heart Association (AHA) 2006 Diet and Lifestyle Recommendations for Cardiovascular Disease Risk Reduction

- Balance calorie intake and physical activity to achieve or maintain a healthy body weight
- Consume a diet rich in vegetables and fruits
- Choose whole grain, high-fiber foods
- Consume fish, especially oily fish, at least twice a week
- Limit your intake of saturated fat to < 7% of energy, *trans* fat to < 1% of energy, and cholesterol to < 300 mg per day by:

  ► Choosing lean meats and vegetable alternatives;
  ► Selecting fat-free (skim), 1%-fat, and low-fat dairy products; and
  ► Minimizing intake of partially hydrogenated fats

- Minimize your intake of beverages and foods with added sugars
- Choose and prepare foods with little or no salt
- If you consume alcohol, do so in moderation
- When you eat food that is prepared outside of the home, follow the AHA Diet and Lifestyle Recommendations

---

Source: Data are from reference 11.

Table 8.4 ✦ Lifestyle Patterns Counseling Considerations in Patients with Cardiovascular Disease or Hypertension

Pattern	Reason for Concern
Eating patterns	
Convenient Diner	More than 75% of salt in the diet comes from processed foods; the remainder is from salt added at the table or while cooking, and naturally occurring (12).
Fruitless Feaster	Inclusion of fruits and vegetables and other sources of potassium is an important component of the Dietary Approaches to Stop Hypertension (DASH) diet (13,14).
Exercise patterns	
Couch Champion, Uneasy Participant, Rain Check Athlete	Physical activity is associated with improved health outcomes for individuals at risk for or suffering from cardiovascular disease. Engaging in regular aerobic physical activity such as brisk walking (for at least 30 minutes per day, on most days of the week), reduces blood pressure and overall cardiovascular risk (15).
Fresh Starter, Tender Bender	Improperly performed resistance training, which may involve breath-holding (Valsalva maneuver), can significantly increase blood pressure. Exercise should also not be recommended if resting systolic blood pressure > 200 mmHg or if diastolic blood pressure > 110 mmHg. Some patients with cardiovascular disease require physician clearance (16).
Coping patterns	
Fast Pacer, Overreaching Achiever, Doubtful Dieter, Self Scrutinizer	Psychological stress exerts independent adverse effects on cardiovascular health (17). Traits linked with type A behavior (time urgency, impatience, achievement-striving, and competitiveness) are associated with risk of developing hypertension and coronary heart disease (17,18).

Source: Data are from references 12-18.

Metabolic Syndrome

Overweight and obese patients should be assessed for metabolic syndrome because it is a risk factor for type 2 diabetes mellitus and cardiovascular disease. The Third Report of the National Cholesterol Education Program's Adult Treatment Panel (ATP III), released in 2001, identified metabolic syndrome as a multifactorial risk factor for cardiovascular disease with clinically defined criteria that include abdominal obesity, increased triglycerides, low high-density lipoprotein cholesterol, increased blood pressure, and impaired fasting glucose (19). See Table 8.5 (19).

Using this definition, approximately 24% of US adults are estimated to have metabolic syndrome, with higher prevalence rates among older individuals and Mexican Americans (20). The treatment recommendations outlined previously for diabetes and hypertension can be used for patients with metabolic syndrome.

Very-Low-Calorie Diets

Occasionally, VLCDs are prescribed as a form of aggressive dietary therapy. The primary purpose of prescribing a VLCD is to promote a rapid and significant (13 to 23 kg) short-term weight loss over a 3- to 6-month period. These propriety formulas typically supply fewer than 800 kcal, 50 to 80 g protein, and 100% of the RDI for vitamins and minerals per day. A recent meta-analysis (21) found that after a weight loss of 20 kg or more, individuals maintained significantly more weight loss than after low-calorie diets or weight loss of less than 10 kg. In contrast, other studies have found no difference in long-term weight loss between VLCDs and low-calorie diets (22). According to a review by the National Task Force on the Prevention and Treatment of Obesity (23), indications for initiating a VLCD include well-motivated individuals who are moderately to severely obese (body mass index [BMI] > 30), have failed at more conservative approaches to weight loss, and have a medical condition that would be immediately improved with rapid weight loss (eg, poorly controlled type 2 diabetes, hypertriglyceridemia, obstructive sleep apnea, or symptomatic peripheral edema). Because of the need for close metabolic monitoring, these diets are usually prescribed by physicians specializing in obesity care. Implementation of the Lifestyle Patterns Approach may be delayed until this aggressive treatment approach is completed.

Anti-obesity Medications

Adjuvant pharmacological treatments can be considered for patients with BMI more than 30, and for patients with BMI more than 27 who also have associated obesity-related risk factors or diseases and for whom dietary and physical activity therapy has not been successful (24). There are several potential tar-

Table 8.5 ✦ Clinical Identification of Metabolic Syndrome[a]

Risk Factor	Defining Level
Abdominal obesity	Men: Waist circumference > 102 cm (> 40 in) Women: Waist circumference > 88 cm (> 35 in)
Triglycerides	≥ 150 mg/dL
HDL cholesterol	Men: < 40 mg/dL Women: < 50 mg/dL
Blood pressure	≥ 130/85 mmHg
Fasting blood glucose	≥ 110 mg/dL

[a] Having 3 of 5 risk factors constitutes diagnosis of metabolic syndrome.
Source: Data are from reference 19.

gets of pharmacological therapy for obesity, all based on the concept of producing a sustained negative energy (calorie) balance.

Anorexiants (Phentermine and Sibutramine)

Appetite-suppressing drugs, or anorexiants, effect satiation (the processes involved in the termination of a meal), satiety (the absence of hunger after eating), and hunger (a biological sensation that initiates eating). By increasing satiation and satiety and decreasing hunger, these agents help patients reduce energy intake while providing a greater sense of control without deprivation.

Phentermine and sibutramine (Meridia, Abbott Laboratories, Abbott Park, IL) are the two most commonly prescribed medications in this class. The most commonly reported adverse events of phentermine and sibutramine are headache, dry mouth, insomnia, and constipation. However, these are generally mild and well-tolerated. The principal concern is a dose-related increase in blood pressure and heart rate that may require discontinuation of the medication (25). Table 8.6 identifies eating patterns to review most carefully in patients taking anorexiants (26,27).

Orlistat

In contrast to anorexiants, orlistat is a peripherally acting medication that is a potent, slowly reversible inhibitor of pancreatic and gastric lipases. The drug's activity takes place in the lumen of the stomach and small intestine by forming a covalent bond with these lipases (28). Taken at a therapeutic prescriptive dose (Xenical, Hoffman-LaRoche, Nuttley, NJ) of 120 mg three times daily, orlistat blocks the digestion and absorption of approximately 30% of dietary fat. In 2007 orlistat was approved for over-the-counter (OTC) use under the brand name Alli (GlaxoSmithKline, Philadelphia, PA). The OTC dose of 60 mg three times daily blocks approximately 25% of dietary fat.

Because orlistat is minimally (< 1%) absorbed from the gastrointestinal tract, it has no systemic adverse effects. Tolerability to the drug is related to the malabsorption of dietary fat and subsequent passage of fat in the feces. Six gastrointestinal tract adverse effects have been reported to occur in at least 10% of orlistat-treated patients: oily spotting, flatus with discharge, fecal urgency, fatty/oily stool, oily evacuation, and increased defecation. The events are generally experienced early, diminish as patients control their dietary fat intake, and infrequently cause patients to withdraw from clinical trials (25). When taken concomitantly with orlistat, psyllium mucilloid helps control the orlistat-induced gastrointestinal adverse effects. The manufacturer's package insert for Xenical (29) strongly encourages that patients take a vitamin supplement along with the drug to prevent potential deficiencies; vitamin supplementation is also recommended for individuals using Alli. Table 8.7 identifies eating patterns to review most carefully with patients taking orlistat.

Table 8.6 ✦ Eating Patterns Counseling Considerations for When Patients Are Taking Anorexiants

Eating Patterns	Reason for Concern
Hearty Portioner	Anorexiants work by reducing hunger and/or increasing satiety. Clinicians can help patients focus on the reduced hunger and increased satiety cues brought about by the anorexiant medication.
Meal Skipper, Nighttime Nibbler, Steady Snacker, Swing Eater	Studies have shown that a structured meal plan forms an important foundation for successful use of these medications (26,27).

Source: Data are from references 26 and 27.

Table 8.7 ✦ Eating Patterns Counseling Considerations in Patients Taking Orlistat

Eating Patterns	Reason for Concern
Convenient Diner	Tolerability of the medication is related to following a fat-restricted diet; therefore, careful attention to hidden and visible fats is important.
Meal Skipper, Steady Snacker	Orlistat should be taken with two to three meals per day.

Bariatric Surgery

Bariatric surgery can be considered for patients with severe obesity (BMI > 40) and those with moderate obesity (BMI > 35) associated with a serious medical condition (24). Bariatric surgery leads to weight loss by reducing energy intake and, depending on the procedure, macronutrient absorption.

Weight-loss surgeries fall into one of two categories—restrictive or restrictive-malabsorptive. Restrictive surgeries limit the amount of food the stomach can hold and slow the rate of gastric emptying. The laparoscopic adjustable silicone gastric banding (LASGB) is the most commonly performed restrictive operation (30). The first banding device, the LAP-BAND (Allergan, Irvine, CA), was approved for use in the United States in 2001. The diameter of this band is adjustable by way of its connection to a reservoir that is implanted under the skin. Injection or removal of saline into the reservoir tightens or loosens the band's internal diameter, respectively, thus changing the size of the gastric opening. Because there is no rerouting of the intestine with LASGB, the risk for developing micronutrient deficiencies is entirely dependent on the patient's diet and eating habits.

The restrictive-malabsorptive bypass procedures combine the elements of gastric restriction and selective malabsorption. The roux-en-y gastric bypass (RYGB) is the most commonly performed bypass procedure (30). It involves formation of a 10- to 30-mL proximal gastric pouch by surgically separating the stomach across the fundus. Outflow from the pouch is created by performing a narrow (10 mm) gastrojejunostomy. The distal end of jejunum is then anastomosed 50 to 150 cm below the gastrojejunostomy. "Bypass" refers to the exclusion or bypassing of the distal stomach, duodenum, and proximal jejunum. The RYGB procedure is generally effective in producing a mean weight loss of approximately 30% to 35% of total body weight that is maintained in almost 60% of patients after 5 years. In general, mean weight loss is greater after the combined restrictive-malabsorptive procedure compared with the restrictive procedure (31).

The most common surgical complications of RYGB include strictures and marginal ulcers (32) with symptoms of prolonged nausea and vomiting after eating or inability to advance the diet to solid foods. For patients who undergo LASGB, there are no intestinal absorptive abnormalities other than mechanical reduction in gastric size and outflow. Therefore, selective deficiencies are uncommon unless eating habits remain restrictive and unbalanced. In contrast, the restrictive-malabsorptive procedure produces a predictable increased risk for micronutrient deficiencies of vitamin B-12, iron, folate, calcium, and vitamin D based on surgical anatomical changes (33). The patients require lifelong supplementation with these micronutrients. Table 8.8 identifies the eating patterns most important to review in patients who have had or are considering bariatric surgery.

Table 8.8 ✦ Eating Patterns Counseling Considerations in Patients Who Have Had or Are Considering Bariatric Surgery

Eating Patterns	Reason for Concern
Hearty Portioner	Bariatric surgery substantially reduces the volume of food intake.
Meal Skipper	Patients can only tolerate small portions and should consume 4 to 6 meals/snacks per day.
Nighttime Nibbler, Steady Snacker	Grazing, mindless munching, and nibbling may circumvent the restrictive aspect of the surgical procedure and lead to poor weight loss or to weight regain.

Summing It Up

In this chapter, you have learned how comorbid conditions and other treatment methods can impact a weight-loss treatment plan. Whether your patients have diabetes, heart disease, or metabolic syndrome, or are candidates for VLCDs, medication therapy, or bariatric surgery, you need to know the possible effects these factors can have on using the Lifestyle Patterns Approach. In the next chapter, you will learn how to use the Lifestyle Patterns Approach in a group setting. The chapter covers the benefits of group counseling techniques, our experiences using the Lifestyle Patterns Approach in a group format, and how to run a group.

References

1. Kushner RF, Roth JL. Assessment of the obese patient. *Endocrinol Metab Clin N Am.* 2003;32:915-934.
2. Must A, Spadano J, Coakley EH, Field AE, Colditz G, Dietz WH. The disease burden associated with overweight and obesity. *JAMA.* 1999;282:1523-1529.
3. Decklebaum RJ, Fisher EA, Winston M, Kumanyika S, Lauer RM, Pi-Sunyer FX, St. Joer SS, Schaefer EJ, Weinstein IB. Summary of a scientific conference on preventive nutrition: pediatrics to geriatrics. *Circulation.* 1999;100:450-456.
4. Eyre H, Kahn R, Robertson RM. Preventing cancer, cardiovascular disease, and diabetes. A common agenda for the American Cancer Society, the American Diabetes Association, and the American Heart Association. *Circulation.* 2004;109:3244-3255.
5. Nutrition recommendations and interventions for diabetes—2006. A position statement of the American Diabetes Association. *Diab Care.* 2006;29:2140-2157.
6. Boule NG, Haddad E, Kenny GP, Wells GA, Sigal RJ. Effects of exercise on glycemic control and body mass in type 2 diabetes mellitus: a meta-analysis of controlled clinical trials. *JAMA.* 2001;286:1218-1227.
7. American College of Sports Medicine. Position stand: exercise and type 2 diabetes. *Med Sci Sports Exerc.* 2000;32:1345-1360.
8. American Diabetes Association. Position statement: physical activity/exercise and diabetes. *Diab Care.* 2004;27(Suppl 1):S58-S64.
9. Rubin RR, Peyrot M. Psychological issues and treatments for people with diabetes. *J Clin Psychol.* 2001;57:457-478.
10. Appel LJ, Brands MW, Daniels SR, Karanja N, Elmer P, Sacks FM. Dietary approaches to prevent and treat hypertension. A scientific statement from the American Heart Association. *Hypertension.* 2006;46:296-308.

11. Lichtenstein AH, Appel LJ, Brands M, Carnethon M, Daniels S, Franch HA, Franklin B, Kris-Etherton P, Harris WS, Howard B, Karanja N, Lefevre M, Rudel L, Sacks F, Van Horn L, Winston M, Wylie-Rossett J. Diet and lifestyle recommendations revision 2006. A scientific statement from the American Heart Association Nutrition Committee. *Circulation.* 2006;114:82-96.

12. US Department of Health and Human Services and US Department of Agriculture. *Dietary Guidelines for Americans,* 2005. 6th ed. Washington, DC: US Government Printing Office; 2005. http://www.health.gov/dietaryguidelines/dga2005/document/default.htm. Accessed December 19, 2007.

13. Appel LJ, Moore TJ, Obarzanek E, Vollmer WM, Svetkey LP, Sacks FM, Bray GA, Vogt TM, Cutler JA, Windhauser MM, Lin PH, Karanja N. A clinical trial on the effects of dietary patterns on blood pressure. DASH Collaborative Research Group. *N Engl J Med.* 1997;336:1117-1124.

14. Sacks FM, Svetkey LP, Vollmer WM, Appel LJ, Bray GA, Harsha D, Obarzanek E, Conlin PR, Miller ER 3rd, Simons-Morton DG, Karanja N, Lin PH,: DASH Sodium Collaborative Research Group. Effects on blood pressure of reduced dietary sodium and the Dietary Approaches to Stop Hypertension (DASH) diet. *N Engl J Med.* 2001;344:3-10.

15. Whelton SP, Chin A, Xin X, He J. Effect of aerobic exercise on blood pressure: a meta-analysis of randomized, controlled trials. *Ann Intern Med.* 2002;136:493-503.

16. Whaley MH, Brubaker PH, Otto RM, eds. *American College of Sports Medicine Guidelines for Exercise Testing and Prescription.* 7th ed. Philadelphia, PA: Lippincott Williams & Wilkins; 2006.

17. Das S, O'Keefe JH. Behavioral cardiology: recognizing and addressing the profound impact of psychosocial stress on cardiovascular health. *Curr Atheroscler Rep.* 2006;8:111-118.

18. Yan LL, Liu K, Matthews KA, Daviglus ML, Ferguson TF, Kiefe CI. Psychosocial factors and risk of hypertension: the Coronary Artery Risk Development in Young Adults (CARDIA) study. *JAMA.* 2003;290:2138-2148.

19. National Institutes of Health. Third report of the National Cholesterol Education Program Expert Panel on Detection, Evaluation, and Treatment of High Blood Cholesterol in Adults (Adult Treatment Panel III). Bethesda, MD: National Institutes of Health; 2001. NIH Publication 01-3670.

20. Ford ES, Giles WH, Dietz WH. Prevalence of the metabolic syndrome among US adults: findings from the third national health and nutrition examination survey. *JAMA.* 2002;287:356-359.

21. Anderson JW, Konz EC, Frederich RC, Wood CL. Long-term weight-loss maintenance: a meta-analysis of US studies. *Am J Clin Nutr.* 2001;74:579-584.

22. Wadden TA, Osei S. The treatment of obesity: an overview. In: Wadden TA, Stunkard AJ, eds. *Handbook of Obesity Treatment.* New York, NY: Guilford Press; 2002:229-248.

23. National Task Force on the Prevention and Treatment of Obesity. Very low-calorie diets. *JAMA.* 1993;270:967-974.

24. National Heart, Lung, and Blood Institute. Clinical guidelines on the identification, evaluation, and treatment of overweight and obesity in adults. The evidence report. *Obes Res.* 1998;6(Suppl 2):51S-210S.

25. Yanovski S, Yanovski JA: Obesity. *N Engl J Med.* 2002;346:591-602.

26. Wadden TA, Berkowitz RI, Sarwer DB, et al: Benefits of lifestyle modification in the pharmacologic treatment of obesity. A randomized trial. *Arch Intern Med.* 2001;161:218-227.

27. Wadden TA, Berkowitz RI, Womble LG, Sarwer DB, et al. Randomized trial of lifestyle modification and pharmacotherapy for obesity. *N Engl J Med.* 2005;353:2111-2120.

28. Lucas KH, Kaplan-Machlis B. Orlistat—a novel weight loss therapy. *Ann Pharmacother.* 2001;35:314-328.

29. Xenical [package insert]. Nutley, NJ: Roche Laboratories; 1999.

30. Buchwald H; Consensus Conference Panel. Bariatric surgery for morbid obesity: health implications for patients, health professionals, and third-party payers. *J Am Coll Surg.* 2005;200:593-604.

31. Buchwald H, Avidor Y, Braunwald E, Jensen MD, Pories W, Fahrbach K, Schoelles K. Bariatric surgery: a systematic review and meta-analysis. *JAMA.* 2004;292:1724-1737.

32. Stocker DJ. Management of the bariatric surgery patient. *Endocrinol Metab Clin North Am.* 2003;32:437-457.

33. Kushner RF. Micronutrient deficiencies and bariatric surgery. *Curr Opin Endocrinol Diabetes.* 2006;13:405-411.

Chapter 9

✦ ✦ ✦

Counseling Groups

Overview

The Lifestyle Patterns Approach can be applied to counseling overweight and obese patients in a group format. Whether the group is recruited within the clinician's health care facility, through a local community center, or as part of a workplace wellness program, the group counseling format offers clinicians an alternative to the traditional, one-on-one client counseling arrangement.

Benefits of Counseling Patients in Groups

The group counseling approach has been used as a way to cost-effectively treat a larger number of overweight and obese people (1). Groups have other benefits as well. Preliminary research in the treatment of obesity suggests that group counseling may be as effective as individual interventions, presumably because of the social support created among group members (2). In one study, group therapy produced greater reductions in body weight than individual therapy, even among clients who express a preference for individual treatment (3). In another study, group participants who were recruited with friends had greater weight loss both at months 4 and 10 than participants recruited alone (4). Certain modalities may work better in a group setting. Drapkin et al found that behavioral coping responses such as counter-conditioning (substituting new behaviors) may occur more naturally and be more easily taught to participants in a group weight-loss program vs the use of cognitive strategies, which may require more individual sessions (5).

Worksite health promotion programs that include weight-loss and nutrition classes are becoming more common (6). In a 2004 HealthStyles survey, 67% of respondents (adults employed full or part time outside of the home) said that weight-loss programs were one of the preferred health promotion services that can be offered in the workplace (7). A pilot study that tested the effect of financial incentives ($7.00 and $14.00 per percentage point of weight loss) on weight loss among 207 employees found that modest financial incentives can be effective in motivating overweight employees to lose weight (8). Corporate groups can also be used to create fun competition among its members by holding weight-loss or pedometer challenges among departments with incentives/prizes for winners (9).

Our Experience Using the Lifestyle Patterns Approach in a Group Format

We used the Lifestyle Patterns Approach in a group format as part of a research study, called PPET (People and Pets Exercising Together) (10). Small groups ranging from six to 12 participants (n = 92) met weekly for the first 16 weeks (treatment phase) and then once per month at months 5, 6, 9, and 12 (maintenance phase). Participants in two types of groups were compared: (*a*) overweight and obese people who had obese dogs (PP/people with pets), and (*b*) overweight and obese people without dogs (PO/people only).

All group participants completed the Lifestyle Patterns Quiz, which was then entered into the computer and scored. In addition to giving each group member his or her own Lifestyle Patterns profile graph results, we also looked at the most common patterns within each group. Using 33% or more as the cutoff for a positive pattern, we identified the top three patterns in each of the three categories (eating, exercise, and coping) as the main Lifestyle Pattern topics to be discussed with that group during the course of the study. Each week, a different Lifestyle Pattern was discussed along with the strategies for controlling that pattern. A registered dietitian instructed the groups on recognizing and adopting healthful eating, exercise, and coping patterns. In addition, other modalities were discussed, such as the use of meal-replacement products and activity guidelines that included a walking kit with a pedometer and self-monitoring forms. For ease of organization and to keep participants focused on one dimension at a time, we addressed all dominant eating patterns first, followed by exercise, and then coping. Mean weight losses at 1 year were 4.7% (PP) and 5.2% (PO). Mean weight loss among the dogs was 15%.

Six elements of successful groups, proposed by Yalom (11), have been discussed as being particularly relevant to groups for obesity (2): imparting information, instilling hope, altruism, universality, interpersonal learning, and group cohesiveness. Groups counseled in the PPET study touched on all six:

- **Imparting information**: Week to week, group members gave tips to one another about their experiences implementing some of the strategies for changing their lifestyle patterns into more healthful ones.

- **Instilling hope**: Group members who were losing weight and feeling in control helped motivate other group members who had been less successful.

- **Altrusim**: Members who would offer help to one another each week would be encouraged to stay focused so they wouldn't disappoint fellow members at the next meeting.

- **Universality**: Members were able to understand that others shared the same Lifestyle Patterns or habits that they had. The Lifestyle Pattern names helped group members address their habits and patterns of behaviors in a nonjudgmental way, rather than focusing on personal flaws.

- **Interpersonal learning**: Members were able to give their own personal strategies and keys to success to others who struggled with that same pattern.

- **Group cohesiveness**: The pet-owner group was more cohesive than the non–pet owners as they shared stories of buddying up with their pets for exercise.

How to Run a Group Using the Lifestyle Patterns Approach

The Lifestyle Patterns Quiz and pattern-specific patient handouts offer clinicians a ready-made weight-management program that can be used in a group setting. Clinicians have a few options for administering the quiz in a group setting:

- They can give participants the complete 50-question quiz; answers will then need to be either entered into the computer to have personalized Lifestyle Patterns results printouts for each individual or manually scored to give each participant their pattern percentage scores. (See Appendix C for how to grade the quiz manually.)
- They can give participants the three mini-quizzes as a way to quickly gauge the top group patterns of concern in eating, exercise, and coping.

Using the different quiz methods, clinicians would explain the program during session 1, administer the quiz, and then at session 2 the clinician would share the quiz results with the group, including a discussion of the most significant Lifestyle Patterns for that group. The discussion topics for subsequent group sessions would be selected based on the most common Lifestyle Patterns shared by group members.

Table 9.1 is an example of a 10-week Lifestyle Patterns weight management program in which the most common Lifestyle Patterns were three eating patterns (Meal Skipper, Hearty Portioner, Steady Snacker), two exercise patterns (Couch Champion, Rain Check Athlete), and two coping patterns (Emotional Eater, Self-Scrutinizer). Having clear guidelines for group members will help groups function better. The guidelines in Box 9.1 are adapted from the *Learn Program for Weight Management* (12). Group guidelines and expectations should be discussed on the first session.

Table 9.1 ✦ Example of a 10-Week Schedule for Group Counseling Using the Lifestyle Patterns Approach

Session	Objectives
Week 1	• Review program and group guidelines. • Administer quiz.
Week 2	• Hand out and explain individual profile graphs (if 50-question quiz was given) or discuss most common patterns found in mini-quiz results. • Discuss realistic goal setting. • Hand out food and activity tracking logs. • Discuss self-monitoring: bringing completed logs to future sessions, and weighing self weekly.
Week 3	• Review completed tracking logs. • Discuss eating regularly (Meal Skipper eating pattern and handout). • Discuss being portion-savvy (Hearty Portioner eating pattern and handout).
Week 4	• Discuss Meal Skipper and Hearty Portioner strategies from previous week. • Discuss taking control of emotional eating (Emotional Eating coping pattern and handout).
Week 5	• Discuss Emotional Eating coping strategies from previous week. • Discuss healthy snacking (Steady Snacker eating pattern and handout).
Week 6	• Discuss Steady Snacker eating strategies from previous week. • Discuss moving more (Couch Champion exercise pattern and handout).
Week 7	• Discuss Couch Champion exercise strategies from previous week. • Discuss overall eating strategies from past weeks. • Discuss making time to exercise (Rain Check Athlete exercise pattern and handout).
Week 8	• Discuss Rain Check Athlete strategies from previous week. • Discuss being kind to yourself (Self-Scrutinizer coping pattern and handout).
Week 9	• Discuss Self-Scrutinizer coping strategies from previous week. • Discuss progress with eating, exercise, and coping patterns.
Week 10	• Discuss other topics of interest to group such as night eating, dining out; use Nighttime Nibbler and Convenient Diner handouts when needed. • Summarize Lifestyle Patterns program and discuss follow-up resources.[a]

[a]See Appendix F for resources.

Box 9.1 ✦ Guidelines for Being a Good Group Member

- Attend meetings and be on time.
- Pay attention to those speaking and really listen to what they're saying.
- Accept your fellow group members and don't judge them.
- Be an active participant and share ideas.
- Let everyone have their turn to talk.
- Be nice, helpful, and supportive.
- Share similar experiences that show your understanding.
- Be a team player who motivates and encourages fellow group members.

Source: Data are from reference 12.

Summing It Up

In this chapter, you have learned how to apply the Lifestyle Patterns Approach in a group setting. Whether the group is small or large, part of a corporate wellness program, or a series of educational classes, clinicians should have the basics they need for leading this approach in a group format.

References

1. Wing RR. Behavioral interventions for obesity: recognizing our progress and future challenges. *Obes Res.* 2003;11(Suppl):3S-6S.

2. Hayaki J, Brownell KD. Behaviour change in practice: group approaches. *Int J Obes Relat Metab Disord.* 1996;20(Suppl 1): S27-S30.

3. Renjilian DA, Perri MG, Nezu AM, McKelvey WF, Shermer RL, Anton SD. Individual versus group therapy for obesity: effects of matching participants to their treatment preferences. *J Consult Clin Psychol.* 2001;69:717-721.

4. Wing RR, Jeffrey RW. Benefits of recruiting participants with friends and increasing social support for weight loss and maintenance. *J Consult Clin Psychol.* 1999;67:132-138.

5. Drapkin RG, Wing RR, Shiffman S. Responses to hypothetical high risk situations. Do they predict weight loss in a behavioral treatment program or the context of dietary lapses? *Health Psychol.* 1995;14:427-434.

6. Gates D, Brehm B, Hutton S, Singler M, Poeppelman A. Changing the work environment to promote wellness: a focus group study. *AAOHN J.* 2006;54:515-520.

7. Kruger J, Yore MM, Bauer DR, Kohl HW. Selected barriers and incentives for worksite health promotion services and policies. *Am J Health Promot.* 2007;21:439-447.

8. Finkelstein EA, Linnan LA, Tate DF, Birken BE. A pilot study testing the effect of different levels of financial incentives on weight loss among overweight employees. *J Occup Environ Med.* 2007;49:981-989.

9. Associated Press. Md. workers compete in $1,000 weight loss challenge. July 25, 2007. http://www.foxnews.com/printer_friendly_story/0,3566,290673,00.html. Accessed September 28, 2007.

10. Kushner RF, Jackson Blatner D, Jewell DE, Rudloff K. The PPET study: People and pets exercising together. *Obesity.* 2006;14:1762-1770.

11. Yalom ID. *The Theory and Practice of Group Psychotherapy.* New York, NY: Basic Books; 1985.

12. Brownell KD. *The Learn Program for Weight Management.* 10th ed. Dallas, TX: American Health Publishing; 2004:227-230.

Final Note

◆ ◆ ◆

It is important to stay at the forefront of the obesity epidemic and continue to offer high-quality care to our patients, and we know that the process of counseling overweight adults is ever-changing as new guidelines are developed and new research discoveries are made. Pattern recognition of diet and lifestyle behaviors that contribute to chronic disease is becoming well recognized. We envision that more evidence-based research will be published in this area.

In our hopes of helping clinicians adapt the Lifestyle Patterns Approach most smoothly to their practices, Dr. Kushner is inviting readers to stay in touch through e-mail communications to doctorkushner@aol.com and through his Web site, http://www.counselingoverweightadults.com. We invite readers to share their feedback with Dr. Kushner and feel free to ask questions about the Lifestyle Patterns program. Together, we can make a difference and improve the delivery of health care to our overweight patients.

Appendix A

◆ ◆ ◆

Lifestyle Patterns Quiz

This quiz will help to pinpoint your lifestyle patterns or habits that have been preventing you from losing weight. The quiz results will help us personalize and prioritize a weight management program to best meet your needs.

Quiz Directions

Read each statement and then place a check next to the answer that best reflects your level of agreement. Record your *current* feelings and behaviors (not how you used to feel or act).

Eating Inventory

1. If I "cheat" on my diet, I feel guilty afterward.
   - ☐ Not me at all.
   - ☐ This is true some of the time.
   - ☐ This is me most of the time.
   - ☐ That's me!

2. If there's food around me, I'll probably eat it.
   - ☐ Not me at all.
   - ☐ This is true some of the time.
   - ☐ This is me most of the time.
   - ☐ That's me!

3. I'm someone who regularly skips meals.
   - ☐ Not me at all.
   - ☐ This is true some of the time.
   - ☐ This is me most of the time.
   - ☐ That's me!

Adapted from *Dr. Kushner's Personality Type Diet*. Copyright 2009 Robert Kushner, MD.

4. Most meals are take-out or eaten in restaurants.

☐ Not me at all.

☐ This is true some of the time.

☐ This is me most of the time.

☐ That's me!

5. Fruits and vegetables are my least favorite foods.

☐ Not me at all.

☐ This is true some of the time.

☐ This is me most of the time.

☐ That's me!

6. I rarely eat fresh foods or home-cooked meals.

☐ Not me at all.

☐ This is true some of the time.

☐ This is me most of the time.

☐ That's me!

7. Hungry or not, I snack on foods at home.

☐ Not me at all.

☐ This is true some of the time.

☐ This is me most of the time.

☐ That's me!

8. Given a choice, I seldom choose fruits and vegetables.

☐ Not me at all.

☐ This is true some of the time.

☐ This is me most of the time.

☐ That's me!

9. Hungry or not, I snack on foods brought into the workplace.

☐ Not me at all.

☐ This is true some of the time.

☐ This is me most of the time.

☐ That's me!

10. I eat a fast-food meal most days of the week.

☐ Not me at all.

☐ This is true some of the time.

☐ This is me most of the time.

☐ That's me!

Adapted from *Dr. Kushner's Personality Type Diet.* Copyright 2009 Robert Kushner, MD.

11. I eat little during the day and am most hungry at night.
    - ☐ Not me at all.
    - ☐ This is true some of the time.
    - ☐ This is me most of the time.
    - ☐ That's me!

12. I have two eating styles: the "good" one I show in public and the "bad" one I use in private.
    - ☐ Not me at all.
    - ☐ This is true some of the time.
    - ☐ This is me most of the time.
    - ☐ That's me!

13. I rarely take the time to plan my meals.
    - ☐ Not me at all.
    - ☐ This is true some of the time.
    - ☐ This is me most of the time.
    - ☐ That's me!

14. I eat most of my food in the evening, at dinner and after.
    - ☐ Not me at all.
    - ☐ This is true some of the time.
    - ☐ This is me most of the time.
    - ☐ That's me!

15. I never feel full until it's too late.
    - ☐ Not me at all.
    - ☐ This is true some of the time.
    - ☐ This is me most of the time.
    - ☐ That's me!

16. I have difficulty controlling my portion sizes.
    - ☐ Not me at all.
    - ☐ This is true some of the time.
    - ☐ This is me most of the time.
    - ☐ That's me!

17. Eating is always a battle between what I would like to eat and what I think I should eat.
    - ☐ Not me at all.
    - ☐ This is true some of the time.
    - ☐ This is me most of the time.
    - ☐ That's me!

Adapted from *Dr. Kushner's Personality Type Diet.* Copyright 2009 Robert Kushner, MD.

Physical Activity Inventory

18. I really don't know the first thing about how to get started with an exercise program.
    - ☐ Not me at all.
    - ☐ This is true some of the time.
    - ☐ This is me most of the time.
    - ☐ That's me!

19. I exercise regularly but I may be in a rut because my routine doesn't vary much.
    - ☐ Not me at all.
    - ☐ This is true some of the time.
    - ☐ This is me most of the time.
    - ☐ That's me!

20. It hurts when I exercise.
    - ☐ Not me at all.
    - ☐ This is true some of the time.
    - ☐ This is me most of the time.
    - ☐ That's me!

21. I want to exercise but have little time to devote to being more active.
    - ☐ Not me at all.
    - ☐ This is true some of the time.
    - ☐ This is me most of the time.
    - ☐ That's me!

22. I'm too embarrassed by my body to go to the gym.
    - ☐ Not me at all.
    - ☐ This is true some of the time.
    - ☐ This is me most of the time.
    - ☐ That's me!

23. I have physical limitations that make it difficult for me to be active.
    - ☐ Not me at all.
    - ☐ This is true some of the time.
    - ☐ This is me most of the time.
    - ☐ That's me!

24. Being physically active has never been one of my priorities.
    ☐ Not me at all.
    ☐ This is true some of the time.
    ☐ This is me most of the time.
    ☐ That's me!

25. I limit my exercise because I fear injury or stress on my heart.
    ☐ Not me at all.
    ☐ This is true some of the time.
    ☐ This is me most of the time.
    ☐ That's me!

26. I don't exercise because frankly I don't like it.
    ☐ Not me at all.
    ☐ This is true some of the time.
    ☐ This is me most of the time.
    ☐ That's me!

27. I alternate between being sedentary and working out excessively.
    ☐ Not me at all.
    ☐ This is true some of the time.
    ☐ This is me most of the time.
    ☐ That's me!

28. Once my week-to-week exercise routine is interrupted, I find it very hard to get back on track.
    ☐ Not me at all.
    ☐ This is true some of the time.
    ☐ This is me most of the time.
    ☐ That's me!

29. I'm someone who has never exercised and will need direction.
    ☐ Not me at all.
    ☐ This is true some of the time.
    ☐ This is me most of the time.
    ☐ That's me!

30. My heightened awareness of other people's and my own body size and shape prevents me from exercising.
    - ☐ Not me at all.
    - ☐ This is true some of the time.
    - ☐ This is me most of the time.
    - ☐ That's me!

31. If I can't do my full workout, I typically do nothing at all.
    - ☐ Not me at all.
    - ☐ This is true some of the time.
    - ☐ This is me most of the time.
    - ☐ That's me!

32. I have been doing the same workout for the past 3 months or more.
    - ☐ Not me at all.
    - ☐ This is true some of the time.
    - ☐ This is me most of the time.
    - ☐ That's me!

33. Despite trying, I can't seem to fit exercise into my hectic schedule.
    - ☐ Not me at all.
    - ☐ This is true some of the time.
    - ☐ This is me most of the time.
    - ☐ That's me!

34. I don't usually vary the type, intensity, length, or frequency of my exercise routine.
    - ☐ Not me at all.
    - ☐ This is true some of the time.
    - ☐ This is me most of the time.
    - ☐ That's me!

Stress and Coping Inventory

35. I do a lot to help others but not enough to help myself.
    - ☐ Not me at all.
    - ☐ This is true some of the time.
    - ☐ This is me most of the time.
    - ☐ That's me!

36. Negative self-talk makes me my own worst enemy.

☐ Not me at all.

☐ This is true some of the time.

☐ This is me most of the time.

☐ That's me!

37. My pace of life is out of control and I don't know how to slow it down.

☐ Not me at all.

☐ This is true some of the time.

☐ This is me most of the time.

☐ That's me!

38. I feel ashamed of my body.

☐ Not me at all.

☐ This is true some of the time.

☐ This is me most of the time.

☐ That's me!

39. I know I need to lose weight, but I keep putting it off and can never seem to get started.

☐ Not me at all.

☐ This is true some of the time.

☐ This is me most of the time.

☐ That's me!

40. I find myself eating instead of expressing my emotions.

☐ Not me at all.

☐ This is true some of the time.

☐ This is me most of the time.

☐ That's me!

41. I avoid social situations because of my weight.

☐ Not me at all.

☐ This is true some of the time.

☐ This is me most of the time.

☐ That's me!

42. My own high expectations lead me to feel disappointed even when I'm making progress.
    - ☐ Not me at all.
    - ☐ This is true some of the time.
    - ☐ This is me most of the time.
    - ☐ That's me!

43. I am usually doubtful that a new weight loss program will work for me.
    - ☐ Not me at all.
    - ☐ This is true some of the time.
    - ☐ This is me most of the time.
    - ☐ That's me!

44. I often find myself eating when I'm stressed, lonely, anxious, or depressed.
    - ☐ Not me at all.
    - ☐ This is true some of the time.
    - ☐ This is me most of the time.
    - ☐ That's me!

45. I've had a high degree of success in my work and home life and expect the same of my weight loss.
    - ☐ Not me at all.
    - ☐ This is true some of the time.
    - ☐ This is me most of the time.
    - ☐ That's me!

46. I feel like I'm juggling too many things at once and have little time for myself.
    - ☐ Not me at all.
    - ☐ This is true some of the time.
    - ☐ This is me most of the time.
    - ☐ That's me!

47. I often put myself last on my "to do" list.
    - ☐ Not me at all.
    - ☐ This is true some of the time.
    - ☐ This is me most of the time.
    - ☐ That's me!

48. I'm doubtful that I will ever find someone who can help me lose weight.

    ☐ Not me at all.

    ☐ This is true some of the time.

    ☐ This is me most of the time.

    ☐ That's me!

49. I spend more time thinking about what I need to do to lose weight than actually doing something about it.

    ☐ Not me at all.

    ☐ This is true some of the time.

    ☐ This is me most of the time.

    ☐ That's me!

50. Food is my trusted friend and comfort source.

    ☐ Not me at all.

    ☐ This is true some of the time.

    ☐ This is me most of the time.

    ☐ That's me!

Appendix B

✦ ✦ ✦

Grading the Quiz Manually

Step 1: Assign Scores to Each Quiz Answer

After a client has completed the 50-question Lifestyle Patterns Quiz (see Appendix A), the clinician can manually score it. The first step is to circle the point score next to each of the client's 50 responses. **Note:** Each question has four possible answers. The choices are the same for every question, as are the scores assigned to them:

- Not me at all (0 points)
- This is true some of the time (1 point)
- This is me most of the time (2 points)
- That's me! (3 points)

Step 2: Use the Scoring Algorithm

The questions that pertain to each Lifestyle Pattern have been jumbled within the different quiz sections. Therefore, the clinician must use an algorithm to correctly calculate the total scores and percentage scores for each of the 21 Lifestyle Patterns.

Meal Skipper

To calculate the Meal Skipper total score, add the scores from questions 3 and 13: _____

To calculate the Meal Skipper percentage score, divide the Meal Skipper total score by 6 (maximum possible points): _____

Nighttime Nibbler

To calculate the Nighttime Nibbler total score, add the scores from questions 11 and 14: _____

To calculate the Nighttime Nibbler percentage score, divide the Nighttime Nibbler total score by 6 (maximum possible points): _____

Convenient Diner

To calculate the Convenient Diner total score, add the scores from questions 4, 6, and 10: _____

To calculate the Convenient Diner percentage score, divide the Convenient Diner total score by 9 (maximum possible points): _____

Fruitless Feaster

To calculate the Fruitless Feaster total score, add the scores from questions 5 and 8: _____

To calculate the Fruitless Feaster percentage score, divide the Fruitless Feaster total score by 6 (maximum possible points): _____

Steady Snacker

To calculate the Steady Snacker total score, add the scores from questions 2, 7, and 9: _____

To calculate the Steady Snacker percentage score, divide the Steady Snacker total score by 9 (maximum possible points): _____

Hearty Portioner

To calculate the Hearty Portioner total score, add the scores from questions 15 and 16: _____

To calculate the Hearty Portioner percentage score, divide the Hearty Portioner total score by 6 (maximum possible points): _____

Swing Eater

To calculate the Swing Eater total score, add the scores from questions 1, 12, and 17: _____

To calculate the Swing Eater percentage score, divide the Swing Eater total score by 9 (maximum possible points): _____

Couch Champion

To calculate the Couch Champion total score, add the scores from questions 24 and 26: _____

To calculate the Couch Champion percentage score, divide the Couch Champion total score by 6 (maximum possible points): _____

Uneasy Participant

To calculate the Uneasy Participant total score, add the scores from questions 22 and 30: _____

To calculate the Uneasy Participant percentage score. divide the Uneasy Participant total score by 6 (maximum possible points): _____

Fresh Starter

To calculate the Fresh Starter total score, add the scores from questions 18 and 29: _____

To calculate the Fresh Starter percentage score, divide Fresh Starter total score by 6 (maximum possible points): _____

All-or-Nothing Doer

To calculate the All-or-Nothing Doer total score, add the scores from questions 27, 28, and 31: _____

To calculate the All-or-Nothing Doer percentage score, divide the All-or-Nothing Doer total score by 9 (maximum possible points): _____

Set-Routine Repeater

To calculate the Set-Routine Repeater total score, add the scores from questions 19, 32, and 34: _____

To calculate the Set-Routine Repeater percentage score, divide the Set-Routine Repeater total score by 9 (maximum possible points): _____

Tender Bender

To calculate the Tender Bender total score, add the scores from questions 20, 23, and 25: _____

To calculate the Tender Bender percentage score, divide the Tender Bender total score by 9 (maximum possible points): _____

Rain Check Athlete

To calculate the Rain Check Athlete total score, add the scores from questions 21 and 33: _____

To calculate the Rain Check Athlete percentage score, divide the Rain Check Athlete total score by 6 (maximum possible points): _____

Emotional Eater

To calculate the Emotional Eater total score, add the scores from questions 40, 44, and 50: _____

To calculate the Emotional Eater percentage score, divide the Emotional Eater total score by 9 (maximum possible points): _____

Self-Scrutinizer

To calculate the Self Scrutinizer total score, add the scores from questions 36, 38, and 41: _____

To calculate the Self Scrutinizer percentage score, divide the Self Scrutinizer total score by 9 (maximum possible points): _____

Persistent Procrastinator

To calculate the Persistent Procrastinator total score, add the scores from questions 39 and 49: _____

To calculate the Persistent Procrastinator percentage score, divide the Persistent Procrastinator total score by 6 (maximum possible points): _____

People Pleaser

To calculate the People Pleaser total score, add the scores from questions 35 and 47: _____

To calculate the People Pleaser percentage score, divide the People Pleaser total score by 6 (maximum possible points): _____

Fast Pacer

To calculate the Fast Pacer total score, add the scores from questions 37 and 46: _____

To calculate the Fast Pacer percentage score, divide the Fast Pacer total score by 6 (maximum possible points): _____

Doubtful Dieter

To calculate the Doubtful Dieter total score, add the scores from questions 43 and 48: _____

To calculate the Doubtful Dieter percentage score, divide the Doubtful Dieter total score by 6 (maximum possible points): _____

Overreaching Achiever

To calculate the Overreaching Achiever total score, add the scores from questions 42 and 45: _____

To calculate the Overreaching Achiever percentage score, divide the Overreaching Achiever total score by 6 (maximum possible points): _____

Manual Grading Examples

Example 1

If the point score for question 3 is 2 points ("This is me most of the time") and the point score for question 13 is 3 points ("That's me!"), here is how the clinician would fill in the scores for the Meal Skipper:

- To calculate the Meal Skipper total score, add the scores from questions 3 (2 points) and 13 (3 points): 5 points
- To calculate the Meal Skipper percentage score, divide the Meal Skipper total score (5) by 6 (maximum possible points): 83%

Example 2

If the point score for question 11 is 0 points (Not me at all) and the point score for question 13 is 0 points (Not me at all), here is how the clinician would fill in the scores for the Nighttime Nibbler:

- To calculate the Nighttime Nibbler total score, add the scores from questions 11 (0 points) and 14 (0 points): 0 points
- To calculate the Nighttime Nibbler percentage score, divide the Nighttime Nibbler total score (0) by 6 (maximum possible points): 0%

Appendix C

Lifestyle Patterns Mini-Quizzes

Eating Lifestyle Patterns Mini-Quiz

Patient name: _____ **Date:** _____

Directions: For each question, read the pattern description. If a pattern seems to describe you, put a check in the Yes box. When you finish, look at your quiz. If you checked Yes for more than one pattern, go back and put a star by the two patterns that you think best describe you.

Eating Pattern	Pattern Description	This Describes Me
1. Are you a Meal Skipper?	You don't plan your meals or eat on a set schedule, and you often end up skipping meals.	Yes ☐ No ☐
2. Are you a Nighttime Nibbler?	You eat little during the day, and have most meals and snacks from dinnertime onward.	Yes ☐ No ☐
3. Are you a Convenient Diner?	You eat foods that are convenient, ready-made, packaged, frozen, and microwavable; many of these foods are ordered in or taken out from a restaurant.	Yes ☐ No ☐
4. Are you a Fruitless Feaster?	You eat few fresh fruits and vegetables.	Yes ☐ No ☐
5. Are you a Steady Snacker?	You mindlessly snack on foods throughout the day, whether you are hungry or not.	Yes ☐ No ☐
6. Are you a Hearty Portioner?	You eat too much food too fast; you don't know when to stop eating until it's too late and you feel stuffed.	Yes ☐ No ☐
7. Are you a Swing Eater?	You swing between eating "good" foods in public and overeating "bad" foods in private, and this diet leaves you never feeling satisfied.	Yes ☐ No ☐

Exercise Lifestyle Patterns Mini-Quiz

Patient name: _____ **Date:** _____

Directions: For each question, read the pattern description. If a pattern seems to describe you, put a check in the Yes box. When you finish, look at your quiz. If you checked Yes for more than one pattern, go back and put a star by the two patterns that you think best describe you.

Exercise Pattern	Pattern Description	This Describes Me
1. Are you a Couch Champion?	You don't like to exercise and spend most of your leisure time doing sedentary activities or relaxing on the couch.	Yes ☐ No ☐
2. Are you an Uneasy Participant?	You are not comfortable exercising around others, and this keeps you from going to a gym or exercising in public.	Yes ☐ No ☐
3. Are you a Fresh Starter?	You don't know the first thing about how to start an exercise program, but you are willing to learn with the proper instruction.	Yes ☐ No ☐
4. Are you an All-or-Nothing Doer?	You're either "on" or "off" when it comes to exercise—sometimes you work out excessively, sometimes you are completely sedentary.	Yes ☐ No ☐
5. Are you a Set-Routine Repeater?	You've been doing the same exercise routine for the past 3 months (or longer) without varying the type, duration, or intensity of exercise.	Yes ☐ No ☐
6. Are you a Tender Bender?	You have pain, an injury, or a condition that restricts what you can and cannot do in an exercise program.	Yes ☐ No ☐
7. Are you a Rain Check Athlete?	You know you need to exercise and you want to, but you can't seem to find the time to fit it into your busy schedule.	Yes ☐ No ☐

Coping Lifestyle Patterns Mini-Quiz

Patient name: _____   **Date:** _____

Directions: For each question, read the pattern description. If a pattern seems to describe you, put a check in the Yes box. When you finish, look at your quiz. If you checked Yes for more than one pattern, go back and put a star by the two patterns that you think best describe you.

Coping Pattern	Pattern Description	This Describes Me
1. Are you an Emotional Eater?	You turn to food for comfort when you're stressed, anxious, lonely, or depressed.	Yes ☐ No ☐
2. Are you a Self-Scrutinizer?	You feel ashamed of your body and can be your own worst enemy in terms of thinking negative thoughts about yourself.	Yes ☐ No ☐
3. Are you a Persistent Procrastinator?	You keep putting off losing weight and can never seem to get started.	Yes ☐ No ☐
4. Are you a People Pleaser?	You keep saying yes to everyone else, which keeps your own needs at the bottom of your "to do" list.	Yes ☐ No ☐
5. Are you a Fast Pacer?	You are juggling so many things in your hectic pace of life and don't know how to slow it down and take time for yourself.	Yes ☐ No ☐
6. Are you a Doubtful Dieter?	You doubt that any new weight loss approach will work because nothing has helped in the past.	Yes ☐ No ☐
7. Are you an Overreaching Achiever?	You feel disappointed even when you're making progress, and you have a hard time living up to your own high expectations.	Yes ☐ No ☐

Appendix D

✦ ✦ ✦

Lifestyle Patterns Name Changes

Former Names (used in *Personality Type Diet*)	Current Names (used in this book and on Diet.com)
Eating Patterns	
Unguided Grazer	Meal Skipper
Nighttime Nibbler	Nighttime Nibbler
Convenient Consumer	Convenient Diner
Fruitless Feaster	Fruitless Feaster
Mindless Muncher	Steady Snacker
Hearty Portioner	Hearty Portioner
Deprived Sneaker	Swing Eater
Exercise Patterns	
Hate-to-Move Struggler	Couch Champion
Self Conscious Hider	Uneasy Participant
Inexperienced Novice	Fresh Starter
All or Nothing Doer	All-or-Nothing Doer
Set Routine Repeater	Set-Routine Repeater
Aches and Pains Sufferer	Tender Bender
No Time to Exercise Protester	Rain Check Athlete
Coping Patterns	
Emotional Stuffer	Emotional Eater
Low Self-Esteem Sufferer	Self-Scrutinizer
Persistent Procrastinator	Persistent Procrastinator
Can't Say No Pleaser	People Pleaser
Fast Pacer	Fast Pacer
Pessimistic Thinker	Doubtful Dieter
Unrealistic Achiever	Overreaching Achiever

Appendix E

◆ ◆ ◆

Sample Patient Education Handouts

The CD-ROM includes 21 patient education handouts, one for each of the Eating, Exercise, and Coping Patterns. These handouts are printer-ready PDF files.

This appendix presents three sample handouts:

- The Meal Skipper (an Eating Pattern)
- The Couch Champion (an Exercise Pattern)
- The Emotional Eater (a Coping Pattern)

The Meal Skipper

☑ Your Goal: Plan Three Meals Each Day

- Set your meal times:
  - ► Breakfast should be no more than 2 hours after waking up.
  - ► Lunch should be 4 to 6 hours after breakfast.
  - ► Dinner should be 4 to 6 hours after lunch.
- Write down your set meal times:
  - ► I will eat breakfast each day at _____
  - ► I will eat lunch each day at _____
  - ► I will eat dinner each day at _____
- If you're short on time, grab a meal replacement drink, bar, or frozen meal. The box below gives advice about how to pick the best products.

How to Choose a Meal Replacement Bar, Shake, or Frozen Meal

Use the Nutrition Facts label and select products that have:

- 220 to 350 calories per serving
- Less than 4 grams saturated fat per serving
- At least 10 grams protein per serving
- At least 3 grams of dietary fiber

☑ Your Goal: Focus on Your Meal

- Eat meals at a **table**, from a **plate**, while sitting in a **chair**. Try not to eat from a package, while standing in front of the fridge, or while sitting on the couch.
- Limit distractions while you are eating.
- Eat more slowly, so you can enjoy your meal and be more aware of when you feel full. See the box below for ways to slow down.

How to Eat More Slowly

- Put less food on each forkful.
- Chew each bite more thoroughly.
- Put your fork down between bites.
- Have a sip of water between bites.

☑ Your Goal: Track Your Hunger and Fullness

- Keep a journal and before each meal, write down your **hunger** level on a scale of 0 to 4, where 0 = not hungry; 1 = slightly hungry; 2–3 = moderately hungry; 4 = starving. Have a plan in mind:
  - ▸ To eat when your hunger level is between 2 and 3.
  - ▸ To drink a glass of water or try another activity when your hunger level is 1 or less.
  - ▸ To prevent yourself from letting your hunger level climb to 4.
- After eating, use your journal to write down your **fullness** level on a scale of 0 to 4, where 0 = not full; 1 = slightly full; 2–3 = moderately full; and 4 = stuffed. Have a plan in mind to:
  - ▸ Take midmeal breaks to gauge your level of fullness.
  - ▸ Stop eating when your fullness level is between 2 and 3.
- Eat planned snacks to stop yourself from getting overly hungry. See the snack ideas in the box below.

Healthy Snack Ideas Between 100 and 200 Calories

- A 6-ounce container of light yogurt topped with 1/4 cup high-fiber cereal
- A piece of fruit with 1 stick of string cheese
- 1 ounce (23) almonds
- Vegetables (such as peapods, grape tomatoes, celery, cucumber, carrots) dipped in 4 tablespoons low-fat salad dressing or hummus

---

☑ Your Goal: Fill Up on Water and Fiber

- Carry a water bottle to remind yourself to drink water. Aim to drink 9 to 13 cups (72 to 100 ounces) each day.
- Try to eat 25 to 30 grams of fiber each day. If you aren't used to eating that much fiber, take time to *gradually* increase the daily amounts (it may take a few weeks to reach your fiber goal). Gradual increases will help your body adapt and avoid gas.
- Read Nutrition Facts labels to find foods that have at least 3 grams of dietary fiber per serving.
- See the How to Add Fiber box for snack and meal ideas.

How to Add Fiber

- At breakfast, top whole grain cereal or oatmeal with 1/2 cup berries.
- At lunch, add 1/4 cup garbanzo or kidney beans to a salad, or choose a lentil- or bean-based soup with a sandwich made with whole grain bread.
- At dinner, eat 1 to 2 cups of raw or cooked nonstarchy vegetables, such as green beans, broccoli, carrots, and bell peppers.
- At snack-time, choose a piece of fruit, or vegetables dipped in low-fat ranch dressing, or whole grain crackers with more than 3 grams of fiber per serving and a piece of string cheese.

The Couch Champion

☑ Your Goal: See Benefits

- Write a list of the benefits (other than weight loss) of engaging in more physical activity.
- Make the connection between being more active and boosting your energy level. For example, rate your energy level after a walk by asking yourself, "Do I feel more energetic, less energetic, or the same after walking?"
- Understand that you can be more active without sweating or feeling uncomfortable. Daily activities don't have to be strenuous to provide benefits.

☑ Your Goal: Move More

- Sneak activity into your daily routine by:
  - ▶ Taking stairs instead of elevators
  - ▶ Parking your car farther away
  - ▶ Walking to a coworker's desk instead of e-mailing
  - ▶ Walking during your lunch hour
  - ▶ Getting off the bus or train one stop earlier
  - ▶ Walking to mail a letter
  - ▶ Walking a child to school
  - ▶ Walking your dog longer
- Build toward long-term goals. You could begin with a commitment to walk 5 to 10 minutes each day and work up to a longer-term goal of at least 30 minutes of walking each day. (Walking for 60 minutes would provide even greater weight-loss benefits.)
- Write down a plan (such as waking up earlier or going to the park after work) that will fulfill your daily walking goals. Include whether you will aim for one 30-minute walking session or several shorter sessions each day.
- Understand that all activities burn calories, but some burn more. For example, check the Calorie-Burning Activities chart to compare the calories burned during 30 minutes of various activities. (Note that people with different body weights will burn calories at different rates.)

Calorie-Burning Activities		
Activity	**Calories Burned by a 150-Pound Person**	**Calories Burned by a 220-Pound Person**
Sleeping	31	45
Reclining and reading	34	50
Sitting, playing with children	85	125
Vacuuming	119	175
Very brisk walking (4 miles per hour)	170	250
Biking, moderate effort	273	400
Running at a pace of 1 mile in 9 minutes	374	550

☑ Your Goal: Count Steps

- Wear a step counter (pedometer) daily to track how many steps you take:
  - ► Choose a pedometer that counts steps, not miles.
  - ► Clip the pedometer to your waistband in line with the front midline of your thigh.
  - ► Check to see whether your pedometer is working correctly by setting it to zero and then counting while you walk 100 steps. If the pedometer number is between 90 and 110 steps when you finish walking, it is working fine. If the number is not in that range, try moving the pedometer closer to or farther from your belly button and then checking it again. If it is still not counting correctly, you may want to return it and try another brand.
  - ► Use your pedometer for three days to calculate, on average, how many steps you walk each day.
- Write down your average daily steps in an activity log, or use an online exercise tracker.

Tips for Setting Walking Goals

- Each week, set a goal to increase your daily steps. In the first week, aim to add 250–500 steps each day. Each week that follows, increase the goal by another 250–500 steps per day.
- Set a long-term goal to take 10,000 steps (the equivalent of about 3 to 5 miles) per day. This may take you weeks or months depending on your starting point.
- Set a goal to increase the pace that you walk. To make your heart and lungs stronger, you need to be walking at a brisk pace, not strolling.
- Even after you meet goals, continue to record your daily steps taken, and bring in logs to discuss at future appointments.

☑ Your Goal: Buddy Up

- Think about the people (or pets) in your life who can be your walking buddies, tennis or bowling friends, or exercise partners.
- Think about hiring a personal trainer who can help you become more active.
- Write a specific plan for buddying up that includes:
  - ► Who you will buddy up with?
  - ► What type of activity you will do together?
  - ► When and where you will do the activity?
  - ► For how long?

The Emotional Eater

☑ Your Goal: Track Your Feelings

- Keep an ABC food and mood diary for a few days. Start by drawing a chart with three columns, similar to the sample diary in this handout. Fill in the ABCs:
  - ▶ **A** is for Antecedents—the trigger situations or emotions that come before eating.
  - ▶ **B** is for the Behavior of eating—what you ate and how much.
  - ▶ **C** is for Consequences—the feelings and attitudes that occur after eating.
- Bring your completed diary to future appointments.

Sample ABC Food/Mood Diary		
Antecedents	**Behavior**	**Consequences**
Got yelled at by boss; felt stressed.	Grabbed candy and soda from vending machine.	Felt better at first, but left work still feeling stressed.
Home alone Saturday night; felt lonely.	Ate 1/2 bag of cookies and 1/2 bag of chips.	Food improved my mood initially, but then I felt guilty.

☑ Your Goal: Know Your Triggers

- Identify the emotions that you've typically been soothing with food, such as:
  - ▶ Anxiety
  - ▶ Loneliness
  - ▶ Stress
  - ▶ Sadness
- Ask yourself:
  - ▶ "How much of my eating is emotionally related?" (You can measure in percentages or count the number of eating occasions per week.)
  - ▶ "What triggers can I identify from my diary?"
- Write down your trigger situations and emotions:

_____

_____

_____

☑ Your Goal: Cope Without Food

- Practice "mood surfing" as a way to keep your moods from getting worse. In other words, try to "ride out" your emotion or the desire to eat just as a surfer would ride out a wave. Instead of giving in to your desire to eat, observe and feel the emotion. Chances are the emotion or trigger to eat will slowly diminish.
- Develop an emotional eating action plan. Write your plan on an index card and carry it with you so you can refer to it when needed (see sample plan).
- Know that exercise is an effective way to boost your mood.

Sample Emotional Eating Action Plan	
When Feeling Lonely:	**When Feeling Stress at Work:**
Call a friend.	Take slow, deep breaths.
Log onto an Internet chat group.	Talk it out with someone you trust.
Write a letter to someone.	Take a walk outside.
Visit the health club.	Put thoughts in a journal.

☑ Your Goal: De-stress

- Explore stress management techniques, such as:
  - ► Progressive muscle relaxation
  - ► Deep breathing exercises
  - ► Meditation
  - ► Visualization
  - ► Yoga
  - ► Tai chi
  - ► Massage
  - ► Stretching
  - ► Exercise
  - ► Humor
- You can learn these techniques by finding a class in your community or buying a book, video, DVD, or audio CD.
- Pay attention to your stress level before and after you try these techniques; think about how different activities can lower your stress level.
- Other ways to reduce stress include:
  - ► Seeking out friends who make you laugh or seeing funny movies
  - ► Working with a qualified therapist who understands stress and eating issues
- Write down the stress management techniques that interest you:

_____

_____

_____

Appendix F

◆ ◆ ◆

Additional Resources

Eating-Focused Resources

Web Sites

American Dietetic Association Evidence Analysis Library
http://www.adaevidencelibrary.com
A user-friendly Web site, the American Dietetic Association's Evidence Analysis Library presents a synthesis of the best, most relevant nutrition research on important dietetics practice questions.

American Dietetic Association Position Papers
http://www.eatright.org (Click "Position Papers" on the left navigation menu)
Explains the association's stance on issues that affect the nutritional status of the public. Positions, which consist of a position statement and a support paper, are based on sound scientific data.

American Institute for Cancer Research
http://www.aicr.org
Offers information about diet, obesity, and cancer; includes free recipes.

Calorie King
http://www.calorieking.com
The Calorie King food database covers nearly 50,000 food products, including food offered by fast-food restaurants. The site also sells books, such as *The Calorie, Fat, & Carbohydrate Counter,* a pocket-size resource that patients can use to look up calories of foods, including fast-food items.

Diet.com Nutrition on the Go Text Messaging Service
http://diet.com/mobile
Using a cell phone and texting DIET1 (34381) with a menu item and restaurant name, individuals can get nutritional information on more than 36,000 menu items at 1700 restaurants. This service is free aside from the costs of text messaging. An online demonstration of this tool is available at http://diet.com/mobile.

Food and Nutrition Information Center
http://fnic.nal.usda.gov
A part of the US Department of Agriculture, FNIC provides credible, accurate, and practical resources for nutrition and health professionals, educators, government personnel, and consumers.

Institute of Medicine
http://www.iom.edu
Provides unbiased, evidence-based information on health. The Food and Nutrition section contains information and reports on issues such as food safety, dietary supplements, adequate nutrition, and guidelines for nutrient intake.

International Food and Information Council
http://www.ific.org
Communicates science-based information on food safety and nutrition to health and nutrition professionals, educators, journalists, government officials, and others who provide information to consumers. Supported primarily by food, beverage and agricultural industries.

National Fruit and Vegetable Program (Fruits & Veggies—More Matters)
http://www.fruitsandveggiesmatter.gov
Sponsored by the Centers for Disease Control and Prevention and public and private partners, this public health initiative replaces the "5 A Day" program. The National Fruit & Vegetable Program supports initiatives to provide education on the health benefits of fruit and vegetable consumption and to improve access to fruits and vegetables.

National Heart, Lung, and Blood Institute (NHLBI) Portion Distortion Quiz
http://hp2010.nhlbihin.net/portion/keep.htm
Offers a food quiz with pictures comparing food portions and calories from 20 years ago to today; quiz takers guess how many calories are in today's food portions.

Print Publications

Cooking Light Magazine
The magazine and Web site (http://www.cookinglight.com) emphasize light cuisine, include recipes with photos, and explore food and nutrition news as well as fitness and health issues.

Craighead L. *The Appetite Awareness Workbook.* Oakland, CA: New Harbinger Publications; 2006.
Offers a self-monitoring technique to help people understand hunger and fullness cues and to regulate eating behavior.

Green A. *The Field Guide to Produce.* Philadelphia, PA: Quirk Books; 2004.
Gives detailed descriptions of, selection tips for, and guidelines on peeling, blanching, cooking, and eating popular fruits and vegetables.

Wansink B. *Mindless Eating: Why We Eat More than We Think.* New York, NY: Bantam Books; 2006.
Exposes the hidden psychology of eating based on Wansink's innovative research.

Exercise-Focused Resources

Web Sites

Accusplit
http://www.accusplit.com
Sells pedometers; online catalog.

American College of Sports Medicine
http://www.acsm.org
Promotes and integrates scientific research, education, and practical applications of sports medicine and exercise science to maintain and enhance physical performance, fitness, health, and quality of life.

American Council on Exercise
http://www.acefitness.org
Helps the public to make informed decisions about the safety and effectiveness of fitness products and trends through its research and independent comparative studies.

Collage Video
http://www.collagevideo.com
Sells exercise videos and DVDs; free catalog.

Exercise TV
http://www.exercise.tv
Offers online and video-on-demand workouts with digital cable.

Fit Day Activity Tracker
http://www.fitday.com
Offers online tracking (with graphic analyses) of calories burned from basal, lifestyle, and activities expenditures.

Video Fitness
http://www.videofitness.com
Has a consumer guide to exercise videos. Contains reviews of more than 1,000 exercise videos. The site does not sell videos but offers a long list of places that do.

Print Publication

Anderson B. *Stretching: 20th Anniversary Revised Edition*. Bolinas, CA: Shelter Publications; 2000. Presents stretching routines (with pictures) for all muscle groups as well as warm-up and cool-down sequences for common sports.

Coping-Focused Resources

Web Sites

American Psychological Association: Psychologist Locator

http://locator.apa.org
An online locator for psychologists in specific localities. Individuals can also obtain referrals by calling 800/964-2000.

Benson-Henry Institute for Mind Body Medicine

http://www.mbmi.org
The Web site's store sells guided relaxation CDs that may help individuals reduce tension and anxiety and manage stress.

Psychology Today: Find a Therapist

http://www.psychologytoday.com
Choose the Find a Therapist option from the left navigation menu to access detailed listings for psychologists, psychiatrists, therapists, and counselors throughout the United States and Canada.

Print Publications

Beck JS. *The Beck Diet Solution: Train Your Brain to Think Like a Thin Person.* Birmingham, AL: Oxmoor House; 2004.
Teaches dieters how to use cognitive therapy techniques to lose weight and make long-term lifestyle changes.

Cash TF. *The Body Image Workbook: Second Edition.* Oakland, CA: New Harbinger Publications; 2008.
Offers an eight-step program to help individuals discover their own body image and set goals for change and improvement.

Young JE, Klosko JS, Weishaar ME. *Schema Therapy: A Practitioner's Guide.* New York, NY: Guilford Press; 2003.
Offers a method for approaching patients with chronic, longer-term patterns of behavior and treatment resistance.

General Weight Management Resources

Web Sites

American Medical Association Roadmaps for Clinical Practice series:
Assessment and Management of Obesity

http://www.ama-assn.org/ama/pub/category/10931.html
Ten downloadable booklets that offer practical recommendations for addressing adult obesity in the primary care setting.

Diet.com

http://www.diet.com

Extensive consumer information on diet, health, and long-term weight control. Includes online tracking tools, recipes, ongoing weight loss challenge groups, diet buddies, expert support, diet blogs, and fitness videos. Also has an online edition of Dr. Kushner's Lifestyle Patterns quiz and lifestyle-based weight loss program.

MyPyramid.gov

http://www.mypyramid.gov

Features information on the new Food Pyramid, its 12 models geared to different populations, and Dietary Guidelines. The site can calculate each individual's calorie needs using five variables (age, gender, weight, height, and activity level) and provide a corresponding specific breakdown of daily food group servings needed for a well-balanced and healthy diet. Other tools include a food and activity tracker and educational pictures of portion sizes.

National Heart, Lung, and Blood Institute: Body Mass Index calculator

http://www.nhlbisupport.com/bmi

Allows you to enter your weight and height and obtain your BMI.

National Heart, Lung, and Blood Institute: We Can! Ways to Enhance Children's Activity and Nutrition

http://www.nhlbi.nih.gov/health/public/heart/obesity/wecan/

Supports families and communities working to help children achieve a healthy weight. The program focuses on three important behaviors: improved food choices, increased physical activity and reduced screen time.

National Weight Control Registry

http://www.nwcr.ws

Developed to identify and investigate the characteristics of individuals who have succeeded at long-term weight loss. The registry tracks more than 5,000 individuals who have lost significant amounts of weight and kept it off for long periods of time. Recruitment for the registry is ongoing.

Print Publications

Kushner RF, Kushner N. *Dr. Kushner's Personality Type Diet.* New York, NY: St. Martin's Griffin; 2004. Presents the original consumer version of the Lifestyle Patterns Approach with a description of the Scaling Up Syndrome, the Lifestyle Patterns quiz, pattern-specific strategies, and scaling down recipes.

Obesity Management Journal

Publishes clinical, practical information on obesity, including prevention and management, patient motivation, and nutrition. Each issue includes original papers, an interview with a leading obesity expert, clinical case reports, clinical Q & A, tools and patient information, reviews of obesity programs, news and literature reviews, and a comprehensive Web watch.

Index